ADAPTIVE 2018

The Tenth International Conference on Adaptive and Self-Adaptive Systems and Applications

February 18 - 22, 2018

Barcelona, Spain

ADAPTIVE 2018 Editors

Andreas Rausch, TU Clausthal, Clausthal-Zellerfeld, Germany

Christoph Knieke, TU Clausthal, Clausthal-Zellerfeld, Germany

Melanie Schranz, EU-H2020 CPSwarm, Lakeside Labs GmbH, Austria

Printed from e-media with permission by:

Curran Associates, Inc.
57 Morehouse Lane
Red Hook, NY 12571

Some format issues inherent in the e-media version may also appear in this print version.

Printed by Curran Associates, Inc. (2018)

International Academy, Research, and Industry Association (IARIA)
412 Derby Way
Wilmington, DE 19810

Phone: (408) 893-6407
Fax: (408) 527-6351

petre@iaria.org

Additional copies of this publication are available from:

Curran Associates, Inc.
57 Morehouse Lane
Red Hook, NY 12571 USA
Phone: 845-758-0400
Fax: 845-758-2633
Email: curran@proceedings.com
Web: www.proceedings.com

ADAPTIVE 2018

Forward

The Tenth International Conference on Adaptive and Self-Adaptive Systems and Applications (ADAPTIVE 2018), held between February 18 - 22, 2018 - Barcelona, Spain, continued a series of events targeting advanced system and application design paradigms driven by adaptiveness and self-adaptiveness. With the current tendencies in developing and deploying complex systems, and under the continuous changes of system and application requirements, adaptation is a key feature. Speed and scalability of changes require self-adaptation for special cases. How to build systems to be easily adaptive and self-adaptive, what constraints and what mechanisms must be used, and how to evaluate a stable state in such systems are challenging duties. Context-aware and user-aware are major situations where environment and user feedback is considered for further adaptation.

The conference had the following tracks:

- Self-adaptation
- Adaptive applications
- Adaptivity in robot systems
- Fundamentals and design of adaptive systems

Similar to the previous edition, this event attracted excellent contributions and active participation from all over the world. We were very pleased to receive top quality contributions.

We take here the opportunity to warmly thank all the members of the ADAPTIVE 2018 technical program committee, as well as the numerous reviewers. The creation of such a high quality conference program would not have been possible without their involvement. We also kindly thank all the authors that dedicated much of their time and effort to contribute to ADAPTIVE 2018. We truly believe that, thanks to all these efforts, the final conference program consisted of top quality contributions.

Also, this event could not have been a reality without the support of many individuals, organizations and sponsors. We also gratefully thank the members of the ADAPTIVE 2018 organizing committee for their help in handling the logistics and for their work that made this professional meeting a success.

We hope ADAPTIVE 2018 was a successful international forum for the exchange of ideas and results between academia and industry and to promote further progress in the area of adaptive and self-adaptive systems and applications. We also hope Barcelona provided a pleasant environment during the conference and everyone saved some time for exploring this beautiful city.

ADAPTIVE 2018 Chairs

ADAPTIVE 2018 Steering Committee

Roy Sterritt, Ulster University, UK
Constantin Paleologu, University Politehnica of Bucharest, Romania
Claudia Raibulet, University of Milano-Bicocca, Italy
Radu Calinescu, University of York, UK
Po-Hsun Cheng, National Kaohsiung Normal University, Taiwan
Marc-Philippe Huget, Polytech Annecy-Chambery-LISTIC | University of Savoie, France
Ryotaro Kamimura, Tokai Univerisity, Japan
Valérie Camps, Paul Sabatier University – IRIT, Toulouse, France

ADAPTIVE 2018 Industry/Research Advisory Committee

Weirong Jiang, Google, USA
Jessie Y.C. Chen, U.S. Army Research Laboratory, USA
Sherif Abdelwahed, Distributed Analytics and Security Institute (DASI), USA
Gregor Grambow, AristaFlow GmbH, Ulm, Germany
Marc Kurz, ecx.io austria GmbH - An IBM company, Wels, Austria
Habtamu Abie, Norwegian Computing Center/Norsk Regnesentral-Blindern, Norway

ADAPTIVE 2018

Committee

ADAPTIVE 2018 Steering Committee

Roy Sterritt, Ulster University, UK
Constantin Paleologu, University Politehnica of Bucharest, Romania
Claudia Raibulet, University of Milano-Bicocca, Italy
Radu Calinescu, University of York, UK
Po-Hsun Cheng, National Kaohsiung Normal University, Taiwan
Marc-Philippe Huget, Polytech Annecy-Chambery-LISTIC | University of Savoie, France
Ryotaro Kamimura, Tokai Univerisity, Japan
Valérie Camps, Paul Sabatier University – IRIT, Toulouse, France

ADAPTIVE 2018 Industry/Research Advisory Committee

Weirong Jiang, Google, USA
Jessie Y.C. Chen, U.S. Army Research Laboratory, USA
Sherif Abdelwahed, Distributed Analytics and Security Institute (DASI), USA
Gregor Grambow, AristaFlow GmbH, Ulm, Germany
Marc Kurz, ecx.io austria GmbH - An IBM company, Wels, Austria
Habtamu Abie, Norwegian Computing Center/Norsk Regnesentral-Blindern, Norway

ADAPTIVE 2018 Technical Program Committee

Sherif Abdelwahed, Distributed Analytics and Security Institute (DASI), USA
Habtamu Abie, Norwegian Computing Center/Norsk Regnesentral-Blindern, Norway
Nadia Acbchiche-Mimouni, University of Evry, France
Jose M. Alcaraz Calero, University of the West of Scotland, UK
Harvey Alférez, Universidad de Montemorelos, Mexico
Richard Anthony, University of Greenwich, UK
Abdalkarim Awad, University of Erlangen, Germany
Charles K. Ayo, Covenant University, Ogun State, Nigeria
Dirk Bade, University of Hamburg, Germany
Nik Bessis, Edge Hill University, UK
Stefan Bosse, University of Bremen, Germany
Darko Bozhinoski, Gran Sasso Science Institute, Italy
Antonio Brogi, University of Pisa, Italy
Radu Calinescu, University of York, UK
Valérie Camps, Paul Sabatier University – IRIT, Toulouse, France
Carlos Carrascosa, Universidad Politécnica de Valencia, Spain
Jessie Y.C. Chen, U.S. Army Research Laboratory, USA
Po-Hsun Cheng, National Kaohsiung Normal University, Taiwan

Enrique Chirivella Perez, University of the West of Scotland, UK
Maher Chaouachi, University of McGill, Canada
François Charpillet, Inria, France
Jose Alfredo F. Costa, Federal University - UFRN, Brazil
Anderson da Silva Soares, Professor at Federal University of Goiás, Brazil
Baudouin Dafflon, Université de Lyon, Université Lyon 1, France
Angel P. del Pobil, Jaume I University, Spain
Mihaela Dinsoreanu, Technical University of Cluj-Napoca, Romania
Ioanna Dionysiou, University of Nicosia, Cyprus
Benedikt Eberhardinger, University of Augsburg, Germany
Holger Eichelberger, University of Hildesheim, Germany
Lukas Esterle, Vienna University of Technology, Austria
Fairouz Fakhfakh, University of Sfax, Tunisia
Ziny Flikop, Consultant, USA
Francisco J. García-Peñalvo, University of Salamanca, Spain
Ilias Gerostathopoulos, Technical University Munich, Germany
Giuseppina Gini, Politecnico di Milano, Italy
Thomas Göthel, Technische Universität Berlin, Germany
Gregor Grambow, AristaFlow GmbH, Ulm, Germany
Hongsheng He, Wichita State University, USA
Alwin Hoffmann, University of Augsburg, Germany
Leszek Holenderski, Philips Lighting Research, Data Science Dept - Eindhoven, The Netherlands
Mohssen Hosseini, KU Leuven, Belgium
Christopher-Eyk Hrabia, Technische Universität Berlin | DAI-Labor, Germany
Marc-Philippe Huget, Polytech Annecy-Chambery-LISTIC | University of Savoie, France
Weirong Jiang, Google, USA
Clarimar José Coelho, Escola de Ciências Exatas e da Computação (ECEC) - Pontifícia Universidade Católica de Goiàs (PUC Goiás), Brazil
Imène Jraidi, University of Montreal, Canada
Ryotaro Kamimura, Tokai Univerisity, Japan
Alexey Kashevnik, SPIIRAS, Russia
Quist-Aphetsi Kester, Ghana Technology University College, Ghana
Verena Klös, Technische Universität Berlin, Germany
Oliver Kosak, Institut for Software & Systems Engineering - University of Augsburg, Germany
Satoshi Kurihara, University of Electro-Communications, Japan
Marc Kurz, ecx.io austria GmbH - An IBM company, Wels Austria
Mikel Larrea, University of the Basque Country UPV/EHU, Spain
Jinoh Lee, Istituto Italiano di Tecnologia (IIT), Italy
Henrique Lopes Cardoso, FEUP/LIACC, Portugal
Maite López-Sánchez, Universitat de Barcelona, Spain
Tamara Lorenz, University of Cincinnati, USA
Ricardo Marco Alaez, University of the West of Scotland, UK
Cesar Marin, The University of Manchester, UK
Mieke Massink, CNR-ISTI, Italy
Dalton Matsuo Tavares, Federal University of Goiás, Brazil
René Meier, Lucerne University of Applied Sciences and Arts, Switzerland
Andreas Metzger, paluno (The Ruhr Institute for Software Technology) / University of Duisburg-Essen, Germany

Copyright Information

Table of Contents

Self-Reconfigurable Manufacturing System For Personalized Mass Customisation 1
Rotimi Ogunsakin, Cesar Marin, and Nikolay Mehandjiev

Low Power Tristate Buffer for Mobile Applications 9
Karol Niewiadomski and Dietmar Tutsch

Adaptive Petri Nets – A Petri Net Extension for Reconfigurable Structures 15
Carl Mai, Rene Schone, Johannes Mey, Thomas Kuhn, and Uwe Assmann

Managing Communication Paradigms with a Dynamic Adaptive Middleware 24
Tim Warnecke, Karina Rehfeldt, and Andreas Rausch

Towards A Cubesat Aautonomicity Capability Model 34
Clement Gama, Roy Sterritt, George Wilkie, and Glenn Hawe

Improvement of Self-optimizing in Selection and Composition of Services Using Reinforcement Learning Algorithm Based on Convex Hull 44
Hadis Khorasaninasab Abbasi and Eslam Nazemi

Conception of a Type-based Pub/Sub Mechanism with Hierarchical Channels for a Dynamic Adaptive Component Model 53
Mohamad Ibrahim, Karina Rehfeldt, and Andreas Rausch

Distributed Simulation for Evolutionary Design of Swarms of Cyber-Physical Systems 60
Micha Rappaport, Davide Conzon, Midhat Jdeed, Melanie Schranz, Enrico Ferrera, and Wilfried Elmenreich

Automated and Connected Driving in Urban Scenarios 66
Maximilian Flormann, Adrian Sonka, and Roman Henze

Highly Accurate Map-based Path and Behavior Planning for Automated Urban Driving 69
Bjorn Reuber, Holger Znamiec, Roman Henze, and Ferit Kucukay

Vehicle Antenna-Footprint Optimization for Efficient MIMO V2X Communications 71
Andreas Pfadler, Christian Ballesteros, Jordi Romeu, and Lluis Jofre

Improving Thermal Management of Electric Vehicles by Prediction of Thermal Disturbance Variables 75
Peter Engel, Sebastian Meise, Andreas Rausch, and Wilhelm Tegethoff Tegethoff

Long-Term Environment Prediction for Model Predictive Control in Vehicles: Pattern Recognition upon Primitive Driving Behavior and Driver Condition 84
Karl-Falco Storm, Daniel Eckardt, Meng Zhang, Jorg Grieser, Michael Prilla, and Rausch Andreas

Towards Cross-domain Release Engineering - Potentials and Challenges for Automotive Industry 93
David Inkermann, Tobias Huth, and Thomas Vietor

Towards Alignment of Processes, Tools, and Products in Automotive Software Systems Development 100
Joachim Schramm, Andreas Rausch, Daniel Fiebig, Oscar Slotosch, and Mohammad Abu-Alqumsan

Barcelona Virtual Mobility Lab -The Multimodal Transport Simulation Testbed for Emerging Mobility Concepts Evaluation 107
Lidia Montero, Maria Paz Linares, Juan Salmeron, Gonzalo Recio, Ester Lorente, and Juan Jose Vazquez

Self-Reconfigurable Manufacturing System For Personalized Mass Customisation

Rotimi Ogunsakin, César A. Marín, Nikolay Mehandjiev
Alliance Manchester Business School
Booth St E, Manchester, M13 9SS
Email: {rotimi.ogunsakin, cesar.marin, nikolay.mehandjiev}@manchester.ac.uk

Abstract— **One of the expected benefits of Industry 4.0 is the ability of production systems to effectively produce personalized products for a relatively small lot size in the same assembly line without trade-offs for cost, delivery time and quality. In this case, individual product will be unique and require a production system that is optimized for single lot size (lot-size-of-one). Reconfigurable Manufacturing System (RMS) is an attractive choice for this. However, reconfiguration processes are not automated and not real-time, which sometimes requiring days, thereby making it economically and functionally unfit for personalized mass customisation. To achieve this, Self-Reconfigurable Manufacturing System (S-RMS) is proposed in this paper and implemented in-silico using nature inspired models and algorithms. In our implementation, resource re-configuration is both automatic and immediate. The system is evaluated by measuring total production output, system stability and average lead-time per order during production and during unexpected changes like resource breakdown. This approach is expected to proffer solution to the batch-size-of-one problem in manufacturing and engender personalized mass customisation.**

***Keywords-** Self-Recofigurable Manufacturing System; Reconfigurable Manufacturing System; Personalised Mass Customisation.*

I. INTRODUCTION

Personalized mass customisation is the mass production of individually customised goods in the same production line [1]. This paradigm requires manufacturing systems capable of producing a relatively high volume of unique product options in the same assembly line without trade-offs in cost, delivery time and quality for both manufacturers and consumers [2]. The major challenge in developing a manufacturing system with such capability is the level of structural, control and software flexibility that is required [3]. Present days manufacturing systems cannot be modified to offer the level of structural, control and software flexibility that is required in such system and therefore requiring a new paradigm approach.

There are proposed manufacturing systems expected to give rise to personalized mass customisation, such as Reconfigurable manufacturing system (RMS), but these systems suffer from structural and control inflexibility and therefore functionally unfit for personalized mass customisation [3]. However, Evolvable assembly system (EAS) is an exception to this; it is demonstrated to achieve personalized mass customisation and address the batch-size-of-one problem, but the system achieves this by producing a single unit at a time [4]. In practice, personalized mass customisation scenarios are more complex. They require multiple products on the shop floor with different designs, styles, shapes and colors going through production process at the same time. EAS at present fails to demonstrate such practical complexity, which should be obtainable in a typical manufacturing system capable of personalized mass customisation.

This research proposes and demonstrates in silico Self-Reconfigurable Manufacturing System (S-RMS), a manufacturing system capable of addressing the batch-size-of-one problem in personalized mass customisation. This is achieved by borrowing natural self-organising rules from natural systems, extending and adapting them to reconfiguration in S-RMS to incorporate adaptive properties, such as self-reconfiguration for multiple product mix and self-recovery during machine (resource) failure.

The system is evaluated by measuring average production output, stability and average lead-time per unit during production and during unexpected changes like resource breakdown. The expected benefit of this approach is that, it will proffer solution to the batch-size-of-one problem in the manufacturing systems and engender personalized mass customisation.

The remaining of this paper is organised as follows. Section II reviews related work in reconfiguration and mass-customisation in manufacturing systems. Section III contains details of the approach used, which include models and algorithms, while Section IV contains the simulation and experimental evaluation of the S-RMS. The final section contains the discussion and conclusion.

II. RELATED WORK

Advancements in manufacturing systems have been mainly to increase efficiency and reduce production cost and lead-time. Two approaches have been dominant in achieving these, which are 1) Resource flexibility and 2) Resource layout.

Resource flexibility is the technological improvement on production machines for faster part production, wastage reduction and ability to produce more than one part variety. Resource layout is the spatial arrangement of resources on the factory floor in such a way as to optimize production process [5].

The proposed S-RMS is based on how personalized mass customization can be achieved through reconfiguration of resource layout in real-time, which is one of the major challenges in manufacturing systems. Therefore, reviewed work will be focused on resource layout and reconfiguration approaches.

Resources in manufacturing system can be arranged based on function or process requirement, which are referred to as functional and cellular layout respectively. Functional layout is a resource layout paradigm that is based on resource function. This implies having resources of the same type placed in the same location [6]. This provides economy of scales and simplicity in workloads allocation, but highly inefficient when there are constant or unpredictable changes in product mix and routings, a common scenario in personalized mass customisation.

Cellular layout is a layout configuration in which the factory is partitioned into cells, and each cell is dedicated to a product or part family with similar processing requirements [6]. This type of configuration simplifies workflow and is generally optimized for producing specific product set with stable demand and long product life cycle. However, reconfiguration process is usually expensive and time consuming, making such layout unattractive for personalized mass customisation [6].

As a result of the inefficiencies in both functional and cellular layouts for dynamic production environment, other layouts have been proposed for a more efficient production output in dynamic production environment [5]. Some examples of the proposed layouts are: Spine layout, Hybrid layout, Multichannel layout, Distributed layout and Modular layout (see Table 1).

TABLE I. LAYOUT TYPES AND DESCRIPTION [5]

Layout types	Description
Spine layout	Usually used by Original Equipment Manufacturers (OEMs). In this type of layout, products move along a main artery through the plant. Mini-assembly lines owned by independent suppliers are linked to the spine where additional modules are attached to the product as needed by these suppliers as it moves through the spine. This allows for change of suppliers without changes to the factory layout.
Hybrid layout	This is a combination of different production modules based on multiple production process. For example, a hybrid facility may contain flow-line component for manufacturing common parts and a job-shop component for customizing final products.
Multichannel layout	This involves having duplicate production lines that are shared across products. Products are allowed to move in and out of neighbouring production lines, thereby creating multiple lines and channels, and minimizing queue and congestion.
Distributed layouts	In a distributed layout, not all equipment of the same type is placed in adjoining location. Instead, equipment of the same type is placed individually throughout the factory, which can be quickly combined to form temporary cells dedicated to specific product line or job order.
Modular layout	This conceptualises layout as a network of basic modules. These basic modules may be based on different production process or layouts. For example, a modular layout may contain a network of flow-line, job-shop, cellular layout and functional layout basic modules.

However, these resource layout types are not optimized for production environment with requirement for single-lot-size production [4]. To address this limitation, a system with highly flexible layout is required, where reconfiguration can be done with a minimal amount of time and at no additional cost to both the manufacturer and the consumer. To achieve this level of manufacturing flexibility, smart, flexible and adaptive manufacturing system is proposed.

Manufacturing companies (such as GE, Airbus, Siemens) are observed to be investigating smart, flexible and adaptive manufacturing systems that are capable of autonomous self-healing, self-adaptation and self-reconfiguration, typified by the "batch-size-of-one" (BSo1) problem [3]. Examples of such system include: Reconfigurable Manufacturing System (RMS), Holonic Manufacturing System (HMS), and Evolvable Assembly System (EAS).

Reconfigurable Manufacturing System is a manufacturing system designed to enable rapid change in hardware and software component for quick response to sudden market changes by adjusting its functionality and production capacity [7]. RMS is engineered for mass production and therefore not effective for managing large product varieties and rapid changes in market. This makes RMS unsuitable for personalized mass customization.

Holonic Manufacturing System, which is inspired by Arthur Koestler's holons concept [8]. Holons are autonomous self-reliant units with degree of independence, such that contingencies can be handled without being instructed by higher authority, and simultaneously subjected to control from single or multiple higher authorities [9]. This implies that Holons can exist in complex systems like manufacturing systems as both a whole and a part simultaneously.

The "whole" property ensures stability of forms in the system, while the "part" property signifies intermediate forms and ensure stability for higher form. Holons concept comparatively provides more flexibility for manufacturing systems, but immediate reconfiguration is still lacking, therefore making it not suitable for personalized mass customisation [9].

Evolvable assembly system is a production system whose components are designed to adapt to changing conditions of operations and also assist in the evolution of the component in time, such that processes utilizing the components will become self-evolvable, self-reconfigurable, self-tuning and self-diagnosing [10]. Examples of EAS implementation are plug and produce system, and Smart Manufacturing and Reconfigurable Technologies (SMART).

Plug and produce system is an implementation of Instantly Deployable Evolvable Assembly System (IDEAS), which is aimed at developing an industrially suitable EAS [10]. The plug and produce system was implemented on a mini scale called MiniProd [11]. It is based on multi-agent control paradigm and capable of real-time self-reconfiguration on the shop floor without higher-level instruction. This shows that real-time self-reconfiguration is possible at machine level using distributed control paradigm.

On the other hand, SMART is a demonstration of the application of adaptive agent control in the transformation of legacy manufacturing system into a RMS. SMART is demonstrated to be capable of addressing the "batch-size-of-one" problem [4].

Both IDEAS and SMART are implemented using distributed control and they both addressed the batch-size-of-one problem, but only based on single unit production. This means the system can only produce one unit at a time. In practice, personalized mass customisation scenarios are more complex. They require multiple products on the shop floor with different designs, styles, shapes and colours going through production process at the same time. IDEAS and SMART failed to demonstrate this type of complexity, which should be obtainable in a typical manufacturing system with capability for personalized mass customisation.

III. SELF- RECONFIGURABLE MANUFACTURING SYSTEM (S-RMS)

Manufacturing systems with capability for personalized mass customisation are characterized by the potential for single-lot-size production [10]. This implies that individual product will require distinct production plan, schedule and process. Concurrent execution of these plans and processes during production suggests that different products will require different resources and routes at same or different time slot, depending on the production stage of the product.

The complexity expressed by this process necessitates the use of distributed coordination mechanism for dynamic and autonomous route selection; resource discovery, selection and negotiation; and scheduling. Therefore, applying the present manufacturing system's design approach that is characterized by stationary machines and rigid conveyor belt with pre-defined route for products will be unfit for this purpose. This is because multiple products will be manufactured concurrently, which are unique with distinct and distributed production plan, schedule, process, resource and route requirement. Therefore, S-RMS is proposed to fill this gap by proffering solution to the batch-size-of-one problem.

S-RMS is a manufacturing concept whereby machines can autonomously move around during production, instead of remaining stationary. In this system, there is no conveyor belts, but instead parts and products are transported using mobile robot referred to as products. The underlying complexity of the proposed production system, which is a characteristic of the distributed and distinct nature of the products and physical mobility of machines, suggest the use of nature inspired approach in the design and implementation of the system.

Nature inspired approach is used in this case because the properties of the problems-space, which is the spatial arrangement of products and resources in the production system change constantly with time. This is as a result of the ability of both the product and resource to move freely without any constraints during production. Also, the process of arriving at optimal production strategy for individual product changes concurrently with the problem-space. This is because the process required by a product to discover the closest resource changes constantly as a result of constant changes in the spatial arrangements of these resources. Therefore, the coordination process has to constantly adapt to the problem dynamics. This suggests that a pure computational approach will be expensive if feasible compare to a heuristic approach proffer by taking inspiration from nature.

Ant colony and flock of birds exhibit one of the closest behaviors to the proposed S-RMS in term of underlying complexity and physical mobility of machines and products. Therefore, inspiration is taken from ants and birds.

In biological systems, such as ant colony and flock of birds, these systems are based on entities that exhibit simple behavior, made up of small set of simple rules, with reduced cognitive abilities, and global system of behavior emerges from a multiplicity and reinforcement of non-linear interactions [12]. In such complex natural systems, coordination emerges without a predicted plan or template, not driven by a central entity or global rules, and only become observable at a macro level when the resultant behavior of the whole are greater and more complex than the sum of the behavior of its part [14]. This makes the application of coordination, self-organization and emergence behavior in biological system to S-RMS for personalized mass customisation a very viable alternative solution to purely computational approach [15].

In some species of ants (social ants), pheromones are used as a coordination mechanism by means of indirect or environmental mediated coordination [13]. Information about food location are embedded in pheromones and when perceived by others, it is interpreted and the result of such interpretation informed the next action to be taking by the perceiving entity. With very limited intelligence, ants are able to effectively coordinate activities regarding foraging and construction. When viewed at a higher level, a well-organized and intelligent social system is perceived. This is purely as a result of indirect or environmental-mediated coordination through the use of pheromones.

On the other hand, some species of birds have to migrate from one region to another in search of food. This instinctive behavior can be viewed as a profit oriented strategy. The birds consumed energy in search or migrating to get food. Therefore, to guarantee survival while searching for food, they must use less energy than they will get from the food. To achieve this, birds have to migrate and stay close to food sources, which lower the cost of foraging in the long term. They also store the locations where foods are available including the time of the year in memory. As food availability changes due to weather conditions, this information is also updated.

S-RMS is modeled as interaction between two distinct entities on the shop floor, which are products and resources (both products and resources are mobile). Products seek resources to execute production task in their production plans just like ants seek for food in their environment. While resources at the same time seek to be close to products just like birds migrate in order to stay close to food source. Resources achieve this by minimizing the average distance between them and corresponding products on the shop floor during production. Applying this model, a natural equilibrium is expected over a period. Natural equilibrium implies a situation where a resource is able to establish a location on the shop floor that is optimal for task execution and the product for plan execution.

A. S-RMS Multi-Agent System (MAS) Interaction

The concept of Multi-Agent System (MAS) is used in the design of S-RMS, where products and resources are both agents operating and interacting on the shop floor. These two agents make different observation about the production environment and therefore have different knowledge and belief about the production environment. The product-agents have knowledge of what to produce, processes required to produce them and type of resources required to carry out such processes. However, individual product-agent has no knowledge of the spatial location of these resources. Instead, product-agents discover resources through interactions with other product-agents and location of resources are communicated using pheromones. This is referred to as indirect or environmental mediated coordination [13].

Resource-agents possess knowledge of what production processes they can execute but have no knowledge of where such production processes are located. Instead, the resource-agents rely on foraging strategy, by following the Circulant Traversal Rule (CTR), which will be explained in later section.

During agent interaction, when a product-agent discovers a resource, it drops pheromones (signals) in the production environment. Other product-agents close-by perceive (sense) these pheromones and if the pheromones lead to a required resource, the perceiving product-agent compute the shortest path to the resource and advance in that direction. If the product-agent is able to execute its plan successfully, it drops more pheromones to intensify the signals as demonstrated in Figure 1(a). The resource-agents on the other hand simultaneously and independently seek to stay close to corresponding product-agents using the CTR.

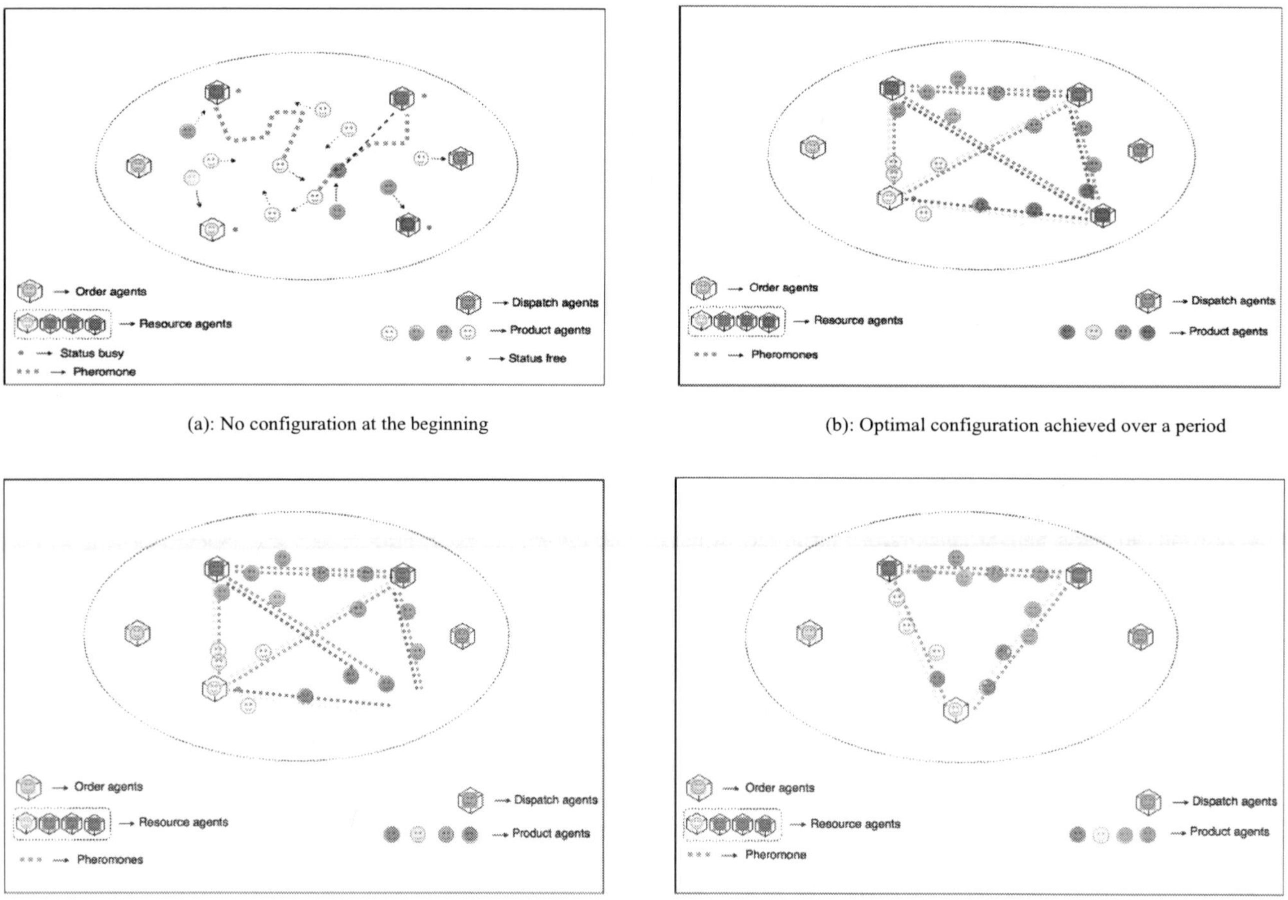

(a): No configuration at the beginning

(b): Optimal configuration achieved over a period

(c): Machine failure during production

(d): Reconfiguration after machine failure

Figure 1: High level observation of S-RMS convergence and reconfiguration after a resource failure

Over a period of interactions, coordination begins to emerge, the system gradually evolve from state of disorder as seen in Figure 1(a), to a state where order is observed as seen in Figure 1(b). Without a physically layout path (conveyor-belt), The system self-organizes itself and form an optimal path for production process using pheromones in the form of virtual marks (virtual conveyor belt) on the shop floor as seen in Figure 1(b). The system is however far from equilibrium as the configuration constantly changes in real time depending on the product mix, resource availability and so on. For example, if a resource suddenly becomes faulty, the system re-configures itself for optimal production from 4 resources as shown in Figure 1(c) to 3 resources as shown in Figure 1(d) without halting production process.

B. *Pheromones For Product Agents in S-RMS*

Applying the concept of pheromone in computational system requires formalization and abstraction of the natural concept into computational concept. To achieve this, we formalize our own concept of pheromones. The following two conditions are necessary for the pheromone properties and behavior in the S-RMS:

C1: Pheromone

$$\forall f_r\ \exists \theta_p \in (R,\theta) : f_r \in F \leftrightarrow \theta_p \in (R,\theta) \qquad \text{(I)}$$

For a particular pheromone fr in all pheromones F in the system leading to a particular Resource R with the capability of executing production plan θ, there exist a production plan θ_p belonging to a product P that is executable by the Resource R, such that f_r will always lead to Resource R. This implies that all pheromones in the system lead to at least one resource, and such resource is capable of executing at least one production plan.

C2: Pheromone decay rate

$$\forall f_r \in F\ \exists\ \delta_{f(t)}: \lim_{\to\infty} \delta_{f(t)} \to \lim_{\to 0} f_r\ , where\ t \in \mathbb{R}^+ \qquad \text{(II)}$$

For a particular pheromone f_r in all pheromones F in the system leading to a particular Resource R, there exist a pheromone decay rate $\delta_{f(t)}$, such that as $\delta_{f(t)}$ increases, the intensity of f_r decreases. This implies that all pheromones in the system have a decay rate, which is inversely proportional to the intensity of the pheromone.

The product-agents use pheromone for resource discovery, that is, to locate resources on the shop floor that is capable of executing their production plan(s) during production. This is achieved by using the pheromone resource discovery algorithm as shown in Figure 2.

PHEROMONE RESOURCE DISCOVERY ALGORITHM (PODUCT-AGENT)

```
Input: product_info, max_x, max_y
Variables: P:Production_Plans; ϕ:shop-floor;
Pa:Product_agent; Pa(x,y):Product_agent_location;
Ra:Resource_agent; Ra(x,y):Required_Resource_agent_loc;
RR:Required_resource; Loc:New_location;
Plan[i]:Production_plans;
Program:
Plans[i] ← create_plans(product_info)
While Pa(x,y) < max (ϕx,y) && i < max Do
  If Pa(x,y) == Ra(x,y);
   Break;
  Else
   Pa → Sense_pheromone (ϕx,y);
   If pheromone → within_range && Leads_to(RR)
      Loc ← shortest_path(Ra(x,y));
      Move_to (Loc);
      Break;
    End if
      Search_for(RR);
     If found(Ra(x,y)) == True && Pa(x,y) == Ra(x,y);
       Break;
     Else
       Continue_search(RR);
     End if
  End if
End While
Execute_plan;
Plan[i] ← Plan[i++];// move to the next plan
End.
```

Figure 2: Algorithm for resource discovery using pheromones

Product-agent P_a generates an array of production plans and corresponding required resources to execute generated plans. It searches for required resources on the shop floor ($\phi_{x,y}$) and if found, it executes production plan and seek resources for the next production plan and leaves pheromones leading to the resource in the environment.

If instead, a pheromone is sensed within the shop floor ($\phi_{x,y}$) while searching for resources and it leads to the location of required resource agent $R_{a(x,y)}$, then P_a computes the shortest path to $R_{a(x,y)}$ and set its destination (Loc) to the location of the resource agent $R_{a(x,y)}$. If the required resource is met at Loc, then P_a executes production plan, seek resources for the next production plan and leaves pheromones leading to the resource in the environment. Else, P_a continues searching for required resource agent. However, if the executed production plan is the last plan to be executed, then P_a ends production and exits system.

C. *Foraging For Resource Agents in S-RMS*

Foraging birds are abstracted as resource-agents. These are resources in the S-RMS for part production. These resource-agents are mobile and use the foraging strategy referred to as CTR for navigation as shown in Figure 3. The CTR provides a heuristic means by which resource-agents are attracted toward areas in the shop floor where there is a higher chance of executing production task. This is achieved computationally by rotating the task execution matrix one element to the right.

The CTR is used for two purposes, first to update spatial location where mobile resource-agents execute production task and secondly, as a tracking mechanism to track locations on the shop floor where chances of order executions are comparatively higher. This rule ensures each resource-agent is positioned close to product-agents with production plans that it can execute. This process is achieved purely by heuristic using the Circulant Traversal Algorithm (CTA) as shown in Figure 4.

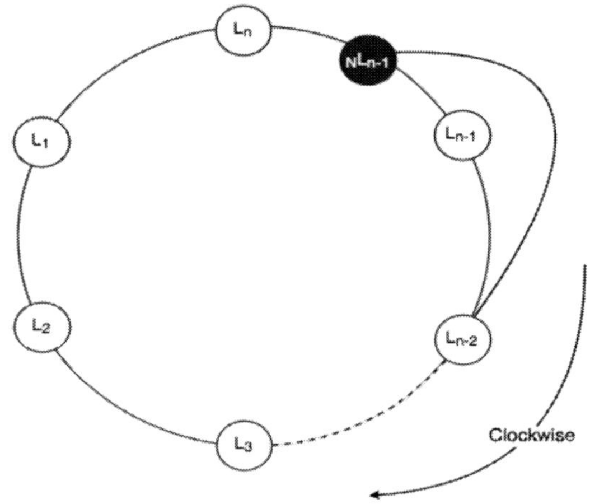

Traversal Rule: If a location **L** *is found between* L_n *and* L_{n-1}, *then set new location as* ${}_{N}L_{n-1}$ *and pop* L_{n-1} *out of memory*

Figure 3: Foraging Strategy: Circulant Traversal Rule

CIRCULANT TRAVERSAL ALGORITHM (RESOURCE AGENT)

```
Input: product_info, max_x, max_y
Variables: P:Production_Plans; ϕ:shop-floor;
Pa:Product_agent; Pa(x,y):Product_agent_location;
Ra:Resource_agent; Ra(x,y):Resource_agent_location;
RSx,y:Resource_agent_saved_location; RR:Required_resource;
Loc:Location; RSx,y[]:Array_of_Previous_locations;
Program:
While Ra(x,y)< max (ϕx,y) Do
 For (i=0, i<= length(RSx,y[]), i++)
  If RSx,y[i]!= NULL && EoF =! True;
    Set Ra(x,y) ← RSx,y[i];
    Move_to_(RSx,y);
     If Pa(x,y) == Ra(x,y)
      Execute_plan;
      Set RSx,y[i] ← RSx,y;
      Set i ← 0
      Repeat;
     Else
     Repeat;
    End if;
  End if;
 End For
Random(i);
Random(j);
Set Ra(x,y) ← Rx+i,y+j
 If Execute_plan == True;
  Set RSx,y[i] ← Rx+i,y+j;
 End if
End while;
End.
```

Figure 4: Algorithm for product discovery using foraging strategy

Resource agent R_a *visits locations stored in memory* `RSx,y[]` *if it is not empty. These locations are previous places where production plans were previously executed. If they do not exist, it creates these locations by first moving randomly and if by chance a plan is executed for a product agent* P_a, *then such location is stored in the memory* `RSx,y[i]` *until the End of File is reached.*

If while attempting to visit these stored locations, it reaches end of file and no production plan is executed, then it generates a random number `i`, `j` *that is added to the present* `x` *and* `y` *coordinates of* R_a *respectively. It sets its next location to* $R_{x+i,y+j}$ *and advances towards this location. This process is repeated until a plan is executed. If a plan is executed this way, the oldest location in memory is replaced with the new location. The resource agent* R_a *defaults back to visiting stored location until End of file is reached before attempting another random movement.*

IV. EXPERIMENTAL EVALUATION

The S-RMS is implemented using agent based simulation software (Netlogo) [16]. Simulation experiment is designed to investigate how changes in product mix, volume and resource unavailability (machine failure) during production process impact the system and its adaptive-behavior.

To evaluate the above, six settings were used. In each setting, maximum numbers of orders that can undergo production process concurrently are kept constant at 50, 100, 150, 200, 250 and 300 respectively. Total number of available product mix is kept constant at 24, and the probability p of a product mix being selected for production is also kept constant for all product mix, $p = \frac{1}{24}$. 30 simulation runs were performed for each of the six settings for 50,000 simulation steps each. At 20,000 simulation steps, a resource failure was introduced and brought back on at 30,000 simulation steps, totaling a period of 10,000 simulation steps. The simulation is allowed to run for an extra 20,000 steps after the resource is brought back. This gives enough time for the system to re-converge.

The following parameters were measured in each of the six settings to investigate how the system adapts to changes in product mix, volume and machine failure during production.

I. **Average lead-time per unit**: This is the average time it takes to manufacture a product, i.e., the average time a product spent in the production system
II. **Production rate:** This is the number of product produced per 1,000 simulation steps during the simulation (a total of 50,000 simulation steps).
III. **Stability:** This is a measure of the system's stability with respect to production input and output. The average distance moved by all resources is measured to quantify stability.

Average lead-time per unit during the simulation is observed to be initially high in all the six settings at approximately 500 simulation steps (see Figure 5(a)). When products and resources start to interact, average lead-time per unit decreases gradually, a sign of system's convergence achieved through the use of pheromone as coordinating mechanism. At 20,000 simulation steps, when resource failure was introduced, lead-time per unit is observed to increase. This is the resultant effect of a machine failure. However, the system re-configures in order to adjust its processes to compensate for the failed resource, which is the rationale behind the continual production process observed in the system, though at a higher lead-time per unit compare to when all resources were present.

Average lead-time per unit is observed to decrease gradually at 30,000 simulation steps when the failed resource was re-introduced into the system. This is as a result of the system's ability to self-reconfigure its resources to integrate the new resource and immediately load-balanced production task. However, the rate of decrease in the lead-time per unit after re-introduction of failed resource (at 30,000 simulation steps) is slower compare to rate of increase when resource failure was initially introduced (at 20,000 simulation steps). This is because the coordination of the process for re-integrating failed resource is achieved through pheromones and thus takes time. On the other hand, introduction of resource failure immediately renders all information embedded in pheromones leading to the failed resource out-dated. Thus, the negative impact immediately propagates through the system, resulting in faster increase in lead-time per unit.

The setting with 50 maximum orders is observed to have the highest average lead-time per unit as a result of fewer product-agents in the system. Product-agents coordinate using pheromones produced by other product-agents. Therefore, the more product-agents that are available in the production environment, the higher the pheromone distribution and intensity, and the more effective the coordination mechanism.

Production rate is observed to increase from zero at about 800 simulation steps into the simulation when the system is observed to move from state of disorder to order (see Figure 5(b)). Production rate decreases between 20,000 and 30,000 simulation steps as a result of resource failure that lead to cascade of changes in the system. Production picks up soon after the failed resource was re-introduced at 30,000 simulation steps. This is because at this point, the system starts to self-reconfigure to accommodate the re-introduced resource and load-balance production task.

Stability of the system is quantified by average distance moved by all resource-agents. The resource-agents are observed to move around more frequently between 20,000 and 30,000 simulation steps when resource failure was introduced. This is to compensate for shortage of resources by moving more frequently to serve more products (see Figure 5(c)). At 30,000 simulation steps, when the failed resource is brought back on, the system is observed to return to its optimal state. This is as a result of the ability of the system to integrate the new resource and immediately load-balanced production task.

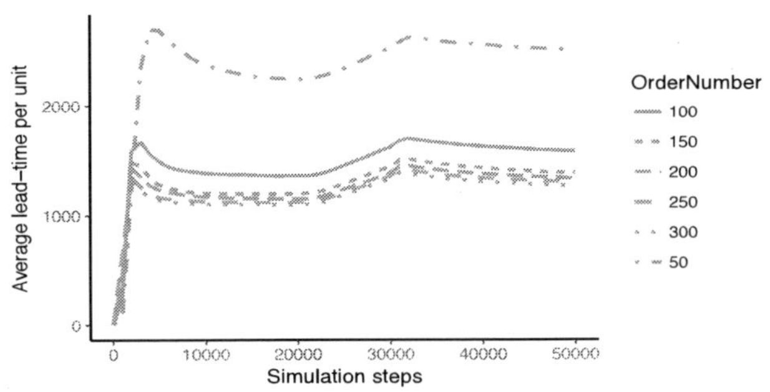

(a): How average lead-time per unit varies during production and resource failure

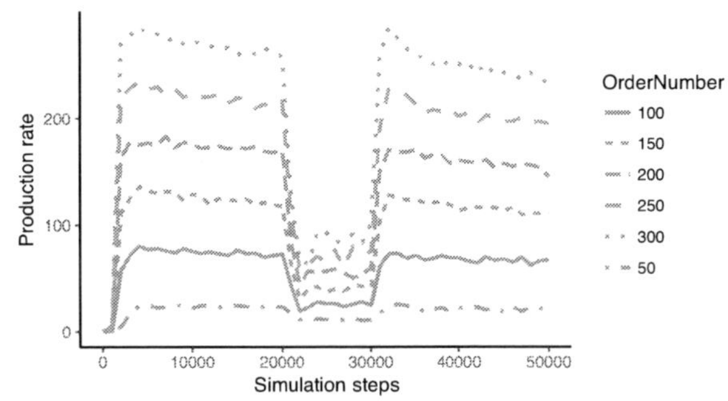

(b): How production rate varies during production and resource failure

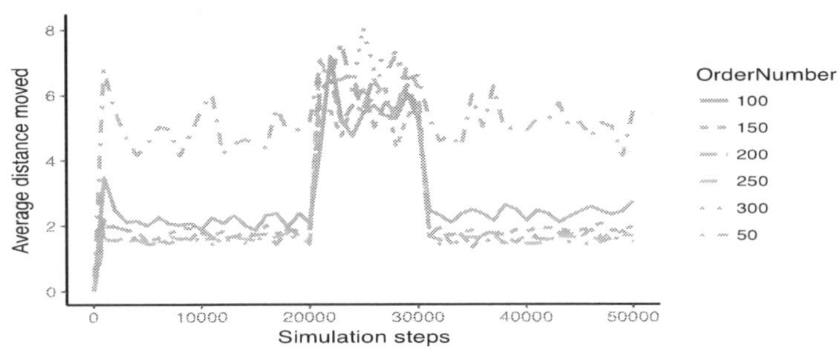

(c): How average distance moved by resource-agent varies during production and resource failure

Figure 5: S-RMS experimental output

V. DISCUSSION AND CONCLUSION

Unexpected changes in the production environment, such as constant changes in product mix, volume and machine failure generate cascades of events that disrupt the system's behavior during production. Such disruptions are recorded in the three observations, which are average lead-time per unit, production rate and stability. The system is observed to be able to keep-up production irrespective of product volume and constantly changing product mix. However, introduction of machine failure disrupts the system, but does not halt production. This shows the adaptive property and self-reconfigurable capability of the proposed S-RMS.

The average lead-time per unit is observed to increase and decrease during and after disruption; this implies that the remaining resources were able to share the task of the failed resource (machine) without halting production. The production rate also decreased and increased during and after disruption instead of production coming to a stop. This implies that the system is capable of re-configuring immediately to compensate for the shortage of resources in the system. The average distance moved by all resource-agents is observed to increase during disruption. This is as a result of three resources executing production task of four resources, therefore requiring resource-agents to cover more distances on the shop floor.

Throughout the simulation, there was no observable instance where production rate equaled zero or resource-agents and product-agents lost coordination, even during unexpected changes in the production environment - like constant changes in product mix and machine failure. This is unlike a typical manufacturing system with reconfigurable capability, where production has to come to a halt for reconfiguration task to be carried out. The result obtained from the demonstration of S-RMS in silico shows that immediate self-reconfiguration of manufacturing system is possible without stopping production process using nature inspired approach. This proven concept will engender a new thinking in the design and implementation of production system with the capability for personalized mass customisation.

A future work for this research will be to compare S-RMS with other implementation of RMS without mobile products and resources, to evaluate efficiency and throughput gain due to product mobility, resource mobility, and self-reconfiguration. Also, the use of nature inspired coordination mechanisms are well known for slow convergence which may impact system performance, hence the use of machine learning algorithm for coordination in S-RMS may be more suitable. Therefore, a comparison of these two approaches based on efficiency and throughput will be explored in future research.

REFERENCES

[1] B. Pine II, Joseph (1993). *Masse Customization - The New Frontier in Business Competition.* Harvard Business School Press. ISBN 0-87584-372-7

[2] S. J. Hu, "Evolving paradigms of manufacturing: From mass production to mass customization and personalization," *Procedia CIRP*, vol. 7, pp. 3–8, 2013.

[3] A. Brusaferri, A. Ballarino, and E. Carpanzano, "Distributed intelligent automation solutions for self-adaptive manufacturing plants," *IFIP Adv. Inf. Commun. Technol.*, vol. 322 AICT, pp. 205–213, 2010.

[4] D. Sanderson, J. C. Chaplin, L. De Silva, P. Holmes, and S. Ratchev, "Smart manufacturing and reconfigurable technologies: Towards an integrated environment for evolvable assembly systems," *Proc. - IEEE 1st Int. Work. Found. Appl. Self-Systems, FAS-W 2016*, pp. 263–264, 2016.

[5] S. Benjaafar, S. Heragu, and S. A. Irani, "Next Generation Challenges Layouts : Factory and Recent Progress," *Interfaces (Providence).*, vol. 32, no. 6, pp. 58–76, 2002.

[6] H. Sarper and T. J. Greene. "Comparison of equivalent pure cellular and functional environments simulation," *International journal of computing, Integrated Manufacturing.*, vol.6, no 4, pp 221-236, 1993

[7] Y. Koren, U. Heisel, F. Jovane, T. Moriwaki, G. Pritschow, G. Ulsoy, and H. Brussel, "Reconfigurable manufacturing systems," *Annals of the CIRP*, vol. 48, pp.527-540, 1999.

[8] A. Koestler, The Ghost in the Machine, Arkana Books, London, 1989.

[9] A. R. Sadik and B. Urban, "A Novel Implementation Approach for Resource Holons in Reconfigurable Product Manufacturing Cell," *Proc. 13th Int. Conf. Informatics Control. Autom. Robot.*, vol. 1, no. Icinco, pp. 130–139, 2016.

[10] M. Onori, N. Lohse, J. Barata, and C. Hanisch, "The IDEAS Project: Plug & Produce at Shop-floor Level," Assembly Automation, vol. 32, no. 2, pp. 124–134, 2012.

[11] M. Onori, D. Semere, and B. Lindberg, "Evolvable Systems: An Approach to Self-X Production," International Journal of Computer Integrated Manufacturing, vol. 24, no. 5, pp. 506–516, 2011.

[12] A. Omicini, "Nature-Inspired Coordination Models: Current Status and Future Trends," ISRN Software Engineering, 2013, pp.1–13.

[13] A. Ricci, A. Omicini, M. Viroli, L. Gardelli, and E. Oliva, "Cognitive stigmergy: Towards a framework based on agents and artifacts," In Weyns, D., Parunak, H. V. D., and Michel, F., editors, Environments for MultiAgent Systems III, volume 4389 of LNAI, pages 124{140. Springer. 3rd International Workshop (E4MAS 2006).

[14] F. Heylighen, "The Science of Self-Organization and Adaptivity," The Encyclopedia of Life Support Systems, vol 5, no 3, pp. 253–280, 2001.

[15] P. Leitão, J, Barbosa, and D. Trentesaux, "Bio-inspired multi-agent systems for reconfigurable manufacturing systems," Engineering Applications of Artificial Intelligence, vol 25, no 5, pp. 934–944, 2012.

[16] U. Wilensky, Center for connected learning and computer-based modeling, Northwestern University, Evanston, IL, 1999, http://ccl.northwestern.edu/ netlogo/ (accessed 08.01.18).

Low Power Tristate Buffer for Mobile Applications

Karol Niewiadomski and Dietmar Tutsch
Chair of Automation and Computer Science - University of Wuppertal
Wuppertal, Germany
Email: {karol.niewiadomski, tutsch}@uni-wuppertal.de

***Abstract*—The adaptiveness of integrated electronics is a key feature in current and future mobile applications. Despite the continuous improvement of battery capacity, reconfiguration capabilities of integrated electronics are an inevitable step to cover the rising demand for processing power. Without any further adjustments for efficiency, power consumption becomes a limiting factor for runtime performance. Field Programmable Gate Arrays (FPGA) provide suitable configuration capabilities, but lack of efficient power saving design measures. To overcome this challenge, different approaches were proposed in recent research activities. A substantial contributor to battery load are General Purpose Input Output (GPIO) circuits, which serve the purpose of connectivity. In this paper, we present a modified tristate buffer, which is a key component in a typical GPIO design. Modifications for active power reduction and standby leakage current suppression are applied at circuit level to achieve a better energy efficiency. This new tristate buffer design is compared to already existing designs.**

***Keywords*–Tristate buffer; GPIO; Power reduction; Leakage suppression; Energy efficiency.**

I. INTRODUCTION

Mobile computing is the driving factor for innovations on the field of instant availability of information. It is expected to have the same computing performance in mobile devices like smartphones, tablets and even sometimes in vehicles, as known from high performance computers in very demandable applications. Vehicles approach a rising degree of functions supporting autonomous driving which require fast evaluation of different driving situations in real time. This comes along with a urgent demand for continuously rising computing power, whilst batteries do not experience comparable proceedings in terms of higher capacities. Field Programmable Gate Arrays (FPGAs) offer vast reconfiguration capabilities way beyond their earlier use case as glue logic [3]. Depending on the size of the FPGA in terms of number of Configurable Logic Blocks (CLBs), different designs can be loaded into the FPGA and therefore synthesized by an intelligent routing of CLBs. However, in most cases implemented designs do not use all resources of reconfigurability, leading to a waste of energy due to leakage currents flowing through blocks in standby mode. Unused blocks inside an integrated circuit, which is intended to be used in mobile applications, should be switched off and only turned on again, if more resources are needed. Different design methodologies can be used on different hierarchical levels to realize a fine-grain and coarse-grain approach for reduction of consumed power. This can be achieved by an efficient combination of design decisions at circuit level, e.g., power gating, clock gating, dynamic voltage scaling, etc [4]. A breakdown of a CLB into its single blocks reveals further possibilities to modify the schematics towards the intended low power purpose, e.g., optimization of configuration random access memory (CRAM) [1] and data flip-flops (D-FFs) [2]. In addition to that, investigations have shown that a noticeable amount of power is dissipated by the General Purpose Input Outputs (GPIOs), which serve as a generic input / output device for integrated circuits [5]. As the number of reconfigurable / adaptive electronics in mobile applications is expected to grow continuously, we beliebe that special attention in terms of improvements or redesign should be allocated to these special circuitry, which can not be neglected for the sake of well interconnectivity in integrated circuits.

In this paper, we investigate a standard tristate buffer design on its most significant characteristics, which are dynamic power consumption, standby leakage current and high Z capabilities. In Section II, we give an overview about related work and key aspects of dependencies between performance and power consumption. In Section III, we introduce a reference design of a tristate buffer and discuss typical characteristics in operation and standy. In Section IV, a newly implemented tristate buffer is presented and its benefits for energy sensitive usage are introduced. In Section V, we compare the simulation results of the different investigated designs. In Section VI, all previous discussions are summarized and concluded.

II. RELATED WORK

GPIOs are used in almost every integrated circuit as an interface to communicate with peripheral circuitry. These elements are designed for receiving data as inputs and to transmit data as output to other connected devices. Therefore tristate buffers are bidirectional circuits with the ability to receive and to transmit logic signals by the same input/output pin. Due to this important functions, GPIO play a major role in consumed area of a chip and power consumption in each complex design [6]. Figure 1 illustrates a simplified block diagram of a FPGA without any additional hard processing cores.

As illustrated in Figure 1, all CLBs of this simplified internal hierarchy are surrounded by GPIO blocks. For the sake of simplicity, all further blocks, e.g., switching matrices, are not displayed there. In complex systems, several FPGAs may drive an internal bus for different purposes, e.g., data exchange, leading to potential conflicts when different circuits try to write different logic values to the same bus line.

Figure 2 highlights the described conflict and depicts a situation, in which two different FPGAs, connected to the same 4 bit data bus, drive the same line with different values: whilst FPGA1 drives one signal line of the bus with a logic 1 or V_{dd}, FPGA2 tries to do same but with a logic 0. The consequence is a floating voltage on the interconnection signal line, which is difficult to predict and an undefined state. For this reason tristate buffers play an important role inside each GPIO, since they offer one special output state beside their functionality to pass a logic value from the input to the output node: $highZ$, also called high impedance. By enabling this state, a tristate

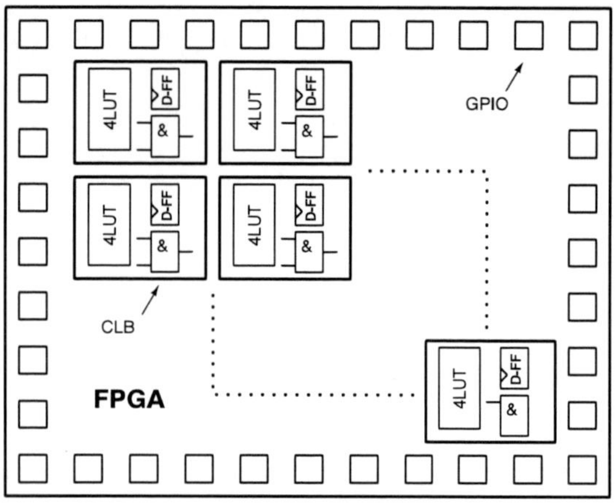

Figure 1. Simplified FPGA structure

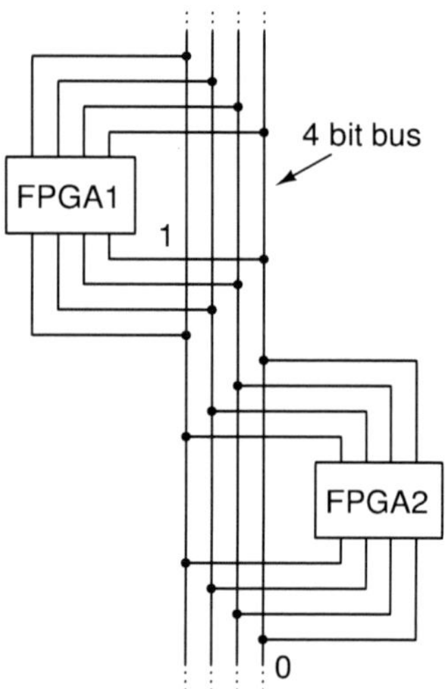

Figure 2. Interconnection bus

buffer cuts off the connection between its input and output node and therefore prevents an undesired throughput from the inputs of the GPIO inside an FPGA to the interconnection bus. So in general, we can identify three aspects to be of relevance for optimization in terms of energy efficiency:

- Subthreshold / standby leakage
- Active power consumption
- $highZ$ behavior

Each of these bullet points has to be adressed by a careful analysis of parameters which are responsible for different behaviour and therefore also different results or performance of the circuit in scope. Subthreshold leakeage current can be characterized by the following equations [7][8]:

$$J_{DT} \propto A\left(\frac{V_{ox}}{T_{ox}}\right)^2 \quad (1)$$

$$I_{leak} \propto \frac{W}{L_{eff}} e^{(V_{GS}-V_{t0}-\gamma V_{SB}+\eta V_{DS})/nV_t}\left(1-e^{-\frac{V_{DS}}{V_t}}\right) \quad (2)$$

Equation (1) explains that a higher oxide thickness T_{ox} will subsequently lead to a lower current density J_{DT}, which is a favored effect for our purposes as we intent to limit undesired current flows as good as possible. On the other hand, (2) highlights the dependency of a subthreshold current I_{leak} to different factors, e.g., the transistor length L_{eff}, the gate-source voltage V_{GS} and the source-body voltage V_{SB}. On the other hand, active power consumption P_{dyn} depends on various factors showed in the following equation:

$$P_{dyn} = \alpha C_{load} V_{dd}^2 f_{Clk} \quad (3)$$

Equation (3) [9] shows that for significant reduction of consumed battery power several factors, e.g., the switching activity α, the load capacitance C_{load}, the supply voltage V_{dd} and the operating frequency f_{Clk} have to be designed in a way to keep P_{dyn} as low as possible. Some factors like C_{load} can not be easily controlled, however other factors can be adapted in a better way directly at circuit level. Last but not least, the $highZ$ attributes of a tristate buffer play an important role due to their ability to decouple this buffer from the remaining signal chain. A careful design of the output transistors inside a tristate buffer offers heavy impact on this ability. Nevertheless it should be stated here, that priority was put on low power characteristics of our newly implemented design. Measurement of the $highZ$ state with different output voltages was done after evaluating power consumption of all investigated designs. Furthermore, all measurements were compared against each other to figure out which design performs best in general.

III. Tristate Buffer Cell Design

The basic purpose of a buffer circuit is to forward the input value with a certain delay to the output node. Some applications might require the addition of a delay time for synchronizing different data paths. The easiest way to understand the basic function of a buffer is to imagine the logic function of two inverter in series. A tristate buffer adds a third, important feature to this functionality: the $highZ$ state. For a better understanding of the circuit's function, a tristate inverter is shown in Figure 3.

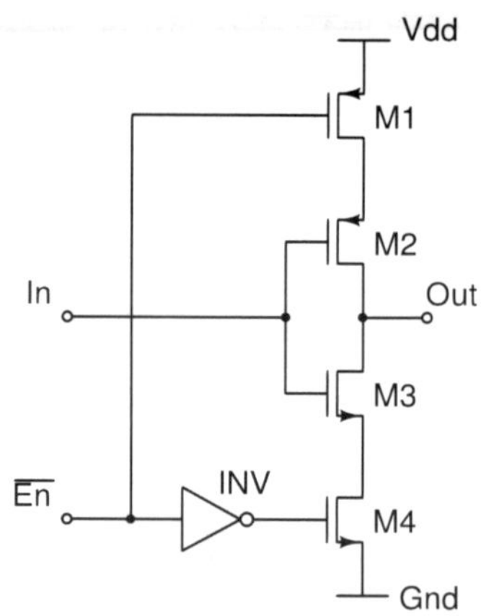

Figure 3. Tristate buffer

As long as $\overline{En}$ provides a logic *LOW* at the respective input node, the transistors *M1* and *M4* are turned on and subsequently provide a direct path to the voltage source V_{dd} and Gnd. As a consequence, the transistors *M2* and *M3* work as an inverter and therefore invert all signals applied to In. On the other hand, if $\overline{En}$ turns to *HIGH*, *M1* and *M4* are turned off and cut-off the internal transistors *M2* and *M3* from the supply voltage and ground path. In this special case, the voltage at the output node *Out* is floating and undefined. This means that in dependence of this floating voltage, only a very small current will flow either as leakage current from the tristate inverter into the circuitry connected to *Out* or from the load into the tristate inverter to Gnd. By adding one additional *nMOS* and *pMOS* transistor, the discussed tristate inverter can be modified to a tristate buffer, which is shown in Figure 4.

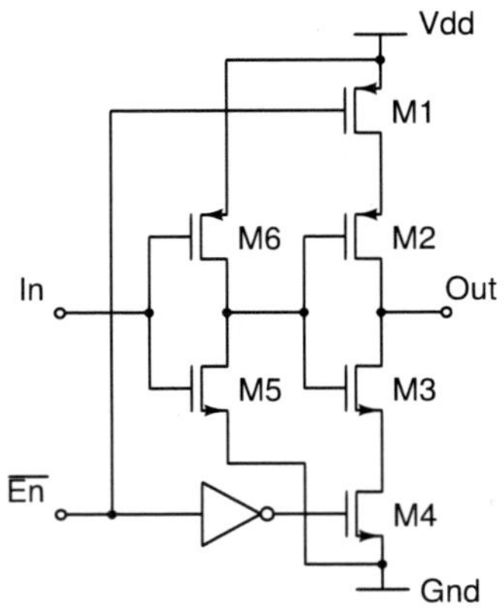

Figure 4. Standard design of a tristate buffer

Different aspects of this tristate buffer's behavior have been investigated during simulations by a $90nm$ TSMC (Taiwan Semiconductor Manufacturing Company) technology and a Cadence toolchain (INCISIVE 6.1.5). All simulations, serving the purpose investigating the circuit's dynamic performance, were done at an operating frequency of $200MHz$ and with standard settings for all transistors' dimensions ($120nm$). Since all analyzed designs are not dynamic logic inheriting a dedicated Clk input, the operating frequency was modulated into the switching events of $\overline{En}$. The results of the first simulation run with active inputs are shown in Figure 5 and also displayed in Table I and Table II . This simulation was followed by further tests for alternative circuit states with the intention to build up a baseline database for further comparisons.

TABLE I. SIMULATION RESULTS (PWR)

Design type	*Average Power nW*	*Max. Power uW*	*Min. Power pW*
Reference	245	56.75	103.8

TABLE II. SIMULATION RESULTS I_{Vdd}

Design type	*Avg. Current nA*	*Max. Current uA*	*Min. Current nA*
Reference	215.2	230.5	261.4

The simulation results display the correct function of this tristate buffer, which directly passes the input value to *Out* whenever $\overline{En}$ is set to *LOW*. Once $\overline{En}$ applies a logic *HIGH* to the cutoff transistors, the voltage level at *Out* starts to float and

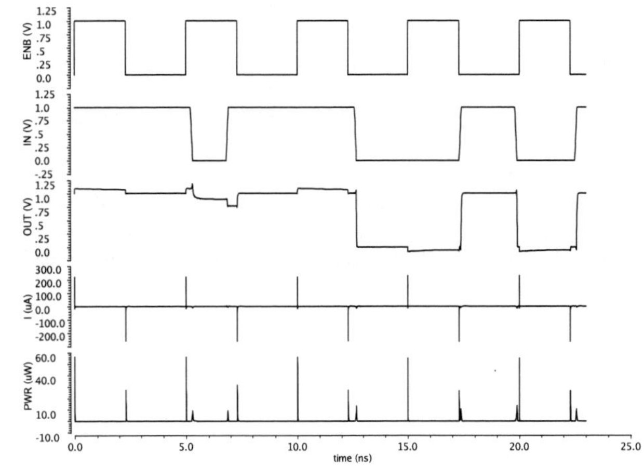

Figure 5. Simulation results of dynamic behavior of a standard tristate buffer

swings between voltage levels above V_{dd} and below $0V$ (Gnd). These floating voltages are not defined and also indicate that the whole circuit is in *highZ* mode. Active power dissipation is of high importance for the estimation of required energy resources, but regardless of these results it is also obligatory to have a closer look on the standby power characteristics when the circuit is lead into an idle phase or put completely into standby mode. This means that the data input is inactive and $\overline{En}$ active. The simulation results are shown in Figure 6.

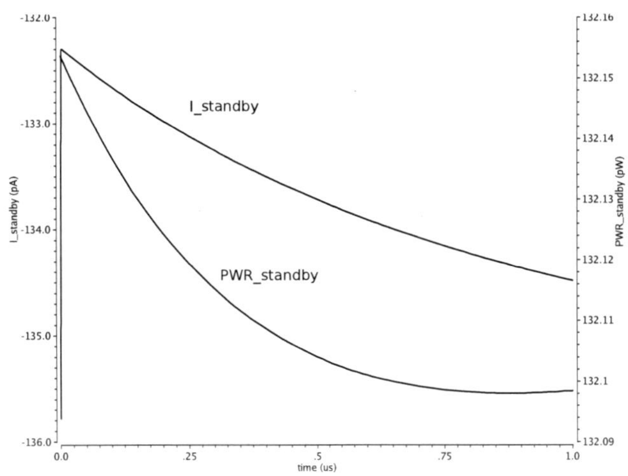

Figure 6. Simulation results of idle standby results

For this analysis and for a better observation of the standby current, the simulation runtime was set to $1\mu s$. The simulation curves of both, standby current and standby power dissipation, show the discharging process of all internal parasitic capacitances after powering on the circuit at the very beginning of the simulation process. Both, standby current and the allocated dissipated power, continuously decrease over time, resulting in an average leakage current I_{leak} of $133.6pA$ and a related average power dissipation of $132.1pW$.

The remaining aspect to be considered at this point is the behavior of the reference tristate buffer in *highZ* mode after setting $\overline{En}$ to *HIGH*. First of all, it should be stated here that there is no unambiguous answer on this question, since this depends on the voltage which will be applied by the load to the output node *Out* of the tristate buffer. In addition to that, there is always a small throughput from the input node on the output in case that the tristate buffer in *highZ* is still stimulated with input date, which might be a realistic situation when the related control logic fails. Thus, two different situations, active and inactive inputs, must be considered. Based on the assumption that the voltage applied to *Out* may vary from $0V$ to$1V$, a dc sweep simulation was done. The results of both test runs are displayed in Figure 7.

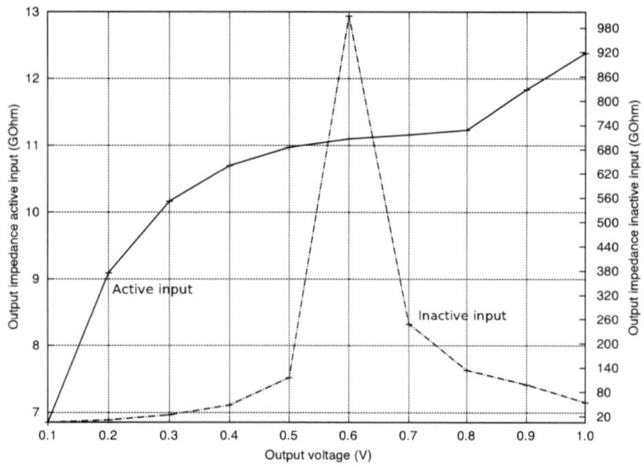

Figure 7. Simulation results of output impedance in *highZ* state

Active input data has a remarkable influence on the circuit's capabilities to decouple its internal switching events to the output node. In case of setting the input node to a $0V$ and therefore making it 'inactive', Figure 7 reveals a sweetspot in terms of output impedance and which is closely allocated to almost $V_{dd}/2$. Having this striking high output impedance ($\approx 1.01T\Omega$) at this voltage range is a desirable situation, since this implements an almost perfect balance between current source and current sink. If input data are applied to *In*, a drop the output impedance can be observed after simulation. Even with turned of decoupling transistors *M1* and *M4*, the throughput originating from the buffer's input is strong enough to lower the impedance at *Out*. Therefore, a stronger decoupling mechanism would probably lead to better results.

IV. MODIFICATIONS

A careful analysis of the reference tristate buffer pointed out that there is still room left for different improvements. Thus, a noticeable adaption of circuits for sensitive low-power application can only be achieved by a synergy of different power savings measures for imaginable operating states.

A. Power Gating

On our way to develop a low-power tristate buffer, the implementation of a *'hold'*-mechanism for standby-phases was an inevitable step. The difficulty here was the fact, that this design does not imply clocked inputs which could have been gated. Instead of this, a more stringent design technique was applied: power-gating. This modification can be applied in different ways, by adding a gating transistor between the supply voltage and the circuit or by inserting a transistor between *Gnd* and all internal nodes. A third alternative comes along with a combination of both design modifications and can be found in Figure 8 (transistors *M5* and *M10*).

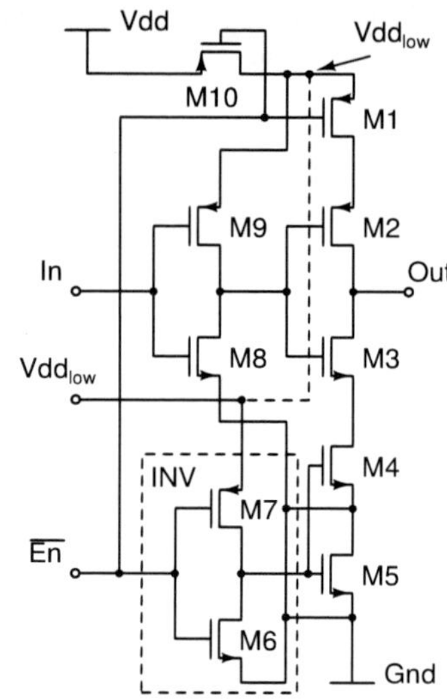

Figure 8. Low-power tristate buffer

The addition of two transistors to a design with a total number of eight transistors before this modification means an increase 20% and a high probability for penalty in terms of area consumption. Regardless of the chosen technology for synthesis and allocated continuous proceedings in technology node shrinking, a higher number of transistors is always considered as a drawback. On the other hand, this modification is responsible for a noteworthy limitation of leakage current running through the design under test (DUT), since we achieve a complete decoupling of the tristate buffer vor V_{dd} and *Gnd* respectively.

B. Leakage Current Reduction

A reasonable extension of power gating is the use of special transistors with a higher oxide thickness T_{ox} which can be also seen in (1), where T_{ox} is in the denominator and therefore has the ability to limit the electrons tunneling through the transistor's gate connector. This results in a reduction of the leakage current in idle / standby state. Despite these benefits it should be mentioned that high T_{ox} transistors have a slower switching frequency than standard T_{ox} do. Hence, adding these transistors should be carefully waived taking a decision upon it. In our case, *M5* and *M10* have an increased T_{ox} than the remaining transistors have for keeping the penalty in performance degradation as low as possible.

C. Subthreshold Current Reduction

Whilst power gating is an effective method for a total shutdown of a circuit, there should be an alternative for measurable reduction of a current flowing through a transistor with an applied gate-source voltage V_{gs} below the threshold. voltage V_{th}. This led to the decision to apply high V_{th} transistors, which have the ability to cut off subthreshold electron tunneling. This method might have a negative impact on the maximum operating frequency and should be carefully applied.

Nevertheless, these special transistors can not be neglected during the design of low power designs. All internal transistors, except the gating transistors, have been replaced by their hight V_{th} counterparts and simulated.

D. Multi Supply Voltage

An operating circuit in low power applications should not only be optimized for static power reduction but also for energy efficiency in active mode. As shown in equation 3, the supply voltage has a vast influence on the overall dissipated power. It's obvious that the best approach would be to decrease the global supply voltage V_{dd}, but might lead to the necessity of additional level restorers for a smooth signal transmission to other circuitry. An alternative is the careful partial supply voltage reduction within a design after analyzing certain parts of a design, which could be powered by a lower V_{dd}. On the other hand, lowering V_{dd} comes along with a slower computation time of the input values, therefore a smaller supply voltage V_{ddlow} was only applied to the internal inverter *M6* and *M7*. In principle, there are two different ways how to generate V_{ddlow}: this can be realized by an external voltage source (illustraed by the additional voltage source V_{ddlow} in Figure 8) or by exploiting internal voltage nodes (illustrated by the dashed line in Figure 8). The second option shows its beauty by an inherent voltage reduction automatism. Once $\overline{En}$ goes *HIGH M10* is turned off and therefore cutting off *M7* from V_{dd}, but keeps the internal inverter still working. Minor adaptions to the width of *M7* have to made due to the decreased internal supply voltage. Nevertheless, both options work well with the low power tristate buffer.

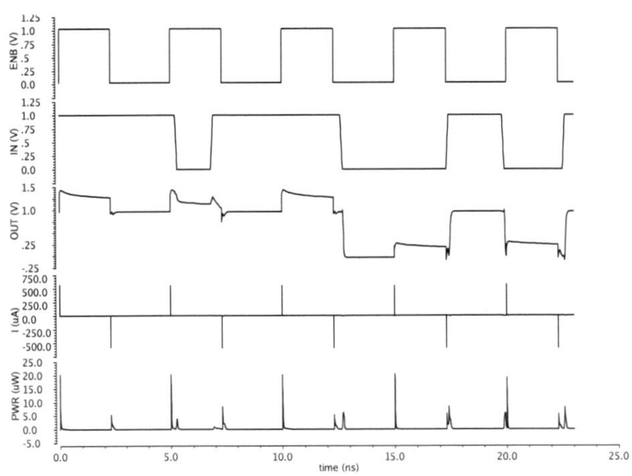

Figure 9. Simulation results of dynamic behavior of the low-power tristate buffer

Figure 9 shows the dynamic behavior of the low power tristate buffer. Compared to the simulation curves shown in Figure 5, it can be seen that the low power tristate buffer is superior in terms of dissipated power during active runtime. The related simulation results are summarized in Table III and Table IV.

Furthermore, an analysis of the standby behavior revealed an improved average leakage current I_{leak} of $24.1pA$ and a related average power dissipation of $22.04pW$. As a final step, the *highZ* characteristic was investigated for having a better comparison to the reference design. The simulation results are displayed in Figure 10.

TABLE III. SIMULATION RESULTS (PWR)

Design type	*Average Power nW*	*Max. Power uW*	*Min. Power pW*
LP tristate	191.3	29.72	22.36

TABLE IV. SIMULATION RESULTS I_{Vdd}

Design type	*Avg. Current nA*	*Max. Current uA*	*Min. Current nA*
LP tristate	225.8	194.8	206.9

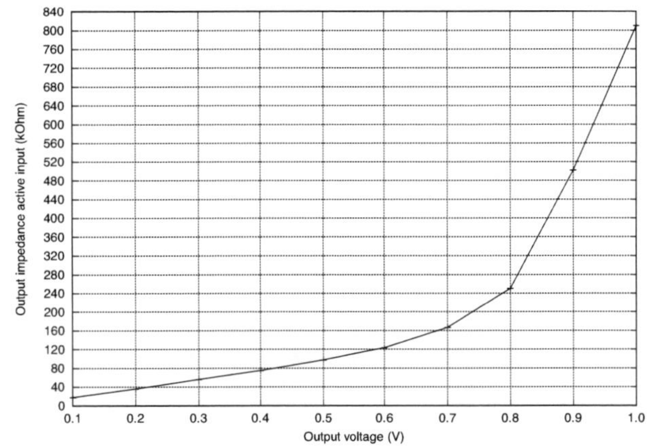

Figure 10. Output impedance in *highZ* state (low power tristate buffer)

In contrast to the reference tristate buffer, the newly implemented tristate buffer shows a different behavior. First of all, the output impedance shows a smaller order of magnitude ($G\Omega \rightarrow k\Omega$) and in addition to this, the output curve strongly depends on the voltage at the output node and reveals a proportional dependency. The higher the voltage at *Out* is, the higher the output impedance will be. Despite the fact that the low power tristate buffer's active *highZ* curve has a smaller order of magnitude, the evaluated results are still acceptable and give an evidence about the appropriateness for the usage as an connecting element in complex designs. These results could be improved by modifying the gate lengths of the output transistors *M2* and *M3*. The downside of this modification would lead to necessary modifications of the manufacturing process, but which can be easily handled by modern technology nodes.

V. RESULTS COMPARISON

For a better comparison of the investigations which have been done, all results were summarized in Table V. The low power tristate buffer outperforms in almost each aspect the reference design, which highlights its appropriateness for use in applications with limited energy resources. Results of dynamic behavior show that power dissipation is reduced significantly, no matter whether the average, maximum or minimum power consumption is in focus of discussion. The most remarkable reduction is allocated to static behavior of both circuits. Here, the standby leakage current and the dissipated power in idle mode are lowered by over 80%, which emphasizes the effect of implemented low power measures.

TABLE V. SIMULATION RESULTS I_{Vdd}

Design type	*Reference buffer*	*Low power buffer*	$\Delta\%$
Av. PWR (nW)	245	191.3	22 ↓
Max. PWR (uW)	56.75	29.72	47.63 ↓
Min. PWR (pW)	103.8	22.36	78.46 ↓
Av. Current (nA)	215.2	225.8	5 ↑
Max. Current (uA)	230.5	194.8	15.49 ↓
Av. Leak. Current (pA)	133.6	24.1	82 ↓
Av. Standby PWR (pW)	132.1	22.04	83.32 ↓
highZ max.	12.38 $G\Omega$	81 $G\Omega$	↑↑
highZ min.	6.85 $G\Omega$	18 $k\Omega$	↑↑

The appropriate choice of process technology due to the multi-oxide requirements as well as careful layout of transistor parameters requires special attention and allows additional improvements. However, the low power tristate buffer delivers remarkable out of the box performance without further detailed optimization. These adaptions are achieved with a small penalty in terms of transistor count and area. Xilinx provides 372 *Maximum User I/O* and 165 *Maximum Differential I/O Pairs* [6], which could be realized in 537 GPIOs. Implementing a new FPGA design by usage of the low power tristate buffer requires 1074 additional transistors. Here it comes to the point where an efficient layout of the overall chip could be a measures to catch up this drawback. In addition to that, the achieved minimum *highZ* state of the new design of about $14k\Omega$ does not perform as good as the result of the reference tristate buffer ($6.85G\Omega$). This could be improved by a further optimization of the transistor parameters in terms of length and width. However, this might lead to a higher energy consumption and should be carefully decided case by case, depending on which characteristic is of higher importance for the respective application. Despite the additional parasitic capacitances which come along by adding transistors, nearly all measured insights does not weaken the positive overall print.

VI. CONCLUSION

We analyzed an existing design of a tristate buffer, which was baselined as a reference design serving for further comparisons. During the analysis we did a deep dive into the characteristics of this design for the evaluation of its active and standby performance in terms of dissipated power, average current consumption and the special ability to enter a *highZ* mode. The outcome of these activities was that we wanted to develop a tristate buffer which is superior in terms of energy savings during runtime and idle state. Due to the lack of a clock signal and therefore the impossibility to apply clock gating, we implemented power gating by choosing special high T_{ox} transistors. These transistors have the ability to decouple the tristate buffer from V_{dd} and *Gnd* as well as the function of gate tunneling mitigation. For subthreshold current reduction we decided to use high V_{th} transistors, being aware of accepting a penalty in the maximum operating frequency, which was not in the focus of our work though. Simulations have shown that the low power tristate buffer delivers outstanding performance in terms of, e.g., average power consumption in active mode, which is decreased by 22% compared to the reference design. This is a noticeable improvement, since it shrinks the losses of energy in active mode of almost a quarter compared to the reference design. In standby mode, our design outperforms the legacy design by 82% related to average I_{leak}, which is a remarkable result. This low power design features the ability to provide the generation of an internal, smaller supply voltage without any extra *enable* signal from external circuitry. The *highZ* mode abilities of the legacy design are better by a higher order of magnitude, nevertheless we consider the achieved results of the new tristate buffer as acceptable. These results come at the cost of a higher transistor count and an additional input for an internal, decreased supply voltage I_{Vddlow} as an option. Several possibilities exist for future investigations and improvements. A very simple but effective method for achieving remarkable power savings would be the choice of a technology library with shorter channel lengths, e.g., $28nm$. A technology shrink usually leads to a measurable reduction of consumed power, however, this comes along with some drawbacks like the short-channel effect. Applying negative V_{GS} voltages is an effective way to suppress subthreshold leakage currents after turning a transistor off. Of course, this requires auxiliary logic for generation of negative V_{GS} gate voltages, but this should be a small amount of additional transistors. Further supporting measures can be applied at a higher hierarchical layer, e.g., at architectural level. Controlled dynamic voltage scaling offers the potential to drive the whole. circuit into a deep sleep mode if a standby mode is not crucial for operation of the whole logic. These suggested measures will be starting points for further elaboration of enhanced energy balance with strong focus on a extended battery lifetime in mobile applications.

ACKNOWLEDGMENT

The authors thank Pierre Mayr, from Ruhr University of Bochum, for giving advice on the aspects of correct signal transmission for bus architectures. We are grateful to Andreas Ullrich, from University of Wuppertal, for his continuous support in tool maintenance.

REFERENCES

[1] K. Niewiadomski, C. Gremzow, and D. Tutsch, "4t loadless srams for low power fpga lut optimization," in Proceedings of the 9th International Conference on Adaptive and Self-Adaptive Systems and Applications (ADAPTIVE 2017), February 2017, pp. 1–7.

[2] K. Niewiadomski and D. Tutsch, "Low power charge recycling d-ff," in The Tenth International Conference on Advances in Circuits, Electronics and Micro-electronics (CENICS 2017), September 2017, pp. 1–6.

[3] C. Maxfield, The Design Warrior's Guide to FPGAs: Devices, Tools and Flows, 1st ed. Newton, MA, USA: Newnes, 2004.

[4] J. M. Rabaey, A. Chandrakasan, and B. Nikolic, Digital integrated circuits- A design perspective, 2nd ed. Prentice Hall, 2004.

[5] T. Tuan, S. Kao, A. Rahman, S. Das, and S. Trimberger, "A 90nm low-power fpga for battery-powered applications," in Proceedings of the 2006 ACM/SIGDA 14th international symposium on Field programmable gate arrays. ACM, 2006, pp. 3–11.

[6] XA Spartan-3A Automotive FPGA Family Data Sheet, Xilinx, 04 2011, rev. 2.0.

[7] C. Piguet, Low-power processors and systems on chips. CRC Press, 2005.

[8] C. Piguet, J.-M. Masgonty, V. von Kaenel, and T. Schneider, "Logic design for low-voltage/low-power cmos circuits," in Proceedings of the 1995 International Symposium on Low Power Design, ser. ISLPED '95. New York, NY, USA: ACM, 1995, pp. 117–122. [Online]. Available: http://doi.acm.org/10.1145/224081.224102

[9] A. Bellaouar and M. I. Elmasry, Low-Power Digital VLSI Design Circuits and Systems, 1st ed., J. Allen, Ed. Norwell, MA, USA: Kluwer Academic Publishers, 1995.

Adaptive Petri Nets – A Petri Net Extension for Reconfigurable Structures

Carl Mai, René Schöne, Johannes Mey, Thomas Kühn and Uwe Aßmann

Technische Universität Dresden
Dresden, Germany
Email: {carl.mai, rene.schoene, johannes.mey, thomas.kuehn3, uwe.assmann} @tu-dresden.de

***Abstract*—Petri nets are used to formally model the behavior of systems. However, when these systems dynamically change, e.g., due to context dependence, modeling gets complex and cumbersome since Petri nets are low-level and can not express dynamic changing parts. Expressing dynamically changing parts of the system directly within Petri nets increases the clarity and allows for modeling complex, context dependent, systems. While various approaches can be found in the literature, their integration into the Petri net ecosystem is often not considered. This restricts the available tools and analysis techniques to those, which can handle that custom net type. We present adaptive Petri nets, an extension to Petri nets, which directly expresses variability within the net. Our approach integrates well with other Petri net extensions, such as colored tokens, inhibitor arcs or hierarchy. Most importantly, it is possible to convert an adaptive Petri net to a semantically equivalent Petri net with inhibitor arcs. This work presents the formalism of adaptive Petri nets, how they can be flattened to Petri nets with inhibitor arcs and their graphical representation. The feasability and usability is demonstrated on two examples that are modeled, flattened and analyzed.**

Keywords–Petri nets; Reconfigurable Petri nets; Inhibitor Arcs; Analysis

I. INTRODUCTION

Petri nets are a mathematical modeling technique used in many areas. Their strengths are especially in modeling concurrent, asynchronous, distributed, parallel, or nondeterministic systems [1]. Based on a mathematical model, they can be analyzed for various properties, such as deadlocks, reachability, or boundedness [2]. While the graphical notation of Petri nets reduces the learning curve and improves communication in teams. In general, Petri nets tend to get large, making it difficult to work on them. Various syntactic additions exist to improve readability and their expressiveness, while still allowing to flatten the net into a semantically equivalent Petri net without these additions. Examples are hierarchical structuring [3], composition [4], or colored tokens [5].

Our approach, adaptive Petri nets, is a Petri net extension allowing a net designer to model structures, which change at runtime. These nets are reconfigured by configuration places that enable or disable parts of the net. Consequently, the net designer can express his/her intentions directly. Additionally, it might open the door for analysis techniques, which utilize the added semantic information.

The paper is structured as follows. In Section II, the related work is reviewed. Next, in Section III-A the formal models of Petri nets and Petri nets with inhibitor arcs are introduced. Two examples from the literature motivate the need for adaptive Petri nets in Section IV. Section V explains the concept of adaptive Petri nets together with a formal semantic and graphical syntax. An algorithm for flattening will show how adaptive nets can be reduced to Petri nets with inhibitor arcs. After that, the two examples from Section IV are reimplemented with our notation. Here, we show that the Petri net analyzers LoLa [2] and Tina [6] can analyze the flattened version of adaptive nets.

II. RELATED WORK

Reconfigurable Petri nets can be seen as composition at runtime. In [4], this is called dynamic composition and is characterized as "*rare*", because it "*radically changes the Petri net semantics* and *complicates the available analysis techniques*". Regardless, several approaches to implement *dynamic composition* exist.

Object Petri nets [7] are Petri nets with special tokens. A token can be a Petri net itself and therefore nets can be moved inside a main net. This type of net can be used for modeling multiple agents, which move through a net representing locations. The agents change their internal state and have different interactions based on the location inside the net. This approach extends the graphical notation of Petri nets. Analysis of object Petri nets is possible with the model checker Maude [8] and by conversion to Prolog. It was not shown that object Petri nets can be flattened to standard Petri nets though.

Reconfiguration with graph-based approaches is a topic of Padberg's group. They developed the tool **ReConNet** [9], [10] to model and simulate reconfigurable Petri nets. A reconfiguration is described as pattern matching and replacement that are evaluated at runtime. This notation is generic and powerful, but can not be represented in the standard notation of Petri nets. It was also not a goal to flatten them into standard Petri nets. Verification is possible with Maude.

Another graph-based reconfiguration mechanism is **net rewriting systems** (NRS) [11]. The reconfiguration happens in terms of pattern matching and replacements with dynamic composition. The expressive power was shown to be Turing-equivalent by implementation of a Turing machine. Additionally, an algorithm for flattening to standard Petri nets was provided for a subset of net rewriting systems called reconfigurable nets. This subset constrains NRS, to only those transformations, which leave the amount of places and transitions unchanged, i.e., only the flow relation can be changed. Flattening increases the size of transitions significantly, i.e., by the amount of transitions multiplied by the number of reconfigurations. With **improved net rewriting systems** [12], the NRS were applied in logic controllers. The improved version of NRS constrains the rewrite rules to not invalidate important structural properties, such as liveness, reversibility, and boundedness.

Self-modifying nets [13] were already introduced in 1978 to permit reconfiguration at runtime. Arcs between places and transitions are annotated with a weight specifying the amount of tokens required inside the place until the transition becomes enabled. To achive reconfiguration, these weights are made dynamic by linking them to a place. The number of the weight is then determined by the amount of tokens inside this referenced place. This mechanism allows the enabling and disabling of arcs and therefore can change the control flow at runtime. However, the authors state that reachability is not decidable [13].

Guan et al. [14] proposed a dynamic Petri net, which creates new structures when firing transitions. The net is divided in a control and a presentation net. The control net changes the structure of the presentation net by annotations on its nodes. Verification and reducibility were explicitly excluded by the authors.

A practical example was shown in **Bukowiec et al.** [15], who modeled a dynamic Petri net, which could exchange parts of the net based on configuration signals. Defining reconfigurable parts was done with a formalism of hierarchical Petri nets. The dynamic parts of the nets were modeled with subnets to generate code for a partially reconfigurable Field Programmabe Gate Array (FPGA). Since this work was of more practical nature, the reconfiguration and transformation was not formalized. Although, it was shown by Padberg et al. [9] that this kind of net can be transformed into a representation, which can be verified using Maude.

Dynamic Feature Petri nets (DFPN) [16] support runtime reconfiguration by annotating the Petri net elements with propositional formulas. These elements are then enabled or disabled based on the evaluation of these formulas at runtime. The formulas contain boolean variables, which can be set dynamically from transitions of the net or statically during initialization. Their model extends the graphical notation with textual annotations. It was shown that they can be flattened to standard Petri nets [17]. Compared to adaptive Petri nets, this type of net is problem specific and has the limitation of indirection by boolean formulas. A boolean formula can not express numbers easily, only by encoding them in multiple boolean variables. In DFPN the net is modified by firing transitions, while in adaptive Petri nets the net is modified by the amount of tokens inside a place.

With **Context-adaptive Petri nets** [18], ontologies were combined with Petri nets to model context dependent behavior in Petri nets. These nets are included in an existing Petri net editor. By this, context-adaptive Petri nets support modeling, simulation and analysis. It was not detailed how the analysis is implemented, therefore scalability is unclear. Additionally, the flattening of these nets is not supported.

Hybrid Adaptive Petri Nets [19] are a Petri net extension coming from the field of biology. These nets extend non-standard Petri nets with a special firing semantic. A transition can fire discrete, which will consume and produce a single token and then wait a specified delay for the next firing. In continuous mode a transition will not have a delay. This Petri net is adaptive by switching between those two modes. Compared to our work this is out of scope since non-standard Petri nets are used and adaptivity is restricted to transitions only.

We found that most of the existing work lacks a good integration in the Petri net ecosystem. The reconfiguration is either written as graph rewrite rules or external descriptions, which fit Petri nets more from a theoretical point of view but not for modelling. Flattening these nets to a lower level Petri net is often not the goal of the approaches, hence existing Petri net tools can not be used, e.g., for efficient model checking or code generation.

III. PRELIMINARIES

In this section, definitions and notations are introduced, which are used throughout the paper.

A. Petri Net Definitions

This section recalls the definition of Petri nets and establishes the notation.

Definition 1: A **Petri net** [1] is a directed, bipartite graph and can be defined as a tuple $\Sigma = (P, T, F, W, M_0)$. The two sets of nodes are P for places and T for transitions, where $P \cap T = \emptyset$ and $P \cup T \neq \emptyset$. F is a set of arcs, describing the flow relation with $F \subseteq (P \times T) \cup (T \times P)$. $W : F \to \mathbb{N}$ is a weight function. $M_0 : P \to \mathbb{N}$ is the start marking.

Referencing a tuple element is done in dot notation: for a Petri net Σ, we reference the places P by $\Sigma.P$.

Definition 2: For an element $x \in P \cup T$, $\bullet x = \{y|(y,x) \in F\}$ and $x\bullet = \{y|(x,y) \in F\}$.

For example, $t\bullet$ with $t \in T$ refers to the set of places, which are connected with an arc originating from t. We call those preset and postset, respectively.

Definition 3: A **marking** is defined as a function $M : P \to \mathbb{N}$.

Definition 4: A transition $t \in T$ is **enabled** if all places $p \in \bullet t$ have a marking of at least $W(p,t)$ tokens, where $W(p,t)$ is the weight for the arc between p and t.

Definition 5: Iff a transition t is enabled, it can **fire** and the marking of each $p \in t\bullet$ is incremented by $W(t,p)$ and the marking of each $p \in \bullet t$ is decremented by $W(p,t)$.

Definition 6: If there exists a $k \in \mathbb{N}$ for a $p \in P$ such that, starting from an initial marking, every reachable marking $M(p) \leq k$, we speak of p as **k-bounded**. This place never contains more than k tokens. If k equals 1, this place is called **safe**.

B. Inhibitor Arcs

Inhibitor arcs extend the flow relation in Petri nets by an arc, which will disable a transition when the connected place has a specified amount of tokens in it. A Petri net with inhibitor arcs is more expressive than a normal Petri net. For example, a Petri net with inhibitor arcs can implement a Turing machine [20], while this is not possible with standard Petri nets. This affects the available tools for model checking, for example, the halting problem can not be solved in general for Turing-complete languages.

Definition 7: The set of **inhibitor arcs** $I \subseteq (P \times T)$ is added to Def. 1. An **Inhibitor Petri net** is a tuple

$\Sigma = (P, T, F, I, W, M_0)$. $P \cap T = \emptyset$ and $P \cup T \neq \emptyset$. $F \subseteq (P \times T) \cup (T \times P)$, $I \subseteq (P \times T)$. $W : (F \cup I) \to \mathbb{N}$, $M_0 : P \to \mathbb{N}$.

Definition 8: The weight W is extended to also include the inhibitor arcs $W : (F \cup I) \to \mathbb{N}$.

To simplify notation we define the inhibiting set of a transition t as $\circ t = \{p \in P | (p, t) \in I\}$.

Definition 9: A transition t is **enabled**$_i$, iff all places connected by an inhibitor arc are below the weight $M(p) < W(p, t)$ for all $p \in \circ t$ and the transition is enabled as defined in Def. 4.

C. Graphical Notation

Places are drawn as circles: ◯, their marking is drawn as black dots ⊙. Transitions are drawn as black rectangles (horizontal or vertical) ❙. The flow relation is drawn with directed arcs between places and transitions ⟶. Inhibitor arcs are only drawn from places to transitions and get a circle head: —○.

IV. Motivating Examples

This section will show examples from the literature to both motivate the need for reconfiguration inside Petri nets and use them to demonstrate adaptive Petri nets in Section VI. The first example shows an informal reconfiguration model of a controller [15] and the second example is a coffee machine implemented with Dynamic Feature Nets [16].

A. Dynamic Control Structures

Control structures for circuits are typically modeled with finite state machines. However, if parallelism or asynchronism is needed, Petri nets are employed [21], [22]. The modeled Petri net gets converted into a hardware description language to load it onto an FPGA. To support modern FPGA with partial dynamic reconfiguration, in which parts of the FPGA can be reconfigured at runtime, the Petri net should support reconfiguration at runtime, too. This is not directly possible with standard Petri nets but requires a reconfigurable addition.

In [15], a proposal was made to model the reconfiguration by two subnets (pages), which are exchanged based on an incoming signal. Their use case is a cement mixing machine, which can be configured with and without a water heating element. The type of Petri net they use is called control interpreted Petri net. These nets are specifically made for use in electronic circuits, so that they can send and receive signals, modeled in terms of variables. Each transition is annotated with a variable, which inhibits the firing until its value becomes true. A place can be annotated by a name, representing a variable, which will be set to true when the place contains a token. The net is compiled into a hardware description language that can be used to synthesize the circuit on the FPGA. An example for control interpreted Petri nets is shown in Figure 1b: the place *P9* enables the output signal *YV2*, if it contains a token, the transition *t9* fires only, if the input signal *XF2* is active and a token is inside *P9*.

We depict the example from the paper of Bukowiec et al. [15] here to show how their reconfigurable Petri nets are implemented. In their work, a cement mixing machine was modeled with a Petri net. Each transition will trigger valves or motors to support the cement mixing. The exact working is irrelevant here, except that the cement can be mixed with

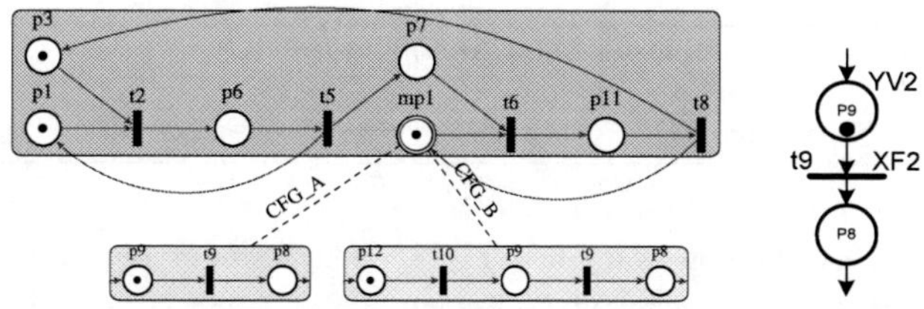

(a) Simplified net of Bukowiec (without annotations, added CFG_* arcs)

(b) Control Interpreted Petri net

Figure 1. Dynamic control structures from [15]

either heated or cold water. These two features are mutually exclusive and should replace the corresponding logic on the FPGA by partial dynamic reconfiguration. A simplified version of the Petri net for the cement mixing machine can be seen in Figure 1a. As simplification the annotations and non-branching structures were removed. This was only done for readability. The pages of Figure 1a are chosen by configuration signals *CFG_A* and *CFG_B*. *CFG_A* enables the default behavior of the water element, while *CFG_B* is the behavior of the water heater. The configuration signals can be found in Figure 1a, while in the original paper, they were part of the informal description. The *CFG*-signals are either sent by an algorithm of the controler or comes from the manual input of a human supervisor.

The resulting net was synthesized to an FPGA specification with a reserved reconfigurable area, in which the pages corresponding to *CFG_A* and *CFG_B* are synthesized.

B. Dynamic Features

Product line engineering is an important topic in software development. A software product line (SPL) is a collection of software systems with a shared set of assets. Typically, there exists a core component in a product line, which gets enriched by various features. These features can be either applied at compile time (static) or at runtime (dynamic). Modeling an SPL with a Petri net requires representing the core and its features, so that they can be enabled or disabled based on the configuration.

In [23], (dynamic) Feature Oriented Petri nets (FOP) were proposed to model an SPL with Petri nets. The activation of a feature is encoded as a boolean variable. The nodes and arcs in the Petri net are annotated by logical formulas containing the feature variables. If the formula evaluates to *false*, the node or arc is temporarily removed from the net until the formula evaluates to *true* again. For static features the variable assignment comes from the outside and does not change while the Petri net gets executed. Therefore, all formulas with static features can be evaluated at first. To model dynamic features, a transition can be annotated by assignments to feature variables. For that, the annotation is split into a formula and an assignment part, illustrated in Listing 1. This transition fires only if the feature *Milk* is deactivated and *Coffee* activated. When the transition fires, it enables the feature *Milk*. This transition is then temporarily removed from the net, as its formula no longer evaluates to true.

Listing 1 Example Formula Annotation

1: $\frac{\texttt{¬Milk∧Coffee}}{\texttt{Milk On}}$

The running example for [23] is a configurable coffee machine, showcased in Figure 2. This net models a coffee machine, which can get a milk module added at runtime. Adding the milk module is done as a dynamic feature inside the net and triggered by the *connect* and *disconnect* transitions.

V. Concept of Adaptive Petri Nets

With adaptive Petri nets, we propose a concept, which supports a Petri net developer to enable and disable a subset of nodes based on the amount of tokens in a set of places. Ultimately, our goal is to support the development of Petri nets with dynamic changing behavior while still supporting the flattening to inhibitor Petri nets to allow the use of standard Petri net tools.

An adaptive Petri net extends the Petri net definition by a set of configuration points $C = \{c_1, c_2, \ldots\}$. A configuration point will enable or disable parts of a Petri net Σ.

Definition 10: An **adaptive Petri net** is a tuple $\Sigma = (P, T, F, W, M_0, C)$, based on Petri nets of Def. 1, with $C = \{c_1, c_2, \ldots\}$ as the set of configuration points.

Definition 11: A **configuration point** is a tuple $c = (p, w, N)$ referencing the nodes of a containing Petri net Σ.

- $p \in \Sigma.P$, a place that we will call *configuration place*.
- $w : \mathbb{Z} \setminus \{0\}$, a weight
- $N \subseteq (\Sigma.P \cup \Sigma.T)$, the nodes that are configured

Definition 12: The set of **external nodes** ($E \subseteq N$) are nodes of N which are connected to nodes outside of N. $E = \{x | x \in N \wedge (\exists y \in ((P \cup T) \setminus N)(\{(x,y),(y,x)\} \cap F \neq \emptyset)\}$

Definition 13: The set of **internal nodes** for a configuration point is calculated by $I = N \setminus E$.

An example for an adaptive Petri net can be seen in Figure 3. The configuration points are $c_1 = (pc1, 1, \{p1, t1, p2, t3\})$ and $c_2 = (pc2, 1, \{p1, t2, p3, t4\})$. The set of externel nodes for c_1 is $c_1.E = \{p_1, t_3\}$, while the set of internal nodes is $c_1.I = \{t_1, p_2\}$.

Definition 14: A configuration point $c \in C$ is **enabled**, iff $(c.w > 0 \wedge M(c.p) \geq c.w) \vee (c.w < 0 \wedge M(c.p) < |c.w|)$. With *M* being the marking function of Def. 3. As a shorthand we will refer to the set of enabled configuration points as $C_e \subseteq C$.

An enabled adaptive Petri net will not change the behavior of the net, while a disabled adaptive Petri net stops the flow of tokens from E to N. This changes the firing definition of Def. 5 and the enabling definition of Def. 4. This is defined in Defs. 17 and 18.

We want to navigate from a place or transition to all configuration points, which are containing this node. For this we define the following functions.

Definition 15:
- The set of configuration points a node belongs to is defined by the function $B^N : (P \cup T) \rightarrow \mathbb{P}(C)$ with $B^N(n) = \{c | c \in C \wedge n \in c.N\}$.
- The set of configuration points, in which a node is external, is defined by the function: $B^E : (P \cup T) \rightarrow \mathbb{P}(C)$ with $B^E(n) = \{c | c \in C \wedge n \in c.E\}$.
- The set of configuration points, in which a node is internal, is defined by the function: $B^I : (P \cup T) \rightarrow \mathbb{P}(C)$ with $B^I(n) = \{c | c \in C \wedge n \in c.I\}$.

Definition 16: The *configured postset* and *configured preset* of a transition t is defined as $t\bullet_c = t\bullet \setminus \{p | c \in (B^E(t) \setminus C_e) \wedge p \in c.N\}$ and $\bullet_c t = \bullet t \setminus \{p | c \in (B^E(t) \setminus C_e) \wedge p \in c.E\}$, respectively.

Definition 17: Iff a transition t with $B^E(t) \neq \emptyset$ is enabled, it can **fire**$_a$ and the marking of each $p \in t\bullet_c$ is incremented by $W(t,p)$ and the marking of each $p \in \bullet_c t$ is decremented by $W(p,t)$. The fire semantics of all other transitions follows Def. 5.

Definition 18: A transition $t \in T$ is **enabled**$_a$, iff it is enabled according to Def. 4 and the following condition holds true $\{p | p \in \bullet t \wedge p \in c.E;\ \forall c \in (B^I(t) \setminus C_e)\} = \emptyset$.

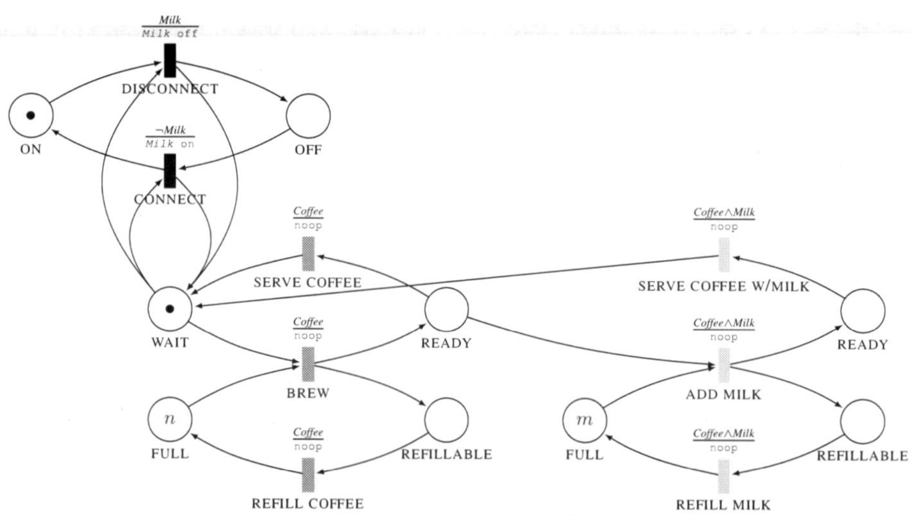

Figure 2. Dynamic Feature Petri net from [16]

Figure 4: DFPN (initial state) of a dynamically reconfigurable product line. Whenever transition DISCONNECT fires, feature *Milk* is switched off, disabling all transitions that are conditioned on *Milk*. It is enabled again by firing CONNECT.

Algorithm 1 Flattening of an Adaptive Petri net

1: **procedure** FLATTEN((P, T, F, W, M, C, I))
2: **for** $\forall c \in C$ **do**
3: **for** $\forall p \in c.E \cap P$ **do**
4: **for** $\forall t \in p \bullet \cap c.I$ **do**
5: $ConnectByArc((\top, c, t, F, I, W))$
6: **end for**
7: **end for**
8: **for** $\forall t \in c.E \cap T$ **do**
9: **if** $(t \bullet \cap c.N \neq \emptyset) \vee (\bullet t \cap c.E \neq \emptyset)$ **then**
10: $t_2 \leftarrow Duplicate(t, P, T, F, W, C, I)$
11: $F \leftarrow F \setminus ((t_2 \times c.N) \cup (c.E \times t_2))$
12: $ConnectByArc((\top, c, t, F, I, W))$
13: $ConnectByArc((\bot, c, t_2, F, I, W))$
14: **end if**
15: **end for**
16: $C \leftarrow C \setminus \{c\}$
17: **end for**
18: **end procedure**

Algorithm 2 Helper method to enable or disable a transition by a configuration place

1: **procedure** CONNECTBYARC((e, c, t, F, I, W))
2: **if** $(c.w > 0 \wedge e = \top) \vee (c.w < 0 \wedge e = \bot)$ **then**
3: $F \leftarrow F \cup \{(c.p, t), (t, c.p)\}$
4: $W(c.p, t) \leftarrow |c.w|$
5: $W(t, c.p) \leftarrow |c.w|$
6: **else**
7: $I \leftarrow I \cup \{(c.p, t)\}$
8: $W(c.p, t) \leftarrow |c.w|$
9: **end if**
10: **end procedure**

In Def. 18, we prohibit that new tokens enter from E to N. For the case, when the external node is a place ($p \in E$) and targets an internal transition ($t \in I$), by inhibiting the transition. For all other cases, Def. 17 changes the places from which tokens are removed and where tokens are added after firing. A transition, which belongs to a disabled configuration point, can not remove tokens from any place in E of this configuration point ($p \in c.E$) and can not create any tokens in any place of N of this configuration point ($p \in c.N$).

A. Flattening Algorithm

Special attention was given to the ability to remove the configuration point structure and replace it with Petri net structures of lower level Petri nets to be compatible with existing Petri net tools. This feature reduction is also called flattening and was already shown for different concepts. Colored Petri nets were introduced by Jensen [5] and are reducible to standard Petri nets by net duplication. Huber [3] published a paper enhancing colored Petri nets with hierarchy and showed how they can be transformed to standard Petri nets with flattening. Portinale [24] describes an or-transition, which, contrary to the standard transition, contains or-logic instead of and-logic. This transition can be reduced to Petri nets with inhibitor arcs.

Theorem 1: An adaptive Petri net can be flattened to a semantically equivalent Petri net with inhibitor arcs $\Sigma = (P, T, F, W, M_0, I)$.

Algorithm 3 Helper method to duplicate a transition

1: **procedure** DUPLICATE((t, P, T, F, W, C, I))
2: $T \leftarrow T \cup \{t_2\}$ with $t_2 \notin (P \cup T)$
3: $F \leftarrow F \cup \{(t_2, p) | p \in P \wedge (t, p) \in F\}$
4: $F \leftarrow F \cup \{(p, t_2) | p \in P \wedge (p, t) \in F\}$
5: $I \leftarrow I \cup \{(p, t_2) | p \in P \wedge (p, t) \in I\}$
6: $W \leftarrow W \cup \{(t_2, p) | p \in P \wedge (t, p) \in W\}$
7: $W \leftarrow W \cup \{(p, t_2) | p \in P \wedge (p, t) \in W\}$
8: **for** $\forall c \in C$ **do**
9: **if** $t \in c.N$ **then**
10: $c.N \leftarrow c.N \cup \{t_2\}$
11: **end if**
12: **end for**
13: **end procedure**

The flattening of Theorem 1 is described in Algorithm 1. We have to show that flattening will respect Defs. 17 and 18.

Lemma 1: ConnectByArc of Algorithm 2 with $e = \top$ will disable t when the configuration point c is disabled.

Proof: We show the correctness of Lemma 1 for the if-branch with $c.w > 0$ in lines 3-5 of Algorithm 2 and the else-branch with $c.w < 0$ in lines 7-8. The if-branch will disable t when $M(c.p) < c.w$, which is the same condition when c is disabled according to Def. 14 ($M(c.p) \geq c.w$). The else-branch will disable t when $M(c.p) \geq |c.w|$, which is the same condition when c is disabled according to Def. 14 ($M(c.p) < |c.w|$) $\square$.

Lemma 2: ConnectByArc of Algorithm 2 with $e = \bot$ will disable t when the configuration point c is enabled.

Proof: The correctness of Lemma 2 is analogous to Lemma 1. It has to be shown for the if-branch with $c.w < 0$ in lines 3-5 of Algorithm 2 and the else-branch with $c.w > 0$ in lines 7-8. The if-branch will disable t when $M(c.p) \geq |c.w|$, which is the same condition when c is disabled according to Def. 14 ($M(c.p) < |c.w|$). The else-branch will disable t when $M(c.p) < c.w$, which is the same condition when c is disabled according to Def. 14 ($M(c.p) \geq c.w$) $\square$.

Lemma 3: A disabled configuration point will disable the firing of all internal transitions, which are in the postset of an external place. According to Def. 18.

Proof: The set of places and transitions, which are referred by Def. 18, are selected in lines 3-4 of Algorithm 1 ($\forall p \in c.E \cap P$ and $\forall t \in p \bullet \cap c.I$). On Line 5, *ConnectByArc* will disable the transition when c is disabled as shown with Lemma 1$\square$.

Lemma 4: The algorithm will transform all transitions, which have a configured postset or preset as defined in Def. 16 and utilized in Def. 18, i.e., $t\bullet \neq t \bullet_c \vee \bullet t \neq \bullet_c t$.

Proof: Def. 17 only changes external transitions, which is implemented in Line 8 of Algorithm 1. Only those transitions have to be changed, which have $t \bullet_c \neq t\bullet$ or $\bullet_c t \neq \bullet t$. This is implemented in Line 9 with a logical *or*. The left part of the *or* is $t \bullet \cap c.N \neq \emptyset$, which is equivalent to the definition of $t \bullet_c$. The right part of the *or* is $\bullet t \cap c.E \neq \emptyset$, which is equivalent to the definition of $\bullet_c t\square$.

Lemma 5: A flattened transition will only produce tokens in $t \bullet_c$. According to Def. 17.

Lemma 6: A flattened transition will only consume tokens from $\bullet_c t$. According to Def. 17.

Proof: As shown in Lemma 4, the set of transitions is selected correctly. We will now proof that the tokens are produced and consumed according to Def. 17.

The code in Line 10 of Algorithm 1 duplicates the transition according to Algorithm 3. This will take the original transition t and create a new transition t_2 with the same properties, connected arcs and inhibitor arcs together with their weights. Additionally, t_2 is added to all N in which t was contained.

The flow relation of t_2 is updated in Line 11, to remove all $c.E$ from its preset and all $c.N$ from its postset, as defined in Def. 16. On Line 12 the transition t without the altered flow relation will fire only when the configuration point is enabled (see Lemma 1). Transition t_2 with the altered flow relation will only fire when the configuration point is disabled as defined on Line 13 (see Lemma 2)□.

Proof: By proving *Lemmas* 3, 5 *and* 6, we could show that the semantics of adaptive Petri nets (Defs. 17 and 18) is preserved in a Petri net with inhibitor arcs □.

This shows that we can flatten arbitrary adaptive Petri nets into Petri nets with inhibitor arcs. The flattened net will duplicate transitions and add new arcs and inhibitor arcs to the net.

Lemma 7: When all $c \in C$ fulfill the condition $(c.w > 0) \wedge (c.E \cap T = \emptyset)$, an adaptive Petri net can be flattened without adding inhibitor arcs.

Proof: According to the condition $c.E \cap T = \emptyset$, the changes to the Petri net happen only on Line 5 of Algorithm 1. With the condition $c.w > 0$ only lines 4-5 of Algorithm 2 are executed, adding an incoming and outgoing arc to a transition□.

The expressive power of adaptive Petri nets is generally higher than that of Petri nets, since we flatten it to a Petri net with inhibitor arcs. A higher expressive power will make some properties unsolvable by model checkers. There are two methods to obtain a Petri net without inhibitor arcs from an adaptive Petri net. *Avoiding inhibitor arcs* at all, by fulfilling Lemma 7 or designing a net with only *bounded configuration places*. It was shown in [25] that an inhibitor arc can be replaced by an equivalent structure, if the inhibiting places are bounded. From Algorithm 1, we can see the only inhibiting places generated are the configuration places. Therefore, a Petri net designer can chose those places carefully or add additional structures to make sure these places are bounded.

B. Graphical Notation

To integrate configuration structures well within Petri nets, we can model a Petri net and then define all configuration points. This approach requires the net designer to manually update the configuration points each time a node was added or removed. A better approach is to create a graphical language, which integrates in the existing graphical language of Petri nets.

The graphical language must express each element of the tuple $c = (p, e, N)$. With $N \subseteq (P \cup T)$, we can draw a contour around all connected nodes of a configuration point forming an area. Since it is not required to have all nodes in N connected with each other, this would create multiple areas belonging to one configuration point. For that the areas for each configuration point should get a unique color or a unique

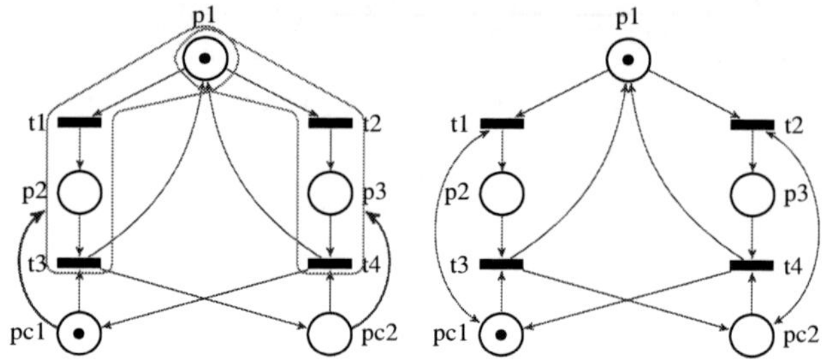

(a) Adaptive Petri net configured by $C = \{c_1, c_2\}$ with configuration points $c_1 = (pc1, 1, \{p1, t1, p2, t3\})$, $c_2 = (pc2, 1, \{p1, t2, p3, t4\})$.

(b) Adaptive Petri net flattened with Algorithm 1. According to Lemma 7, no inhibitor arcs were added.

Figure 3. Flattening of a simple adaptive Petri net

annotation. To declare the configuration point p together with the weight e, we will draw a bold arc or inhibitor arc from p to all areas of N. This arc can be annotated with a weight, which will become e. When an inhibitor arc is used, the weight must be multiplied with -1 to receive e.

An example for a simple Petri net with two configuration points can be seen in Figure 3. On the left is the adaptive Petri net with two different colored areas representing the nodes N of the configuration points c_1 and c_2. The net will execute alternatingly the net of c_1 and c_2, since the configuration points $pc1$ and $pc2$ are alternating their tokens. When flattening this net, the external nodes are $c_1.E = \{t1\}$ and $c_2.E = \{t2\}$.

VI. USE CASES REVISITED

In this section, adaptive Petri nets are put to work. We will show the implementation of two examples from Section IV. It is shown how these examples can be represented in adaptive Petri net syntax. In the end, we will show how the flattening affects the size and model checking results.

A. Dynamic Control Structures

The converted Petri net of Figure 1a can be seen in Figure 4. The reimplementation in Figure 4 required some changes. Removing the initial token from *p9* and *p12* is necessary, because adaptive Petri nets would evaluate this token. Instead of the tokens, a place and transition (px, tx) were added before *p9* and *p12*. Another change was required for enabling transition *t6*. It should be enabled when either *p8* or *p82* contain a token. To achieve this, the transitions *ty1*, *ty2* and the place *py* were added. We argue, these changes could be automated if a formalization for the hierarchy concept of dynamic control structures was found, which can be flattened to a net with exactly this structure.

With adaptive Petri nets, the reconfiguration can be expressed inside the net. For the configuration variables *CFG_A* and *CFG_B*, two transitions were added, which are annotated according to *control interpreted Petri net* syntax. They can only fire when the signals *CFG_A* or *CFG_B* are active. Both transitions are connected to a single place *Conf*, which configures both configuration points - enabling one and disabling the other.

After modeling the original net with adaptive Petri nets, it is still possible to generate the hardware description language from it, as the annotations of control interpreted Petri nets are not prohibited in our model or modified in its semantics. Besides

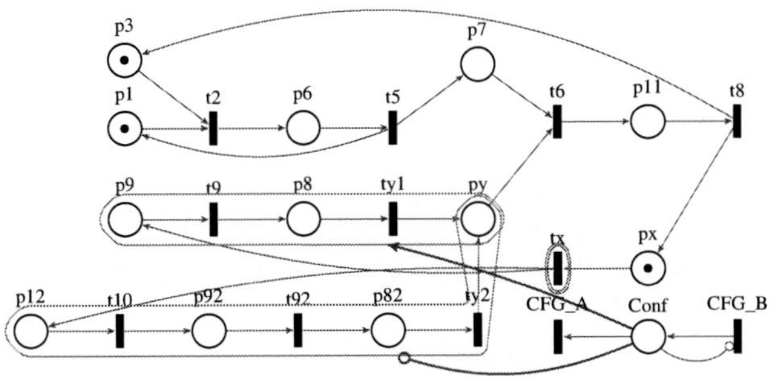

Figure 4. Dynamic control structures of [15] in adaptive Petri net notation. Configured by $C = \{c_1, c_2\}$ with $c_1 = (Conf, 1, \{p9, p8, t9\}, tx, ty1, py)$ and $c_2 = (Conf, -1, \{p12, t10, p92, t92, p82, tx, ty2, py\})$

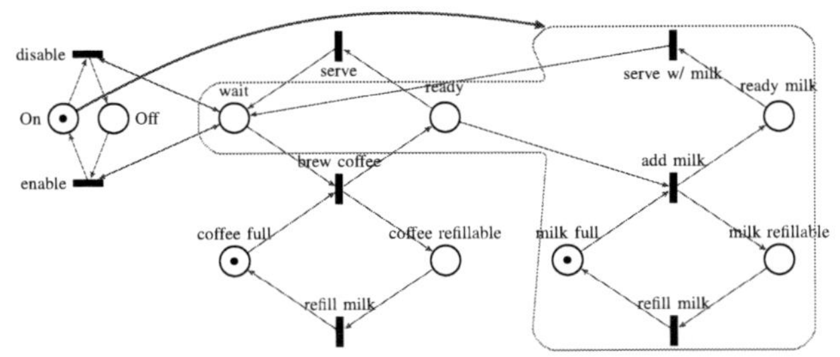

Figure 5. Dynamic Feature Petri net in adaptive Petri net notation Configured by $C = \{(On, 1, \{serve\ w/\ milk, ready\ milk, add\ milk, milk\ full, refill\ milk, milk\ refillable, wait, ready\})\}$.

this, through the net flattening of the configuration points c_1 and c_2, also older FPGA without dynamic reconfiguration can be targeted. Contrary to the original version, where the information regarding the reconfiguration signals was informally inside the description, the runtime semantics of this net is contained in the model. This example shows that adaptive Petri nets can be combined with other formal models of Petri nets (in this case *control interpreted nets*) as they are not imposing any restrictions.

B. Dynamic Features

We will show here how dynamic feature Petri nets [16] from Section IV can be modeled with adaptive Petri nets.

The example from Section IV can be converted straight forward to adaptive Petri nets. For each boolean variable inside a feature annotation we create one *configuration point* with this boolean variable as *configuration place*. All nodes, which are annotated with this boolean variable, are then put into the set N of this configuration point. In our example, the boolean variable *Milk* is mapped to the configuration place *On*. Then all nodes, which contain *Milk* in their annotated formula, are added to N, as well as the nodes bofore and after.

As can be seen in Figure 5, the resulting net has the same size and structure as the original. The annotations were exchanged for the graphical representation of the *configuration point*. Something that can not be expressed in feature nets are configurations based on integers. For example, the places *coffee full* and *milk full* basically are context information to decide whether a net is enabled or disabled. With adaptive nets, such a counting state can be utilized as *configuration place* to disable the net when the amount of token reaches zero.

TABLE I. SIZES OF NETS SHOWN IN SECTION VI

Net	Places	Transitions	Arcs
Original (Figure 4)	13	12	29
Flattened	13	13	32
Flattened (Inhibitor)	14	13	34
Original (Figure 5)	9	8	24
Flattened	9	8	26
Flattened (Inhibitor)	9	8	26

This example had shown that adaptive Petri nets are a feasible alternative for dynamic feature oriented Petri nets. This is especially helpful for cases where adaptivity is required, but no feature orientated development used. Adaptive nets have an advantage over feature Petri nets, which arbitrary places can configure the net, while in dynamic feature oriented Petri nets only formulas over boolean values are possible. Therefore, a layer of indirection is removed. In a recent paper [17], the authors showed how a feature net can be converted to a Petri net, including the formulas. Using this technique, feature nets can also be converted into an equal adaptive net.

C. Flattening and Analysis

One of the goals for adaptive Petri nets is to use existing Petri net tools for model checking. This goal can be reached by flattening all configuration points to Petri nets with inhibitor arcs. Since not all tools support inhibitor arcs, we will also flatten all inhibitor arcs with the algorithm of [25]. The only condition is that the place where the inhibitor arc originates must be bound. This condition holds true for all of our examples.

We flattened the Petri nets of our examples and used LoLa [2] as well as Tina [6] to analyze for common Petri net properties.The tool for flattening and analysis can be found online [26].

The results comparing the size can be seen in Table I. They should give an idea how the size of the nets will increase using flattening. As the size increase depends largely on the net structure, amount of configuration points and which nodes are marked as external, there is no general rule for the size increase. A configuration point consisting only of external places will not increase as much as a configuration point with external transitions. This is due to the fact that external transitions need to be duplicated. A bigger cost is the flattening of inhibitor arcs, which is especially big if the bound is larger than 1 as can be seen in the last row. Flattening an adaptive net will not always yield an inhibitor as can be seen in the row for Figure 5.

In Table II, the results of the model checking tools LoLa and Tina are shown. A short description on the checked properties: reversible (from every state of the net, we can reach the initial marking), deadlock free (starting from M_0, the net can always fire), k-bounded (all places contain at most k tokens) and live (all transitions and places can be reached from the initial marking). The column *markings* corresponds to all unique combinations of markings this net can reach. It is an indicator how long model checking will take, as for some properties (e.g., reversibility), all markings must be calculated.

TABLE II. MODEL CHECKING RESULTS OF NETS SHOWN IN SECTION VI. 1 = TINA, 2 = LOLA

Net	reversible[12]	deadlock[12]	live[1]	k-bounded[1]	markings[12]
Figure 4	yes	no	yes	k=1	44
Figure 5	yes	no	yes	k=1	20

D. Other semantics

There are various alternative approaches to define a semantics for adaptive nets. We settled with a semantics, which requires only few changes to the original net, so that a more complex semantics might build on top of this.

Our semantics orients itself on most imperative programming languages. The exchange of a method (e.g., by pointer in C or by *invoke dynamic* in Java) will happen in a similar fashion. Only new calls to this method are influenced, while current running threads inside this method will still finish. When the program tries to call the method another time it will call its replacement.

Another disabling semantics we considered is to completely stop all token movement within the configured part. This can be implemented as an extension of Def. 18. When flattening this modified version, all transitions inside N have to be connected to the *configuration place*. A use case for this might be freezing an algorithm, e.g., in a single threaded environment, which switches to another thread.

Further extending this semantics, one might reset all tokens of N to an initial state. A similar approach was presented in [27] to implement exceptions in Petri nets.

VII. CONCLUSION

This paper presented a new Petri net extension for modeling dynamic parts inside a Petri net. Contrary to existing proposals this extension puts the least restrictions on the Petri net model. We do neither restrict to a composition model nor the specification language. It was shown that adaptive Petri nets can be specified formally and graphically. The biggest advantage of adaptive Petri nets is the possibility of flattening an adaptive net to a Petri net with inhibitor arcs. By this, existing Petri net tools can be reused for this model, e.g., for code generation or model checking. Because of the specific structure of adaptive nets, inhibitor arcs can be removed in most cases. This was shown on two examples, which were analyzed by low level Petri net tools.

In our ongoing work, adaptive Petri nets are used to convert the control flow of a role-oriented programming language (SCROLL [28]) to Petri nets, as well as generating control structures for hardware / software codesign. Future work will integrate adaptive Petri nets with Petri net composition models and improve tool support.

ACKNOWLEDGMENT

We gratefully acknowledge support from the German Excellence Initiative via the Cluster of Excellence "Center for advancing Electronics Dresden" (cfAED).

This project has received funding from the Electronic Component Systems for European Leadership Joint Undertaking under grant agreement No 692480. This Joint Undertaking receives support from the European Union's Horizon 2020 research and innovation programme and Germany, Netherlands, Spain, Austria, Belgium, Slovakia."

REFERENCES

[1] T. Murata, "Petri nets: Properties, analysis and applications," Proceedings of the IEEE, vol. 77, no. 4, 1989, pp. 541–580.

[2] K. Schmidt, "LoLA a low level analyser," in Application and Theory of Petri Nets, ser. Lecture Notes in Computer Science. Springer, Berlin, Heidelberg, 2000, pp. 465–474.

[3] P. Huber, K. Jensen, and R. M. Shapiro, "Hierarchies in coloured Petri nets," in Advances in Petri Nets 1990, ser. Lecture Notes in Computer Science. Springer, Berlin, Heidelberg, 1989, pp. 313–341.

[4] L. Gomes and J. P. Barros, "Structuring and composability issues in Petri nets modeling," IEEE Transactions on Industrial Informatics, vol. 1, no. 2, 2005, pp. 112–123.

[5] K. Jensen, "Coloured Petri nets and the invariant-method," Theoretical Computer Science, vol. 14, no. 3, 1981, pp. 317–336.

[6] B. Berthomieu, P.-O. Ribet, and F. Vernadat, "The tool TINA – construction of abstract state spaces for Petri nets and time petri nets," International Journal of Production Research, vol. 42, no. 14, 2004, pp. 2741–2756.

[7] R. Valk, "Object Petri nets," in Lectures on Concurrency and Petri Nets, ser. Lecture Notes in Computer Science. Springer, Berlin, Heidelberg, 2003, pp. 819–848.

[8] S. Eker, J. Meseguer, and A. Sridharanarayanan, "The Maude LTL model checker," Electronic Notes in Theoretical Computer Science, vol. 71, 2004, pp. 162–187.

[9] J. Padberg and A. Schulz, "Model checking reconfigurable Petri nets with Maude," in Graph Transformation, ser. Lecture Notes in Computer Science. Springer, 2016, pp. 54–70.

[10] J. Padberg, "Reconfigurable Petri nets with transition priorities and inhibitor arcs," in Graph Transformation. Springer, 2015, pp. 104–120.

[11] M. Llorens and J. Oliver, "Structural and dynamic changes in concurrent systems: Reconfigurable Petri nets," IEEE Transactions on Computers, vol. 53, no. 9, 2004, pp. 1147–1158.

[12] J. Li, X. Dai, and Z. Meng, "Improved net rewriting systems-based rapid reconfiguration of Petri net logic controllers," in 31st Annual Conference of IEEE Industrial Electronics Society IECON., 2005, pp. 2284–2289.

[13] R. Valk, "Self-modifying nets, a natural extension of Petri nets," in Automata, Languages and Programming. Springer, 1978, pp. 464–476.

[14] S.-U. Guan and S.-S. Lim, "Modeling adaptable multimedia and self-modifying protocol execution," Future Generation Computer Systems, vol. 20, no. 1, 2004, pp. 123–143.

[15] A. Bukowiec and M. Doligalski, "Petri net dynamic partial reconfiguration in FPGA," in Computer Aided Systems Theory - EUROCAST, ser. Lecture Notes in Computer Science. Springer, Berlin, Heidelberg, 2013, pp. 436–443.

[16] R. Muschevici, D. Clarke, and J. Proenca, "Feature Petri nets," in Proceedings 1st International Workshop on Formal Methods in Software Product Line Engineering (FMSPLE 2010), 2010.

[17] R. Muschevici, J. Proença, and D. Clarke, "Feature nets: Behavioural modelling of software product lines," Software & Systems Modeling, vol. 15, no. 4, 2016, pp. 1181–1206.

[18] E. Serral, J. De Smedt, M. Snoeck, and J. Vanthienen, "Context-adaptive petri nets: Supporting adaptation for the execution context," Expert Systems with Applications, vol. 42, no. 23, 2015, pp. 9307.– 9317.

[19] H. Yang, C. Lin, and Q. Li, "Hybrid simulation of biochemical systems using hybrid adaptive petri nets," in Proceedings of the Fourth International ICST Conference on Performance Evaluation Methodologies and Tools. ICST (Institute for Computer Sciences, Social-Informatics and Telecommunications Engineering), 2009, pp. 42:1–42:10.

[20] D. Zaitsev and Z. Li, "On simulating turing machines with inhibitor Petri nets," IEEJ Transactions on Electrical and Electronic Engineering, 2017, pp. 147–156.

[21] A. V. Yakovlev and A. M. Koelmans, "Petri nets and digital hardware design," in Lectures on Petri Nets II: Applications. Springer, 1998, pp. 154–236.

[22] N. Marranghello, "Digital systems synthesis from Petri net descriptions," DAIMI Report Series, vol. 27, no. 530, 1998.

[23] R. Muschevici, J. Proença, and D. Clarke, "Modular modelling of software product lines with feature nets," in Software Engineering and Formal Methods. Springer, 2011, pp. 318–333.

[24] L. Portinale, "Behavioral Petri nets: a model for diagnostic knowledge representation and reasoning," IEEE Transactions on Systems, Man, and Cybernetics, Part B (Cybernetics), vol. 27, no. 2, 1997, pp. 184–195.

[25] N. Busi and G. M. Pinna, "Synthesis of nets with inhibitor arcs," in CONCUR'97: Concurrency Theory. Springer, 1997, pp. 151–165.

[26] C. Mai. An implementation of Adaptive Petri nets. [Online]. Available: https://github.com/balrok/adaptive_pn (10.01.2018)

[27] H. Leroux, D. Andreu, and K. Godary-Dejean, "Handling exceptions in Petri net-based digital architecture: From formalism to implementation on FPGAs," IEEE Transactions on Industrial Informatics, vol. 11, no. 4, 2015, pp. 897–906.

[28] M. Leuthäuser and U. Aßmann, "Enabling view-based programming with SCROLL: Using roles and dynamic dispatch for etablishing view-based programming," in Proceedings of the 2015 Joint MORSE/VAO Workshop on Model-Driven Robot Software Engineering and View-based Software-Engineering, ser. MORSE/VAO '15. ACM, 2015, pp. 25–33.

Managing Communication Paradigms with a Dynamic Adaptive Middleware

Tim Warnecke, Karina Rehfeldt, Andreas Rausch

Technische Universität Clausthal
38678 Clausthal-Zellerfeld, Germany
email: {tim.warnecke, karina.rehfeldt, andreas.rausch}@tu-clausthal.de

Abstract—**Autonomous systems, such as self-driving cars, are an emerging but very complex class of systems designed to relieve people of many unpleasant tasks. However, in the industry software architectures and frameworks that have been developed for non-autonomous systems are often used for such autonomous systems. These architectures and frameworks are rigid, very close to the hardware platform and offer little room for extensions. In this paper, we present a dynamic-adaptive middleware for autonomous systems, which is based on a formal component model and supports several communication paradigms independent of the actually used communication technologies. The presented middleware has already been implemented as a prototype and tested with an electric model vehicle.**

Keywords–dynamic adaptive system; component model; decentralized configuration; middleware; communication paradigm

I. Introduction

Autonomous driving starting at level 3 of the Society of Automotive Engineers (SAE level 3) [1] is one of the biggest technological challenges of our current time. But, to be able to provide flexible and safe autonomous driving, a range of challenges have to be tackled. To scale new functions such as autonomous driving and to reduce the complexity of integrating new functions, the electrical/electronic architecture (E/EA) will change to fewer central (domain-specific) computers and increased data preprocessing directly in sensors and actuators. The development approach will shift from "new functions as Electronic Control Unit (ECU)" to "new functions as software".

The typical development process of an embedded system, or any system strongly dependent on hardware/ software, starts with the definition of functionalities. In a next step, these functionalities are divided in hardware and software requirements, which are used for the development of hardware and software solutions. Although, the development of the two domains is strongly interconnected, they often differ with regard to the time needed for their realization, their innovation cycles and their specific technological advancements [2] [3].

While developers may use a hardware platform for quite some time, innovations and new functionalities like autonomous driving are often driven by software improvements [4]–[6]. Additionally, it is desirable to re-use those new software solutions in form of components in a range of different hardware variants of a product line [7]. The changes in the vehicle architecture and the realization of new functions like autonomous fleet management also require to include backend-systems and Car2X communication.

Another aspect, which is especially true for autonomous driving, is that a software system must maintain its functionality and safety in every situation [8]. Therefore, the software urgently needs the ability to adapt to context changes. In some circumstances, a reduction in quality is acceptable but the safety of the autonomous vehicle has to be guaranteed. To do this, safe adaptation during runtime even in uncertain environments and unforeseen situations must be possible [8], [9]. The best case is if both, proactive adaptation and reactive adaptation, are implemented within a safety critical system. Proactive adaptation is used to prevent failures from happening, while reactive adaptation is used to recover from changes or errors in the technical resources or context of the system.

The mentioned challenges have to be tackled to realize flexible and safe autonomous driving. Our solution is to change from rigid and inflexible systems to adaptive systems which adapt to the provisioned hardware and the context of the system. To build such an adaptive system exist different solutions which we will discuss in Section II. In our concept, we decided to construct a programming framework, which relieves the developer of the work of the adaptive mechanisms and optimizes various aspects of the system globally such as performance and communication.

As mentioned before, it will be a crucial part of the new vehicle architecture to be able to work on various hardware platforms and even migrate software components during runtime. Therefore, we are dealing with distributed systems connected by possibly diverse technical communication channels. Even nowadays exist a huge variety of communication busses, middlewares and paradigms within a vehicle [4].

In this paper, we will introduce a new middleware for autonomous systems which builds up on our experiences in adaptive component models and in software architectures. In Section II, we introduce the current state of the art of self-adaptive systems and communication paradigms and taxonomies. We describe our own communication taxonomy for distributed systems in Section III, followed by an introduction in Section IV to our dynamic adaptive middleware currently under development. Motivated by a small example, in Section V, we show which adaptive mechanisms and communication paradigms have to be considered for an adaptive middleware in the autonomous domain. Based on the previous Sections, we explain in Section VI how we integrated the presented communication paradigms into our middleware using fitting concepts. We conclude our paper in Section VII with possible future work and a conclusion in Section VIII.

II. Related Work

As motivated in the introduction, a middleware suitable for flexible autonomous driving scenarios has to deal with adaptive mechanisms and different communication middlewares and paradigms. It has to provide the right tools for the developer for building a robust but flexible system. In this section, we give an overview of current self-adaptive system approaches and communication paradigms.

A. Self-Adaptive Systems and Frameworks

A self-adaptive system is capable of monitoring its operating environment and automatically adapt to changes [10]. It provides self-x properties like self-configuration, self-optimization, self-healing or self-protection [11]. A comprehensive and exhaustive study by Krupitzer et al. has attempted to structure the field of self-adaptation with the help of their own taxonomy [8]. Krupitzer et al. ask a total of six questions related to self-adaptation and map these to five different properties of a self-adaptive system shown in Table I. In their study, they shed light on the individual dimensions of adaptability in detail and evaluate a large number of self-adaptive approaches.

TABLE I. ADAPTION TAXONOMY [8]

Question	Dimension of taxonomy
When to adapt?	Time
Why do we have to adapt?	Reason
Where do we have to implement change?	Level
What kind of change is needed?	Technique
Who has to perform the adaptation?	N/A because of self-adaptation
How is the adaptation performed?	adaptation Control

Self-adaptation can be achieved by many different means and procedures. Adaptation can be managed internally or externally, it can be reactive or proactive, centralised or decentralised and many other criteria play a role. In the field of large-scale systems, component-based development is a solid and state-of-the-art approach [12]–[14]. One example for component based development are middlewares, which not only define services and establish an infrastructure, but also specify a formal component model [15]. In our approach, we opted for a component model and middleware solution that frees the application developer from the task of self-adaptation and is able to hide the underlying specific platform and provide a unified high-level interface.

One well known component model is the CORBA Component Model (CCM) [16] from the Common Object Request Broker Architecture (CORBA) [17], a component based middleware. Building up on CORBA, *dynamicTAO* [18] introduces a reflective Object Request Broker (ORB) to support dynamic reconfiguration by maintaining an explicit representation of the internal structure of the system. Another well-known framework is the Rainbow framework [19] which divides the self-adaptive system in an architecture layer and a system layer with the managed resources. To realize adaptation, an external manager is used, which exploits the architecture model to monitor the running system and in case of constraint violations it performs adaptation accordingly.

In recent years, attempts have also been made in the automotive domain to introduce adaptability as a development approach. One example is the Dynamically Self-Configuring Automotive Systems (DySCAS) project [20], in which a policy-driven middleware was developed. The introduced policies describe a desired high-level behavior, which is then executed by the underlying middleware. This procedure makes it possible that the policy writer does not have to be a self-adaptive expert. One of the focal points of DySCAS is the limited resources of the ECUs and the resulting resource-optimized performance.

Becker et al. describe a model-based extension of the AUTomotive Open System ARchitecture (AUTOSAR) that introduces reconfiguration mechanisms at the architectural level [21]. They present a toolchain, which allows the developer to describe configuration alternatives and transitions between different configurations. These models are translated into executable code. The system's reconfiguration capabilities are limited by the developer's specifications created at design time, but can be verified because of the model-based approach.

B. Communication Paradigms

In our middleware, the focus is not only on adaptivity but also on communication. The application developer should be provided with exactly the right communication paradigms to develop a good architecture. For this reason, we will take a closer look at various well-known communication paradigms in this section.

For communication in distributed systems exist a variety of different paradigms, each suited for special cases. Tanenbaum and van Sten discussed various communication paradigms in [22]. They structured these in four categories: Remote Procedure Call (RPC), message-oriented communication, stream-oriented communication and multicast communication. RPC was further broken down into synchronous and asynchronous RPC, whereas message-oriented communication was separated in transient and persistent communication. Examples for transient communication are Berkeley Sockets or Message-Passing Interfaces. Persistent communication is realized through message broker architectures or message queues.

According to Tanenbaum and van Sten [22], stream-oriented communication is mainly used for continuous media. Important aspects of stream-oriented communication are the quality of service, and, in case of multiple streams, the time synchronization.

Multicast communication includes all communication from one sender to a group of receivers [22]. This could be done by directly addressing a group and sending the message to all of them at once or by using gossip-based protocols where each node receiving a message shares the message with a group of other nodes until all nodes have received the messages.

Another comprehensive summary of communication paradigms is found in Schill and Springer [23]. They structure communication paradigms similar to Tanenbaum and van Sten in Remote Procedure Calls, message-oriented and stream-oriented communication but also include data-based communication. Unlike Tanenbaum and van Sten, they do not have clear sub-categories but highlight individual aspects of communication.

In RPC, they particularly emphasize the synchronous bidirectional call [23]. For message-oriented communication, they focus on unidirectional communication channels such as those used in Publish/Subscribe systems. In the case of stream-oriented communication, they mainly consider periodic, synchronous data streams that can be either uni- or bidirectional.

Data-based communication is divided into mobile objects and shared space or information sharing [23]. Mobile objects are known, for example, as a part of Java RMI (Remote Method Invocation). These refer to data that is packed into an object and exchanged between sender and receiver instead of using messages for data exchange. They are used mainly for communication between a limited number of participants. Shared space allows a number of components to write and read structured data in a collective space. Another suitable term for this kind of communication, which is more common in embedded systems, is global variables.

III. COMMUNICATION TAXONOMY FOR DISTRIBUTED SYSTEMS

The taxonomy of Tanenbaum and van Sten [22] lacked the data-based communication that is often used in the automotive domain, while the taxonomy of Schiller and Spring [23] did not go into as much detail as Tanenbaum and van Sten and lacked the inner structure. That is why, we derived our own taxonomy based on these two, which is shown in Figure 1. In our opinion, we have combined the best of both and supported it with references to well-known software patterns.

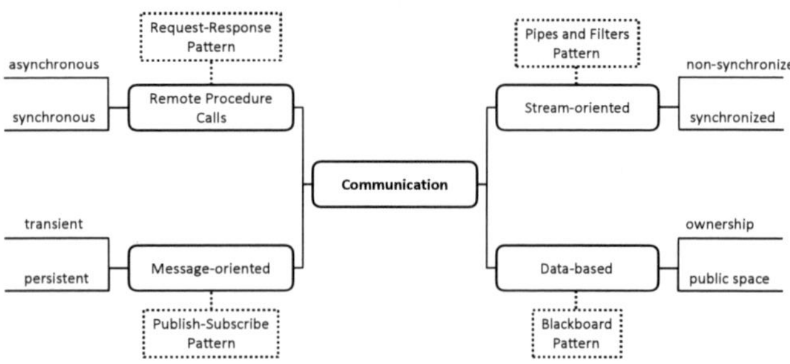

Figure 1. Adapted Communication Taxonomy for distributed Systems based on [22] and [23]

Our taxonomy has four categories: Remote Procedure Calls, message-oriented, stream-oriented and data-based. RPC maps to the classic request-response or client-server pattern [24]. We distinguish it like Tanenbaum and van Sten in asynchronous, non-blocking and synchronous, blocking calls. RPC is mostly used when data has to be transferred irregularly on a request-response (bidirectional) basis.

For message-oriented communication we assign the publish-subscribe [24] pattern. Just like RPC, we follow Tanenbaum and van Sten in our message-oriented communication and further classify messages according to how they are transmitted. In the persistent case, the transmission is carried out using a broker which is able to store messages temporarily, for example. For the transient transmission of messages, we follow the channel pattern [24] that allows the transmission of messages using topics or special channels. An important aspect of topics is that the recipients and senders do not know each other. In both cases, persistent and transient, message-oriented communication is used for either periodic or sporadic data. The transmission is always unidirectional.

In stream-oriented communication, we distinguish between synchronized and non-synchronized communication. By synchronized streams we mean anything where two or more streams have to be synchronized with each other, e. g. internet telephony or video conferences. Non-synchronized communication is used for sensor data streams or continuous media streams. Overall, stream communication maps to the Pipes and Filters pattern [24].

Our last category is based on the taxonomy of Springer and Schill. Data-based communication describes the exchange of structured data that either belongs to a system participant (ownership) or that can be read and processed by everyone in a collective space (public space). Data-based communication matches the blackboard pattern [24]. This communication method is useful when structured data has to be shared between a number of components on a regular basis.

We use the presented taxonomy to divide means of communication. Based on this, we discuss which communication methods should be supported by a dynamic adaptive middleware. In the next section we present our former middleware for dynamic, adaptive systems, which only supported synchronous RPC, followed by the expansion of our middleware to include asynchronous RPC, transient message-oriented and data-based ownership communication.

IV. DYNAMIC ADAPTIVE SYSTEM INFRASTRUCTURE - DAISI

Before we take a closer look at our new concepts for the development of a dynamic-adaptive middleware for autonomous driving, we explain in this section our previous work on a dynamic-adaptive middleware for information systems called Dynamic Adaptive System Infrastructure (DAiSI) [25]. DAiSI is a middleware based on a formal component model.

The model defines each software component in a system as a dynamic adaptive component (*DynamicAdaptiveComponent*), which consists of several component configurations (*ComponentConfiguration*). Each configuration describes in detail which services a component requires (*RequiredServiceReferenceSet* - RSRS) and which services it provides (*ProvidedService* - PS). The PS and RSRS match on service descriptions in the *DomainInterface*. All *DomainInterfaces* are bundled in the *DomainArchitecture*, which describes possible services of a whole domain like autonomous driving.

The provided and required services match via domain interfaces that specify which synchronous method calls the service instances offer. Each component implements the MAPE loop [11]. Each component observes changes to the system and its environment or context (Monitoring), analyses them (Analyze) and plans (Plan) and executes (Execute) necessary adaptations. How these processes work in detail can be found in [25]. For our purposes, a short introduction is sufficient.

A fundamental characteristic of DAiSI is that each component tries to resolve its dependencies in order to be able to offer its services. Each element, briefly explained in the following, implements its own state machine. If a *ProvidedService* is required to run, either because it is needed by the environment (for example GUI or interface to external systems) or because another component in the system has requested the service, this PS informs all *ComponentConfiguration* by which it is provided. The *ComponentConfiguration* then changes to the RESOLVING state. As a result, all RSRSs declared by the *ComponentConfiguration* will also switch to RESOLVING state. This process reflects, that to provide a service, a number of dependencies on other services have to be resolved.

The RSRS is aware of all services available in the system. Either via a central instance, such as a broker or a registry, or via a service discovery. For resolving its dependencies, the RSRS inquires the usage of available matching services. When a PS changes to the RUNNABLE or RUNNING state - meaning its dependencies are resolved - it can be used by an RSRS. After the successful negotiation and connection between PS and RSRS, the RSRS change to the RESOLVED state. When all RSRS of a *ComponentConfiguration* are resolved, the *ComponentConfiguration* itself is considered resolved. The *ProvidedServices* either change to the RUNNABLE state, when they are not needed, or to RUNNING, when they are.

In DAiSI, only one configuration can be active at a time. Therefore, if several configurations are potentially activateable (in RESOLVED state), the "best" one is activated. Each component strives to resolve its "best" configuration to provide the "best possible" service.

Over the last five years, we introduced various new concepts to our component model. The local optimality of the self-adaptive system is complemented in [26] by a global system design that specifies which rules/objectives the overall system should follow. This limits the system configuration resulting from the adaptation process. Likewise, in Klus et al. [26] interface roles were introduced. These extend the concept of domain interfaces with an additional statement about the role of a *ProvidedService* at runtime.

Based on the InterfaceRoles, a quality concept is introduced in [27]. The ability to compare the quality of two interfaces allows to make a more differentiated selection of services for the component. This quality may also include properties at runtime, such as current load, communication latencies or the location of services, due to the runtime evaluation of the InterfaceRole.

Up to this point, the interconnection was based purely on syntactic compatibility. However, in systems developed by several developers, such as in the domain of IoT, it is no longer possible to rely solely on syntactic compatibility. In [28] an additional aspect of interconnections in dynamic adaptive systems was considered - semantic compatibility with syntactic differences.

A semantic description language, on which the developers agree, is used for this purpose. By this, in addition to the syntactical description of the interfaces, a semantic description is given. At runtime, the middleware automatically generates adapters that create syntactic compatibility between interfaces which are semantically compatible.

Although different adaptive concepts have been developed, so far only a few communication paradigms have been considered apart from the synchronous RPC. In the following sections, we will describe our work on further communication paradigms that fit into the DAiSI adaptive component model. First of all, we use an example to motivate which paradigms are essential for the autonomous domain.

V. Motivating Example

In this section, we introduce a motivating example for our adaptive middleware which we keep as simple as possible but still shows the challenges for an adaptive middleware in the autonomous driving domain. The example involves an autonomous electric car, which is equipped with diverse sensors and actuators and some software components as shown in Figure 2. The architecture shown is a combination of hardware components abbreviated with <<HW-C>> and software components abbreviated with <<SW-C>>.

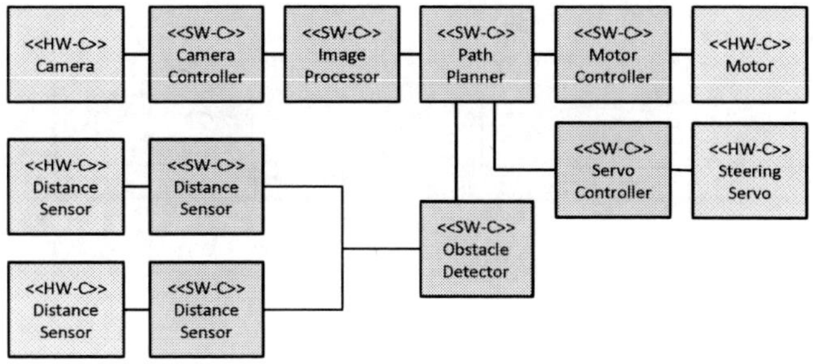

Figure 2. Example Architecture

The task for the car is to follow a lane on the ground and to halt in case of obstacles. A video camera is attached at the front of the car to record a video of the field of vision. The *Camera Controller* component fetches the individual images of the video made available by the camera and the *Image Processor* handles the images to identify the lane. The coordinates of the lane are used by the *Path Planner* to plan the trajectory. The velocity of the motor and the steering angle are controlled by the components *Motor Controller* and *Servo Controller*. These two software components accept the values calculated by the *Path Planner* and control both the motor and the steering servo.

The second simple task for the car is to stop if an obstacle is in front of it. In order to detect obstacles, two distance sensors are attached to the left and right side of the camera. The two software components *Distance Sensor* are responsible for fetching the distance from each sensor. The component *Obstacle Detector* uses these two values to decide whether an obstacle is in front of the car. This in turn is used as an input for the *Path Planner* to determine if the car must halt.

In the next section, we will use this small example to discuss the new communication paradigms in DAiSI.

VI. Extending DAiSI for Autonomous Driving

As we have already indicated in Section III, there are several communication paradigms used in distributed systems. The previous concepts in DAiSI only supported synchronous RPC. It is clear that a modern automotive middleware should offer the application developer more communication methods. Using our taxonomy, we identified three communication paradigms which we included in our component model to account for the needs of the automotive domain. Namely they are asynchronous RPC, ownership data-based communication and persistent message-oriented communication realized through topics. Therefore, we demonstrate how the former component model of DAiSI (see Section IV) can be extended by these three new communication modes. The complete extended model can be seen in Figure 3.

At this point, we will use the example of the autonomous electric car presented in Section V to illustrate our component model.

The elements *DynamicAdaptiveComponent* and *ComponentConfiguration* remain unchanged and still form the basis of the model. The only enhancement at this point is that we have

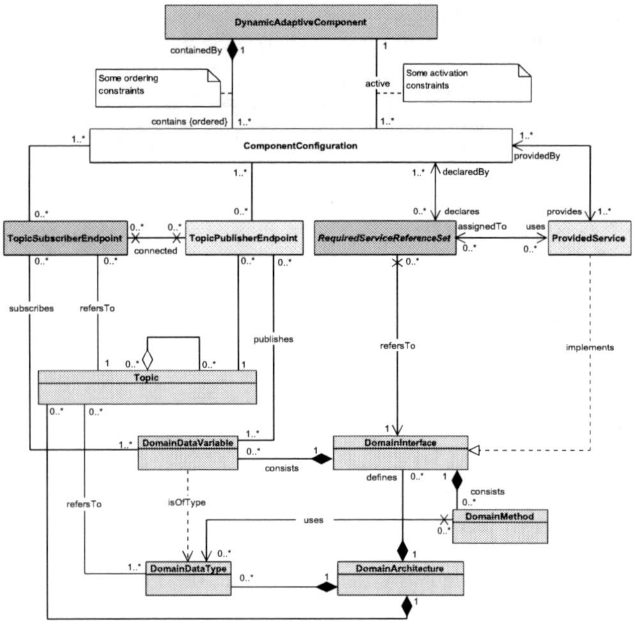

Figure 3. Extended Daisi component model

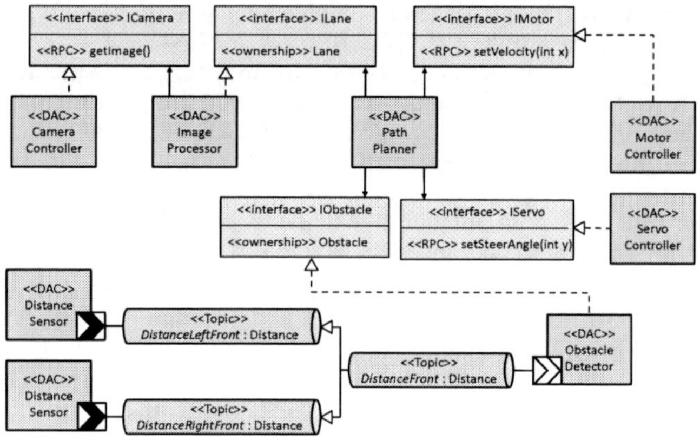

Figure 4. Example Architecture with communication paradigms

granted the possibility that several component configurations can be active at the same time. This should make it easier for developers to combine different configurations.

Each software component shown in the example in Figure 4 corresponds to a *DynamicAdaptiveComponent* annotated with the abbreviation <<DAC>>. However, the communication between the components is now specified by the paradigms RPC, ownership and topics. During runtime, the components can be started and stopped. Thanks to the adaptive concept of the middleware they will connect to the system as shown above. Of course, for every component different *Component-Configurations* might exist. The scope of this paper, however, is on the communication paradigms and therefore these aspects are not further examined here.

In the example shown, the *Path Planner* component uses two different RPCs to control the vehicle based on given sensor information. The component uses on the one hand the interface *IMotor* of the component *Motor Controller* to control the speed of the car and on the other hand the interface *IServo* of the component *Servo Controller* to adjust the steering angle. Both values are set using a call when necessary.

RPCs have always been part of DAiSI. The *RequiredServiceReferenceSet* and *ProvidedService* with the corresponding *DomainInterface* therefore remain identical. The *DomainInterface* is structured in *DomainMethod* and *DomainDataVariable*. *DomainMethod* are (asynchronous) callable methods within the interface. *DomainDataVariable* is introduced for the ownership paradigm.

To determine the speed and steering angle, *Path Planner* uses data from the *Image Processor* and *Obstacle Detector* components using the ownership paradigm. The *Image Processor* provides the *Path Planner* with the *Lane* object of its *ILane* interface. The *Path Planner* also uses the object *Obstacle* of the *IObstacle* interface, which is implemented by the *Obstacle Detector*. Using the ownership paradigm, the *Path Planner* can subscribe to changes of the object, while it still knows exactly to which service the object belongs to.

The ownership communication paradigm is illustrated in the component model in Figure 3 at the bottom left. An ownership object is part of a domain interface, using the *DomainDataVariable* with a data type given by the *DomainDataType*. A domain interface can contain any number of ownership objects and methods.

Transient message-oriented communication is realized using hierarchic topics. In the example, a topic hierarchy is shown in the lower part of the component model. The left distance sensor of the car publishes its data on the topic *DistanceLeftFront* and the right distance sensor correspondingly on the topic *DistanceRightFront*. The naming of the topics generates a certain semantic meaning, in this case a localization of the installation of the sensors. The topic *DistanceFront* merges the data of topics *DistanceLeftFront* and *DistanceRightFront* to describe the distance to objects in front but without further direction. This topic is used by the *Obstacle Detector* component to evaluate whether there is an object in front of the car. In our example, the topics could be used by more than one distance sensor and it would make no difference for the *Obstacle Detector*, as long as the semantic meaning of *DistanceFront* is preserved. In other words, the *Obstacle Detector* does not need to know the exact data sources.

In open and commercial middlewares, it is a common practice for the publisher to define the topic name and data type for the middleware to create a topic based on these definitions. This means that a consumer needs to know which topics are created by the publishers. Although it is often practiced, it is not a good choice in terms of the overall system architecture. Publishers can publish whatever and however they want, and consumers must adapt accordingly.

We propose to decouple the creation of topics from the publishers and to give these rights to the architect on the basis of a formalized description of the topics. For this purpose, we present the concepts *TopicSubscriberEndpoints* and *TopicPublisherEndPoints* in combination with *Topics*. *Topics* are named and typed transport channels for data sent by a publisher. In our concept the middleware itself is responsible for the creation of these topics via a predefined specification by the architect.

The data types that can be published on a topic are determined by the *DomainDatatatype*. Further freedom is given to the architects through the self-aggregation of *Topic*. This relationship allows to design topic hierarchies, that is, one can create topics with names and permitted data types that are inherited from each other, as seen in the example.

In the following sections, we explain the realization of the three used paradigms in details and give a brief introduction to our implementation using code snippets.

A. Remote Procedure Call Paradigm

An RPC can be used in the extended DAiSI, in contrast to its predecessor, both in the synchronous and the asynchronous version.

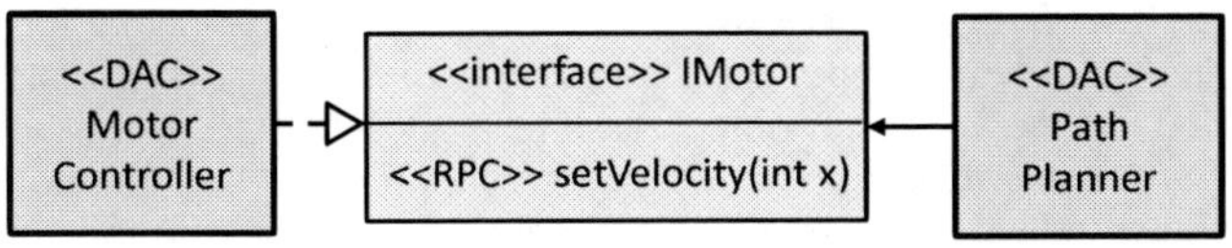

Figure 5. Example RPC

In our example of the electric car, several Remote Procedure Calls have been modeled. At this point, we explain the RPC between the component *Motor Controller* and *Path Planner*, which is shown in Figure 5, in detail. In this case, the component *Motor Controller* is the provider of the interface *IMotor* with the method *setVelocity(int x)* contained in it. It sets the motor speed using the parameter *x*.

```
public class MotorController extends
    DynamicAdaptiveComponent{

  public MotorController() {
    ProvidedService motorSpeed =
    new ProvidedMotor();

    ComponentConfiguration config =
    new ComponentConfiguration() {
      @Override
      protected void
          notifyStateChanged(ConfigurationState
          state) {
        // react to different states
      }
    };
    config.addProvides(motorSpeed);
    this.addConfiguration(config);
  }

  class ProvidedMotor extends ProvidedService
      implements IMotor {
    @Override
    public void setVelocity(int x) {
      // control motor
    }
  }
}
```

Listing 1. Example RPC Callee as Code

In the following, both the *Motor Controller* and *Path Planner* components are shown as simplified Java code. The *Motor Controller* in Listing 1 initially inherits from the *DynamicAdaptiveComponent* of our component model. This allows the application developer to make use of the adaptive mechanism in the middleware. In all of the following examples, the components always inherit from *DynamicAdaptiveComponent*.

To be able to offer a service to other components, a component must first create its own *ProvidedService*. A *ProvidedService*, like *ProvidedMotor* in our example, is created by extending the abstract class *ProvidedService* and implementing a *DomainInterface*, like *IMotor*, with the corresponding methods. In a final step, the service needs to be added to the component configuration to be usable by other components.

A component configuration is created in our middleware using the class *ComponentConfiguration*. The method *notifyStateChanged(ConfigurationState state)* has to be implemented, which informs the component about state changes, e.g. when all dependencies are resolved.

Once the configuration has been created, both provided and required services can be added to it. In the example of *Motor Controller*, the service *ProvidedMotor* is added to the configuration *config* using the method *addProvidedService(ProvidedService ps)*. To add a configuration to a component, the method *addConfiguration(ComponentConfiguration cc)* is used. In the example, *config* is added to the component.

The *Path Planner* component (see Listing 2) wants to use the service *IMotor* and must therefore create a *RequiredServiceReferenceSet* typed with the desired interface. In addition, a RSRS must be given the minimum and maximum number of service instances needed. In the example, both values are set to 1, meaning exactly one service is needed. The RSRS is added to the created configuration using the method *addRequires(RSRS rsrs)*. The process for generating a required service is therefore very similar to the process for creating a provided service. Additionally, the processes for creating a component configurations and adding *ProvidedServices* and *RequiredServiceReferenceSets* to these is the same for each communication paradigm and is therefore not shown again in the following sections on ownership and topics.

```
public class PathPlanner extends
    DynamicAdaptiveComponent{

  public PathPlanner() {
    RequiredServiceReferenceSet<IMotor> m=
    new RequiredServiceReferenceSet(
      IMotor.class, 1, 1);

    ComponentConfiguration config =
    new ComponentConfiguration() {
      @Override
      protected void
          notifyStateChanged(ConfigurationState
          state) {
        // react to different states
      }
    };

    config.addRequires(m);
    this.addConfiguration(config);
    // calculate x
    m.getService().setVelocity(x);
  }
}
```

Listing 2. Example RPC Caller as Code

Once the dependency has been resolved, the service can be used. The RSRS has a *getService()* method, which returns a bound service instance of the given interface *IMotor*. As usual in Java, the methods such as *setvelocity(int x)* can be called here either synchronously or asynchronously using Futures.

B. Data-based Communication Paradigm - Ownership

The biggest disadvantage of the classic, asynchronous or synchronous RPC is the periodic access to data. Each time a component requires a value from another component, an RPC must be sent, a return value calculated and the value returned to the sender. Since the periodic access to data is common in embedded and automotive systems, we have extended our middleware by the communication paradigm ownership.

In our concept, components can create their own data objects and make them available to other components via their *DomainInterfaces*. By making the data available via interfaces, it is clear to the consumer of the data from which component he receives the data. This is extremely important in many cases, as it makes a big difference whether a component receives data from a specific and known sensor or from an arbitrary sensor.

A consumer can subscribe to an ownership object and is thus informed of changes to it. The producer decides when a consumer is informed about data changes. Technically, the consumer is informed about the changes to the object via callback methods of the middleware.

```
public class PathPlanner extends
    DynamicAdaptiveComponent{

  public PathPlanner() {
    private RequiredServiceReferenceSet<ILane> l;
    l = new RequiredServiceReferenceSet(ILane.class,
        1, 1);

    // add required service to config as in Listing 2

    ProvidedService s = l.getService();
    DataObject d = s.getDataObject();
    d.addCallback(new LaneCallback());
  }

  class LaneCallback implements Callback<Lane> {
    @Override
    public void update(Lane lane) {
      // react to new input
    }
  }
}
```

Listing 3. Example Ownership Consumer as Code

We give the producer further freedom in designing the ownership object by allowing to choose between two different types of ownership objects: *ConsumerImmutable* and *ConsumerMutable*. If the producer chooses a *ConsumerImmutable*, he determines that consumers are only allowed to read the data of the ownership object but not to change it. This is especially useful if, for example sensor data is made available to consumers. At this point, it would not be useful or even dangerous if the consumer could change the data. A changed sensor value could lead to fatal consequences for other consumers. By selecting a *ConsumerMutable*, the producer determines that he also allows consumers to change data. Such a setting could be used for example for configuration parameters that are optimized at runtime by different parties.

In relation to our running example Figure 6 shows the components *Image Processor* and *Path Planner*, which exchange their data via ownership communication. As already mentioned, the *Image Processor* offers an object of type *Lane* which stores the exact location. The component updates this object each time it receives a new image from the *Camera Controller*. The component *Path Planner* uses the interface *ILane* to get the ownership object *Lane* from the *Image Processor* and subscribes to it.

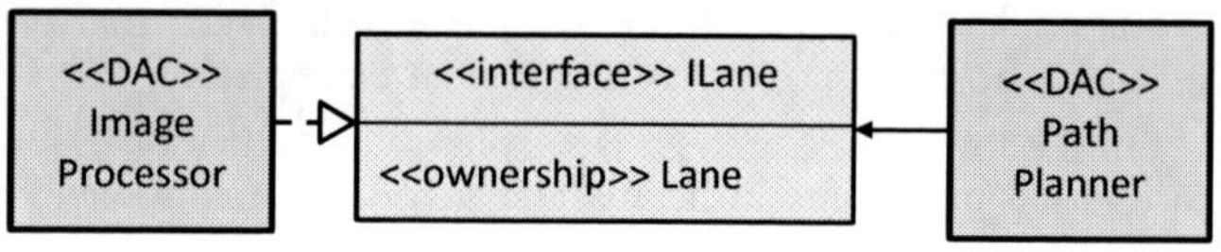

Figure 6. Example Ownership

Based on the simple, small example of the Path Planner and the Image Processor, the two components are shown in Listing 3 and Listing 4 as simplified Java code. In order for the *Image Processor* to be able to offer its *Lane* object to other components, as shown in Listing 4, it must first define such an object and have it inherited by either *ConsumerImmutable* or *ConsumerMutable*. In the example shown, the lane may not be changed by the consumer and therefore it inherits from *ConsumerImmutable*. In the class *Image Processor*, the lane is added within the provided service *ProvidedLane* which implements the DomainInterface *ILane*. The object can be retrieved using the method *getDataObject()*. A consumer is not informed about changes until the producer calls the *publish()* method within the object. This allows the developer to publish updates only for specific events.

```
public class ImageProcessor extends
    DynamicAdaptiveComponent{

  public ImageProcessor() {
    ProvidedService laneLocalisation = new
        ProvidedLane();
    // add provided service to config
  }

  class ProvidedLane extends ProvidedService
      implements ILane {
    private final Lane lane;

    public ProvidedLane() {
      lane = new Lane();
    }

    @Override
    public Lane getDataObject() {
      return lane;
    }
  }
}

public class Lane extends ConsumerImmutable {
  // define lane
}
```

Listing 4. Example Ownership Producer as Code

To be able to use the *Lane* object offered by the *Image Processor*, the *Path Planner*, shown in Listing 3, must first create a *RequiredServiceReferenceSet*, which requires the *ILane* interface. Based on this, the *Path Planner* gets the possibility to access the services of the interface and the method *getDataObject()*, which returns the *Lane* object. A callback is added to this object which is called as soon as the *Lane* is updated by the *Image Processor*.

C. Message-oriented Communication Paradigm - Topics

Topics are the core paradigm for many-to-many communication in DAiSI. We combine already existing concepts for

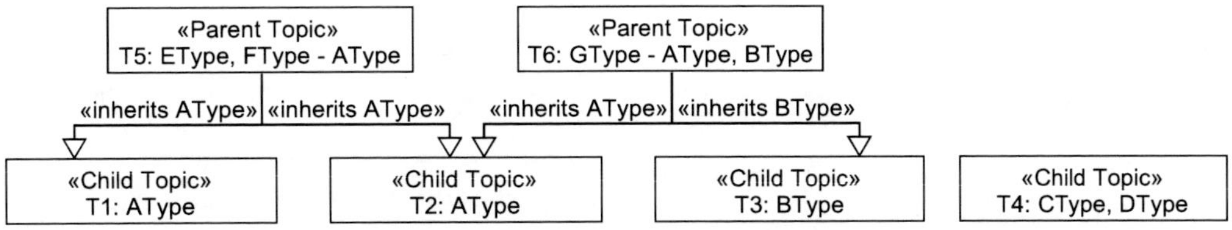

Figure 7. Example Topic Hierarchy

topics with new ideas to a solid and well-structured topic hierarchy. First we use the concept of named and strongly typed topics, which is also already used in middlewares like the Robot Operating System (ROS) [29]. In the case of strongly typed topics, a publisher has to publish data with the correct data type defined by the topic; otherwise the topic refuses transmission. The topics are also defined by a name, so that there can be several topics of the same data type for different purposes.

As already mentioned, we want to further expand the structure of topics so that it is possible to design topics in advance like any other communication and component in the system. We achieve this with a concept that we call *Topic Hierarchy*. The Topic Hierarchy exploits the inheritance relationship of object-oriented programming in such a way that it is possible to combine several smaller topics into larger ones.

Before we delve into the example, we formally define what we mean by the term Topic Hierarchy. First, we define DT as a set of all possible data types which can be used in topics.

A topic hierarchy is a tuple $TH = (CT, PT, IE, src, trg)$ which is defined as a directed acyclic, but not necessarily connected, graph with

- CT (called child topic) is a set of nodes and every node has a label n, a set of own data types $ODT \subseteq DT$ and an arbitrary number of incoming edges
- PT (called parent topic) is a set of nodes and every node has a label n, a set of own data types $ODT \subseteq DT$, a set of inherited data types $IDT \subseteq DT$ and an arbitrary number of incoming and outgoing edges
- IE (called inheritance edge) is a set of directed edges
- $src : IE \to PT$ is a function which maps the source of an inheritance edge to a parent topic
- $trg : IE \to PT \cup CT$ is a function which maps the target of an inheritance edge to a parent topic or a child topic

Furthermore, label n is the name of a topic, $ODT \subseteq DT$ is a set of data types that can be published and subscribed and $IDT \subseteq DT$ is a set of inherited data types that can only be subscribed but not published. This restriction was made because parent nodes should aggregate the data of their child topics but can also introduce additional data types. The own data type could also be identical to the inherited data types.

The topics T1 and T2 represented in Figure 7 are both child topics which support data type AType, but have different names and therefore different semantic meanings. Any publisher wishing to publish the data type AType may choose to publish on both topics. In contrast, T5 is a parent topic inheriting the data types from T1 and T2 by an inheritance edge - AType - and introducing EType and FType as own data types. On the other hand T6 introduces only one additional data type GType and inherits the data type AType from T2 and BType from T3. The last topic T4 is not connected to other topics of the hierarchy, which is also allowed.

In our example of the electric car in Figure 8, the Topic Hierarchy is used to provide data from distance sensors. The Topic Hierarchy is initially described by two child topics *DistanceLeftFront* and *DistanceRightFront*. These are used by both distance sensors individually. In addition, both topics only allow the transmission of data of type *Distance*, i. e. no data of other types can be published on these topics. In order to determine if there are objects directly in front of the vehicle, no matter whether they are to the left or right of it, another channel called *DistanceFront* is used. *DistanceFront* is a parent topic, which subscribes to its two child topics and thus receives all the data sent to them.

As already mentioned, the distance sensors gain access to the two child topics (black arrow in white box) via their *TopicPublisherEndpoints*. The *Obstacle Detector* component subscribes to the parent topic *DistanceFront* using a *TopicSubscriberEndpoint* (white arrow in white box).

```
public class DistanceSensor extends
    DynamicAdaptiveComponent {

  @TopicPublisher(type="topic",
  instance = {"name", "DistanceLeftFront",
    "ownType", "Distance"})
  public TopicPublisherEndpoint publishEndpoint;

  public DistanceSensor() {
    Distance d = new Distance();
    publishEndpoint.addObjectToPublish(d);
    // change d
  }
}

public class Distance extends
    ConsumerImmutableDataObject {
  // define distance
}
```

Listing 5. ExampleTopic Publisher as Code

In Listing 5, the architecture described above for the distance sensor was implemented with the help of our middleware. To gain access to the child topic *DistanceFrontLeft*, the component declares a *TopicPublisherEndpoint*. To specify which topic it has to connect to, it is annotated with @TopicPublisher. This annotation defines two attributes: *type* and *instance*. First of all, the type describes which medium the

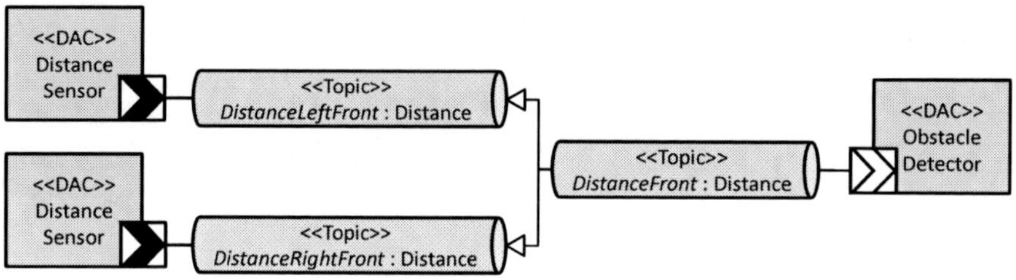

Figure 8. Example Topics

TopicPublisherEndPoint should connect to, which in this case is a topic.

The instance attribute specifies to which concrete instance of the specified type the *TopicPublisherEndpoint* is supposed to be connected. An instance is described by key-value pairs. In this example, a topic named *DistanceLeftFront* which offers the type *Distance* is searched.

```
public class ObstacleDetector {
  @TopicSubscriber(type="topic",
  instance = {"name", "DistanceFront",
  "ownType", "Distance"})
  public TopicSubscriberEndpoint subscriberEndpoint;

  public ObstacleDetector() {
    subscriberEndpoint.addCallback(
      Distance.class,
      new DistanceCallback())
  }

  class DistanceCallback implements
      Callback<Distance> {
    @Override
    public void update(Distance d) {
      // react to new input
    }
  }
}
```

Listing 6. Example Topic Subscriber as Code

After defining the *TopicPublisherEndpoint*, the distance object created can be added to the topic using the method *addObjectToPublish()*. The *TopicPublisherEndpoint* subscribes to this object like a consumer in the Ownership paradigm in the previous section and is informed about updates of this object. The *TopicPublisherEndpoint* automatically sends these updates to the connected topic *DistanceLeftFront*.

To obtain the data provided by the distance sensors, the *Obstacle Detector* component must declare a *TopicSubscriberEndpoint* (see Listing 6). The *TopicSubscriber* annotation is attached to it and uses the same attributes type and instance as seen in the *TopicPublisher* example. However, the *Obstacle Detector* defines that it wants to be connected to the parent topic *DistanceFront*.

Notification of new data on the subscribed topic is handled in the same way as in the ownership paradigm. A callback handler can be added to a *TopicSubscriberEndpoint*, which is called whenever an updated object has been received via the defined topic.

This concludes the presentation of our new component model and middleware. In the next section, we show possible future work within our dynamic adaptive middleware.

VII. Future Work

During interviews with experts in the domain of automotive engineering it quickly became clear that a single communication middleware, such as ROS, would not be sufficient to meet all the requirements of a modern vehicle. Nowadays, most vehicles are equipped with diverse communication middlewares for different purposes and therefore they exchange data with each other by means of adapters. With our middleware DAiSI we would like to offer the possibility that dynamic adaptive components, which run on different DAiSI instances with different communication middleware, can communicate with each other. In order to achieve this goal, a first concept has already been conceived, which will be integrated in a next iteration of DAiSI.

In our interviews, we have also noticed that we need some kind of control mechanism for our adaptation concept, because in safety-critical parts of the system we dont want components to interconnect with each other without a global goal in mind. In this system parts it is often better to give the middleware some kind of blue print on how some of its components have to be connected to guarantee a more deterministic behavior. In this case, we will extend the concept of templates [26] in our new middleware version of DAiSI to have better control over the structure of those critical system parts.

In this paper we have already presented three different types of communication in details: RPC, ownership and topics. However, we noticed that we lacked two crucial communication paradigms for autonomous driving, namely streams and blackboard. We included them in our taxonomy but did not yet implemented them in our DAiSI concept. Streams are used for the transmission of continuous sensor data, e. g. for the transmission of the camera image, since the communication methods described above are not suitable for this type of communication.

Another feature we would like to add to our middleware is a filtering mechanism for the communication methods ownership and topics. In the presented version of these two methods, a consumer of data is informed each time updates were made to the ownership object or new data is published using a topic. We are therefore planning to introduce a filter mechanism that will allow consumers to specify after which kind of changes they would like to be informed. We are still working on a good concept where filtering should take place, whether on the consumer or producer side. Both options have their own advantages and disadvantages in terms of performance.

We are currently persisting the structure of the Topic Hierarchy with an XML document (Extensible Markup Language). We intend to further expand this approach by supplementing semantic information with the help of ontologies. Also, we want to extend the semantic concepts done in [28] to our middleware. With this new feature, we will evaluate whether it is possible to use ontologies effectively and usefully in an autonomous driving scenario. We expect that in very large systems it can make sense to distribute the information about a Topic Hierarchy or general data relation under a common upper ontology. These would be merged at runtime if new components or DAiSI instances are installed in the system and additional topic or data information would be available. We estimate that a semantic reasoner should be able to build the entire Topic Hierarchy.

VIII. Conclusion

In this paper, we have introduced a new kind of dynamic-adaptive middleware for autonomous systems that breaks with many paradigms of classical embedded systems. Components in our middleware are clearly separated from the actual communication technology. The components connect to executable systems on the basis of specified configurations and can be added to or removed from the system at runtime. We have presented three different types of communication: RPC, ownership and topics, which are needed for different requirements of autonomous systems. In addition, we have expanded the classical understanding of topics to structure them into hierarchies.

We are firmly convinced that in a world where autonomous systems such as vehicles, robots, drones or machines are becoming increasingly common, new software architectures and models are also needed. These architectures and models must allow autonomous systems to receive updates and new functions at runtime without having to be installed in workshops by the manufacturer. In this paper we showed a possible way to lay the foundation for dynamic, self-adaptive and autonomous systems with the help of our middleware.

References

[1] SAE J 3016, "Taxonomy and Definitions for Terms Related to Driving Automation Systems for On-Road Motor Vehicles," p. 30, 2016.

[2] C. Brink, E. Kamsties, M. Peters, and S. Sachweh, "On hardware variability and the relation to software variability," in Proceedings - 40th Euromicro Conference Series on Software Engineering and Advanced Applications, 2014, pp. 352–355.

[3] O. Oliinyk, K. Petersen, M. Schoelzke, M. Becker, and S. Schneickert, "Structuring automotive product lines and feature models: an exploratory study at Opel," Requirements Engineering, vol. 22, no. 1, 2017, pp. 105–135.

[4] A. Pretschner, M. Broy, I. H. Krüger, and T. Stauner, "Software engineering for automotive systems: A roadmap," in Future of Software Engineering, 2007, pp. 55–71.

[5] M. Broy, "Challenges in automotive software engineering," in Proceedings of the 28th international conference on Software engineering, vol. 2006, 2006, pp. 33–42.

[6] K. Grimm, "Software Technology in an Automotive Company - Major Challenges," in Proceedings of the 25th International Conference on Software Engineering, 2003, pp. 498–503.

[7] B. Hardung, T. Kölzow, and A. Krüger, "Reuse of software in distributed embedded automotive systems," in Proceedings of the fourth ACM international conference on Embedded software - EMSOFT '04, 2004, p. 203.

[8] C. Krupitzer, F. M. Roth, S. Vansyckel, G. Schiele, and C. Becker, "A survey on engineering approaches for self-adaptive systems," Pervasive and Mobile Computing, vol. 17, no. PB, 2015, pp. 184–206.

[9] M. Bernard et al., Mehr Software (im) Wagen : Informations- und Kommunikationstechnik (IKT) als Motor der Elektromobilität der Zukunft *English Translation: More software in the car: information and communication technology as the motor of electromobility for the future*. ForTISS GmbH, 2011.

[10] P. Oreizy et al., "An architecture-based approach to self-adaptive software," IEEE Intelligent Systems and Their Applications, vol. 14, no. 3, 1999, pp. 54–62.

[11] J. O. Kephart and D. M. Chess, "The vision of autonomic computing," Computer, vol. 36, no. 1, 2003, pp. 41–50.

[12] C. Szyperski, Component Software: Beyond Object-Oriented Programming (2nd Edition), 2nd ed. Addison-Wesley Professional, 2002.

[13] A. MacCormack, J. Rusnak, and C. Y. Baldwin, "The Impact of Component Modularity on Design Evolution: Evidence from the Software Industry," Harvard Business School Technology & Operations Mgt. Unit Research Paper, 2007.

[14] B. Councill and G. T. Heineman, "Definition of a software component and its elements," Component-based software engineering: putting the pieces together, 2001, pp. 5–19.

[15] P. A. Bernstein, "Middleware: a model for distributed system services," Communications of the ACM, vol. 39, no. 2, 1996, pp. 86–98.

[16] N. Wang, D. C. Schmidt, and C. O'Ryan, "Overview of the CORBA Component Model: Component-based Software Engineering," in Component-based software engineering, G. T. Heineman and W. T. Councill, Eds. Boston, MA, USA: Addison-Wesley Longman Publishing Co., Inc, 2001, pp. 557–571.

[17] Object Management Group - OMG, "CORBA Component Model Specification," 2006.

[18] F. Kon et al., "Monitoring, Security, and Dynamic Configuration with the dynamicTAO Reflective ORB," IFIP/ACM International Conference on Distributed systems platforms, 2000, pp. 121–143.

[19] D. Garlan, S.-W. Cheng, A.-C. Huang, B. Schmerl, and P. Steenkiste, "Rainbow: Architecture- Based Self-Adaptation with Reusable Infrastructure," in Proceedings of International Conference on Autonomic Computing, 2004, pp. 46–54.

[20] R. Anthony and C. Ekelin, "Policy-driven self-management for an automotive middleware," in Proceedings of the 1st International Workshop on Policy-Based Autonomic Computing (PBAC 2007), 2007, p. 7.

[21] B. Becker, H. Giese, S. Neumann, M. Schenck, and A. Treffer, "Model-based extension of AUTOSAR for architectural online reconfiguration," Lecture Notes in Computer Science (including subseries Lecture Notes in Artificial Intelligence and Lecture Notes in Bioinformatics), vol. 6002 LNCS, 2010, pp. 83–97.

[22] A. S. Tanenbaum and M. van Steen, Distributed systems: principles and paradigms. Prentice-Hall, 2007.

[23] A. Schill and T. Springer, Verteilte Systeme Grundlagen und Basistechnologien. Berlin; Heidelberg: Springer Vieweg, 2012.

[24] F. Buschmann, R. Meunier, H. Rohnert, P. Sommerlad, and M. Stal, Pattern-Oriented Software Architecture, A System of Patterns: Volume 1 (Wiley Software Patterns Series). Wiley, 2013.

[25] H. Klus and A. Rausch, "DAiSI A Component Model and Decentralized Configuration Mechanism for Dynamic Adaptive Systems," International Journal On Advances in Intelligent Systems, vol. 7, no. 3 and 4, 2014, pp. 27–36.

[26] H. Klus, D. Herrling, and A. Rausch, "Interface Roles for Dynamic Adaptive Systems," in Proceedings of the Seventh International Conference on Adaptive and Self-Adaptive Systems and Applications (ADAPTIVE), 2015, pp. 80–84.

[27] D. Herrling, A. Rausch, and K. Rehfeldt, "Extending Interface Roles to Account for Quality of Service Aspects in the DAiSI," International Journal on Advances in Software, vol. 9, no. 1 & 2, 2016, pp. 37–49.

[28] Y. Wang, D. Herrling, P. Stroganov, and A. Rausch, "Ontology-based automatic adaptation component interface in DAiSi," in Proceedings of the Eighth International Conference on Adaptive and Self-Adaptive Systems and Applications (ADAPTIVE 2016), 2016, pp. 51–58.

[29] M. Quigley et al., "ROS: an open-source Robot Operating System," in ICRA Workshop on Open Source Software, vol. 3, 2009, p. 5.

Towards a Cubesat Autonomicity Capability Model

A Roadmap for Autonomicity in Cubesats

Clement Gama, Roy Sterritt, George Wilkie, Glenn Hawe
School of Computing
Ulster University
Jordanstown Campus, Newtownabbey, County Antrim BT37 0QB, United Kingdom
Gama-C1@ulster.ac.uk, R.Sterritt@ulster.ac.uk, Fg.Wilkie@ulster.ac.uk, Gi.Hawe@ulster.ac.uk

***Abstract* — The paper presents an autonomic / self-managing model, which can be used in cubesat development to make cubesats self-configuring, self-healing, self-optimizing and self-protecting. Autonomous and self-managing systems have emerged in multiple domains, e.g., autonomous ground and aerial vehicles. So far, there is no standard model as to how to design and implement self-managing, autonomous systems. In this paper, we are going to look at how autonomic computing can be applied in unmanned systems and how it can be adapted and applied to the cubesat space industry. Spacecraft always operate in remote environments whereby human intervention is infeasible and therefore making them autonomic is not a niche feature, but a required paradigm change for future satellites. An autonomic capability level model for cubesats is proposed in this paper, which can assist cubesat developers gradually increase the use of autonomic features in satellite and cubesat systems.**

Keywords - autonomic computing; autonomicity; apoptosis; cubesat; capability model.

I. INTRODUCTION

Autonomic Computing (AC) has been adopted in various technical platforms such that it is no longer about the vision that IBM had in 2001 when they first proposed AC for servers [1][2]. Multiple industries, for example the automotive industry, the Ministry of Defence, the freight industry, and space exploration - to mention a few - are all researching and developing self-managing systems specifically to address complex issues within their domains [2]. In some industries, autonomic systems are referred to as Unmanned Systems (UMSs); and examples include Unmanned Underwater Vehicles (UUVs), Unmanned Aerial Vehicles (UAVs), and Unmanned Ground Vehicles (UGVs) [3].

The purpose of this paper is to investigate the applicability of autonomic computing in cubesats, and introduce a roadmap for future autonomic cubesat development (a Cubesat Autonomic Capability Model (CACM)). Autonomicity in cubesats is a new field currently being researched by universities and other stakeholders around the world. The CACM derives inspiration from the IBM 2001 Autonomic Maturity Model, Autonomy Levels Framework, the Automotive Driving Automation Levels model, and the Capability Maturity Model Integration (CMMI).

Cubesats are a type of microsatellites / nanosatellites that came out of a collaborative endeavour between California Polytechnic State University and Stanford University in 1999 [4]. The original vision for developing cubesats and standardizing them was to develop the necessary skills for creating satellites intended for Low Earth Orbit (LEO) and also limit the size and number of science instruments that could go on-board spacecraft. The cubesat form factor specification was standardized to 10cm x 10cm x10cm (1U) with a mass of about 1.33kg [5]. Other form factors include 2U (10cm x 10cm x 20cm), 3U (10cm x 10cm x 30cm), 6U, 12U, etc. The low cost and faster development of cubesats has been the result of accelerated technological advances in spacecraft miniaturization in recent years [6].

Traditionally, spacecraft consist the main payload, which conducts space experiments or tasks, and vehicle support systems, like communications, propulsion, attitude determination and control, electric power system, and data storage [7]. Cubesats, however, can only implement some of the features of monolithic satellites due to their physical size limit, electrical power availability and processing power [7]. Nowadays, these microsatellites are utilised to accomplish LEO missions that were previously performed using monolithic satellites and this has resulted in huge mission cost savings [8].

This paper, in Section 2, delves into the review of published material on autonomic computing, autonomy in cars, Autonomy Levels For Unmanned Systems (ALFUS), CMMI and autonomy in cubesats. In Sub-Section "D. Cubesats", we present a literature review on cubesats as a whole, starting from their inceptions to current development and proposed future use by agencies like NASA. Two hypotheses are presented in Section 3, with specific steps to be followed in investing both hypotheses. Risks in conducting this research are addressed in Sub-Sections 2 and 3. Section 4, outlines the proposed CACM, which will help guide developers who want to design self-managing cubesats. The model is summarised in Table I. Section 5 defines the application of the CACM when developing a kill switch function on cubesats. The kill switch is a de-orbiter feature required to ensure that dead cubesats do not remain in active orbit after their missions are completed or terminated [5].

II. LITERATURE REVIEW

Autonomic computing as defined in the IBM 2001 maturity model, as shown in Figure 1, [1] comprises five maturity levels (Level 1 Basic, Level 2 Managed, Level 3 Predictive, Level 4 Adaptive and Level 5 full Autonomic) [9]. Level 1: At the Basic level, there is heavy reliance on system reports, product documentation, and user intervention to

Levels	Characteristics	Skills	Benefits
Level 5 Autonomic	Integrated IT components are collectively and dynamically managed by business rules and policies	IT staff focuses on enabling business needs	Business policy drives IT management Business agility
Level 4 Adaptive	IT components, individually and collectively, able to monitor, correlate, analyse and take action with minimal human intervention	IT staff manages performance against SLAs	Balanced human / system interaction IT agility and resiliency
Level 3 Predictive	Individual IT components and systems able to monitor, correlate and analyse the environment and recommend actions	IT staff approves and initiates actions	Reduced dependency on deep skills Faster / better decision making
Level 2 Managed	Management software in place to provide consolidation, facilitation and automation of IT tasks	IT staff analyses and takes actions	Greater system awareness Improved productivity
Level 1 Basic	Rely on system reports, product documentation, and manual actions to configure, optimize, heal and protect individual IT components	Requires extensive, highly skilled IT staff	Basic requirements addressed

Human Intervention Decreases

Autonomicity Increases

Figure 1. Derived from the IBM Autonomic Computing Adoption Levels [1].

configure, optimize, recover and protect individual IT components.

Level 2: At the Managed level, management software is used to consolidate, facilitate and automate IT tasks [9]. Level 3: The Predictive level makes limited predictions through monitoring, correlation of individual system [9] components, environmental analysis and recommends user actions. Level 4: Adaptive level, in this level individual and collections of IT components are monitored, correlated and analysed. Corrective action and reconfiguration has minimal human intervention [9]. Level 5: Autonomic level, system components are all integrated and are system managed using business rules and policies stored in a knowledge-base [9].

The lowest level of this capability model is actually not autonomic at all, but instead IT personnel run the show of configuring the AC systems, monitoring them, performing error recovery (healing), fine tuning (optimization) and protecting the systems by anticipating imminent error conditions and taking corrective action before the systems fail [10]. The fifth level, however, in contrast to the basic level, has minimal human intervention, but instead the system is more self-governing and managing. The human actor still intervenes in setting up the policies, which the autonomic system agents use to formulate tasks and goals [10].

A. *Autonomy Levels Framework*

The IBM 2001 autonomic computing maturity model is well suited for environments whereby the systems have ample computing power, enough electric power, have dedicated IT staff. In mobile UMSs, e.g., UAVs, UUVs, and spacecraft, resources are very much limited and therefore a more customised version of autonomic computing is necessary [3].

As a response to the need for a customised autonomic computing model, a voluntary Ad-Hoc Working Group sponsored by the National Institute of Standards and Technology (NIST), comprising government organisations and contractors was formed. The sole purpose of this working group was to develop the ALFUS framework, which was aimed at addressing aerial, underwater and over ground vehicles' autonomic computing issues [11]. The ALFUS framework defines unmanned autonomy using these three categories as shown in Figure 2: Mission Complexity, Environmental Complexity and Human Independence [12].

1) *Mission Complexity (MC)*

Mission complexity depends on the type of unmanned vehicle used in a mission. In ground based vehicles, it could depend on transit systems for both people and goods, which involves moving from one location to another. Mission complexity increases when route distance, optimisation, traffic congestion, and route specificity are taken into consideration [12].

Missions for space exploration and planetary science studies can be complicated by the number of instruments fitted in a vehicle, and also the science tasks and communication latencies. A space mission consists of at least two aspects: the science mission (tasks), and the spacecraft management [12].

2) *Environment Complexity (EC)*

Spacecraft environmental complexities come from space junk, solar flares, and other high energy particles that could damage the spacecraft or some of its instruments. It has to be able to autonomously avoid obstacles, i.e., space debris, other

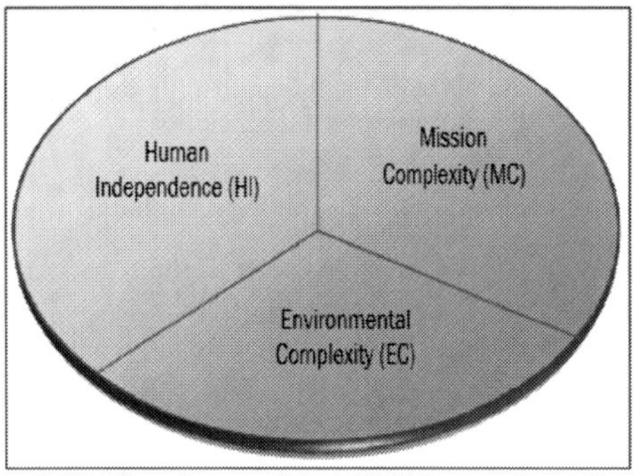

Figure 2. The Three Aspects of the ALFUS framework as defined by the working group [13].

satellites and other objects (meteors, asteroids and comets) [12][13].

In ground based vehicles, complexity comes from the transit network - closed roads, closed lanes, and closed tracks. In some urban areas bus lanes exist to be exclusively used by buses at certain times of the day, and some bus lanes are exclusive to buses all the time, so the vehicle must navigate this complex network at all times. Other constraints come from pedestrians who may or may not adhere to traffic rules and other manned vehicles can pose a threat to UMSs [12].

3) Human Independence (HI)

The measurement of human independence in a UMS ranges from partial human control (Hybrid), e.g., in cars, the use of the auto-cruise, which needs a human to activate it – to fully automated sky-trains and automated trams. The human aspect determines the vehicle's level of autonomy [12].

B. *Autonomy in the Automotive Industry*

The automotive industry has joined the autonomic computing development race in an attempt to make self-driving cars. Autonomy in cars has long been a science fiction phenomenon… as Gao et al [14] puts it *"the Firebird IV concept car, which, as the company explained, "anticipates the day when the family will drive to the super-highway, turn over the car's controls to an automatic, programmed guidance system and travel in comfort and absolute safety at more than twice the speed possible on today's expressways"*. This was in 1964 during the New York World's Fair exhibition by General Motors [14].

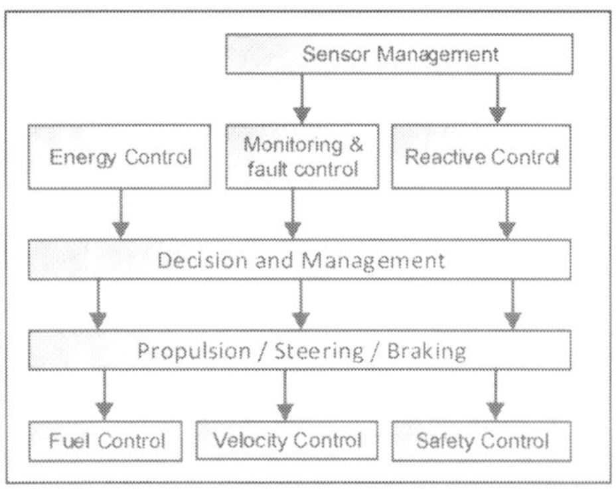

Figure 3. An adapted modular architecture of an autonomous car [16].

The idea of cruising safely on motorways was a far-fetched dream in the 1960s, but that vision is coming closer to a reality, however, there are still problems to overcome. According to the Spectrum IEEE publication [15] an autonomous car failed every 3 hours during test experiments in California in 2016. The Department of Motor Vehicles released a report in January 2017 detailing over 2,500 self-driving car failures in 2016 alone [15].

Autonomous cars control the steering wheel, acceleration, brakes, gears and the clutch using sensory information from multiple sensors. Fig. 3 below shows a diagram of an autonomic car and its various components. Autonomic cars mimic a human driver in that they understand the current situation on the roads from the live streaming of sensory values [16]. An autonomous car modular structure would take the high-level design shown in the figure below, whereby the car controls acceleration through fuel control and braking, steering and implements safety [16].

C. *Capability Maturity Model Integration (CMMI)*

CMMI is a collection of industry best practices designed to help organisations continuously improve their business processes [17]. There are 3 CMMI models comprising CMMI for Development (CMMI-DEV), CMMI for Services (CMMI-SVC) [18] and CMMI for Acquisition (CMMI-ACQ) [19]. CMMI has a framework structure required to produce models within CMMI, appraisal tools and training material [17]. The CMMI framework comprises goals and practices necessary to create CMMI constellation models. The models contain 16 process areas, which are essential to business process improvement [18]. Examples of process areas in CMMI-DEV include: Configuration Management (CM), Integrated Project Management (IPM), Organizational Training (OT), Product Integration (PI), Project Monitoring and Control (PMC), Project Planning (PP), etc. [17]. Each process area has generic goals and practices, and specific goals and practices as shown in the structure below.

CMMI [17] is an integrated approach across an enterprise, which focuses on building tools to support process improvement used to develop software systems. Process improvement helps to reduce the complexity, redundancy and costs associated with the use of separate and multiple capability maturity models (CMMs) [20].

CMMI has two streams of business process improvement (representations), namely: maturity levels – which corresponds to a staged representation, and capability levels, which correspond to a continuous representation. In a staged representation, processes are grouped and improved upon to achieve a specific maturity level. For example, in order to reach Maturity Level 1, an organisation would have to select and improve on these processes: CM, IPM, OT and PP. In continuous representation, a process to be improved on and the desired capability level are selected.

D. *Cubesats*

The original goal for developing cubesats and standardizing them was to develop the necessary skills for creating satellites intended for LEO missions and also limit the size and number of science instruments that could go on-board these spacecraft [21].

Cubesats (see an example of a 1U in Figure 4) [22] are considered low cost spacecraft – by satellite cost standards – because they tend to be designed and constructed from Commercial Off-The-Shelf (COTS) components [4].

Nowadays, such microsatellites are utilised in LEO missions previously performed using monolithic satellites and this has resulted in huge mission cost savings [8]. The International Space Station (ISS) has – among other functions – been used to deploy cubesats into orbit. The ISS uses a standardised deployer called the Poly Picosatellite Orbital Deployer (P-POD) as shown in Figure 5 [23]. Cubesats have gained international interest and adoptions, even NASA has been seriously considering reducing exploration mission costs by automating most of the tasks involved in spacecraft monitoring and control.

Traditionally, monolith spacecraft send their data (instrument data & navigation and health status data) back to earth stations for analysis. The data analysts and engineers send back commands to the craft for the next tasks to be performed. This exercise has a high cost because the number of missions has increased over the years and therefore mission personnel has had to increase [24].

Another issue with traditional satellites is communications lags between earth stations and the satellites in space. This increases the risk of mission failures because it takes more than a few minutes for the ground operators to receive the data and process it before they know what is happening out there, and by that time the spacecraft could be damaged, or the mission could have been jeopardized [24].

Cubesats were meant for the academic environment, but NASA – since the cubesat launch initiative and the Educational Launch of Nanosatellites (ELaNa) [25] - is investing in the advancement and development of the platform with the view to send cubesats into deep space in the near future [26].

NASA Goddard is actively working on propulsion systems, power sources and avionics to use on cubesats.

Figure 4. An example of a 1U cubesat [22].

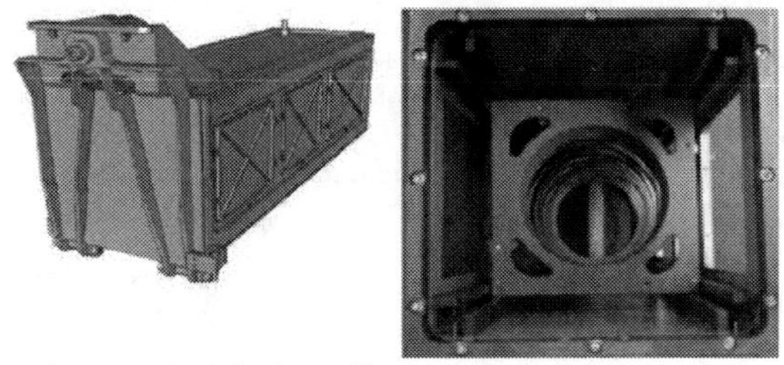

Figure 5. A 3U Poly Picosatellite Orbital Deployer (P-POD) [23].

Currently, cubesats, due to their size have the following limitations [21]:

- No long-range communications for sending data from deep space - however NASA has developed a miniature radio-communication system capable of talking directly to Earth from Mars and beyond.
- Current propulsion systems cannot fit on these small form factor satellites.
- Some scientific instruments cannot fit in the small form-factor frames. Innovators have to design instruments fit for the cubesat platform.

NASA's future strategy is to incorporate cubesats into their long-term plans for deep space exploration once the above limitations have been resolved [27].

The European Space Agency (ESA), since 2013, has had vested interest in cubesats too, mainly to test miniaturised technologies for small payload-driven missions [28]. ESA uses cubesats because of their low cost and high modularity, and therefore allows the demonstration of miniaturised technologies using System-On-Chip (SOC) integration and to demonstrate constellation configurations [28].

Autonomic computing in cubesats as of the writing of this paper is scarcely available – at best. Future endeavours will see cubesats take centre-stage in space missions with monolithic satellites [29] and therefore need to be autonomic. Cubesat design and development is still based on commands being sent from earth stations [30]. An example of a ground station controlled satellite was the SwissCube, which was designed for altitudes of 400km and 1000km and only had ground station access time of between 5 minutes and 10 minutes [31].

This shows another problem in LEO satellites, "access time" is very limited, hence the need for cubesats to be autonomic so they can perform multiple tasks without waiting for instructions from ground stations. There are several projects whereby autonomy is built-in from the beginning like the University Würzburg's Experimental satellite UWE-3, which was designed to address the following challenges [32]:

- Real-time failure detection, identification and recovery on-board, as miniaturization increases susceptibility to noise effects.
- Network control of the multi-satellite system, requiring integration of attitude and orbit control with the communication in order to be tolerant to interruptions of the link.

Current development of autonomic cubesats is still in early stages, e.g., the UWE-4 satellite incorporated orbit determination and control, and it had attitude determination and control [33]. ESA developed a similar autonomic model with levels ranging from E1 to E4 with level E1 being the lowest and level E4 being the highest whereby mission goals are run by the on-board computer.

The level of desired autonomy is not always the highest, it depends on the mission and its goals, and sometimes the best level of AC is adjustable and mixed autonomy [32].

III. RESEARCH HYPOTHESES

Given the young and evolving nature of the cubesat industry and hence the lack of autonomic control in cubesats, the plan in this project is to investigate autonomic computing in cubesats using the following hypotheses:

A. *Hypothesis 1:*

An autonomic capability model can be used as a tool to educate and motivate cubesat developers on the relevance and areas of application of autonomicity in space missions. By following the reasoning and use of the IBM 2001 maturity model and the automotive industry autonomic model, and CMMI, it is possible to develop a CACM that can form the basis for specifying autonomic features of relevance to future cubesat missions.

1) Research Steps

In studying and exploring this hypothesis, the following steps are being followed and used in the development of the CACM:

a. An evaluation of the layered models applied to autonomicity in the car industry and also the IBM 2001 maturity model has been conducted. Parallels have been drawn from the automotive industry autonomic levels and the IBM AC levels and capabilities, and currently investigating how they can be adapted and customised to suit the size and power constrained cubesat platform. This step is being performed through literature reviews of the IBM AC model and the automotive autonomic model, identifying specific capabilities in each level and key features of the progression from one level to the next.

b. Perform an in-depth literature review of the cubesat platform. This will be an intensive study of the cubesat environment, i.e., the components, form factors, current features, feature limitations, current and future cubesat mission types, and projected roadmap for development. Possible alternatives to cubesat components and computing platform will be explored because current "Commercial Of The Shelf" (COTS) components, are too expensive for most schools and universities, and therefore cheaper alternatives are a must to further drive the future of cubesat development.

c. Formulate the capability model (drawing inspiration from CMMI, the IBM Autonomic Maturity Model, the ALFUS and the Automotive Autonomy Model) to be applied to cubesats and to be incorporated in future cubesat developments. This step will involve distilling the best features of the models used as an inspiration for drawing this capability model. Some features and capabilities present in the above-mentioned models will not be applicable to cubesats due to the physical size limitations, component limitation and computing power

d. Develop an expert system to educate cubesat developers on how to use and apply the CACM to their cubesat designs and development. This system will guide developers on how to best develop and deploy the model. The system will be run remotely, and will create space mission profiles based on the interaction with developers as they respond to questions asked by the system to try and determine what level of autonomic computing is required for specific missions.

e. Formulate a set of evaluation questions to test the hypothesis, and to help improve the CACM. The questionnaire will be used to conduct surveys of cubesat developers and professional institutions in the cubesat industry. Such institutions will include private space technology companies, universities and space agencies. The surveys will collect information on how current satellite and cubesat developers think autonomic cubesats could benefit future space missions.

f. Survey a suitable number of cubesat institutions / companies to complete the evaluation. These will be planned in conjunction with the Space Mission challenges for Information Technology (SMC-IT) conference and possibly use the NASA network of contacts to distribute a questionnaire and get enough responses to test the hypothesis. A conference paper will be presented in the SMC-IT conference and delegates will be requested to fill-out the survey questionnaires. The data collected from the questionnaire forms will be used to change and tweak the model to best address any concerns obtained through the questionnaire feedback.

2) Risk Assessment

Perhaps the main risk associated with testing the first hypothesis is in not being able to survey the intended number of cubesat institutions. This could potentially render testing the hypothesis by real-world cubesat developers unachievable. There is another risk that the intended conference paper might not be accepted for presentation at the SMC-IT conference, and that would result in not getting the survey performed as mentioned in the research steps.

3) Risk Mitigation

A workshop will have to be planned and run at one of the SMC-IT conferences if the paper is not accepted. The workshop will be used to show developers how they could benefit from applying autonomic computing in cubesat design and development for individual cubesats and in constellations.

The workshop can also show how space missions can be better managed and made cheaper if cubesats were autonomic. By using a pre-recorded video to cover the use of the CACM, in conjunction with a knowledge-based system, it is hoped that workshop attendees can quickly be brought up to speed with our work and will then be in a position to complete our survey. Participants who need additional time will be able to take the CACM the video and the survey questionnaire away with them, and will be followed-up within two weeks to ensure they complete the survey.

B. *Hypothesis 2:*

An autonomic and apoptotic solution can address the needs of cubesats in complying with the requirements associated with space junk and will act as a suitable demonstrator area to illustrate the architecture of the CACM. Using the tenets of the CACM, cubesats can be designed to comply with the international requirement to clean-up space junk and debris by de-orbiting cubesats at the end of their mission or by executing the kill-switch if a cubesat develops an irrecoverable error condition before the end of its mission. This study will seek to demonstrate an apoptotic architecture through its implementation in a working solution.

1) Research Steps

The research steps to be followed when studying and exploring this hypothesis are as follows:

a. Investigate the space junk / debris problem in light of increased deployed spacecraft, especially cubesats.

b. Investigate available space clean-up solutions both current and those being proposed. Various sizes of space junk may possibly require different methods of clean-up, in this step, we will investigate proposed solutions for cubesat clean-ups.

c. Create a de-orbiter architecture employing apoptosis. The architecture will demonstrate various levels of capability according to the CACM autonomic levels, and therefore will incorporate Self-CHOP (Self-Configuration, Self-Healing, Self-Optimisation and Self-Protection), Monitoring, Analysis, Planning and Execution (MAPE) and communications. The demonstrator will have a number of versions each illustrating specific capabilities and level of sophistication at each of the CACM levels.

d. Perform the de-orbiter evaluation, during and after development and use that outcome to reform, improve and refine the model in step C of the first hypothesis. This is a feedback mechanism to change the model and make it more relevant to actual software development of autonomic cubesats. This provides an internal assessment and fine-tuning of the CACM model.

e. Build a de-orbiter simulator application to demonstrate the kill-switch capabilities of cubesats without propulsion (ground de-orbit simulator).

f. Get feedback from domain experts about the demonstrator / simulator through conference paper presentations and get questions or paper reviewers' feedback.

2) Risk Assessment

The demonstrator application will only test the hypothesis, but getting feedback from domain experts would add weight to the CACM and the apoptotic solution. The risk is in not being able to get the domain expert opinion.

3) Risk Mitigation

A workshop to demonstrate the application of the CACM in an apoptotic solution would have to be held at a conference. The workshop would help to test both the first and the second hypotheses using questionnaires to gather expert opinion on both the CACM and the apoptotic solution.

IV. ROADMAP FOR AUTONOMICITY IN CUBESATS

The roadmap for future cubesat development, as proposed in the CACM, is divided into 2 categories, namely: - the "Inspiration from Existing Models" and the "CACM Functional Areas". These two define both the hierarchy of the model and what modules or functional areas the CACM levels apply to within the cubesat platform.

A. *Inspiration from Existing Models*

Cubesats are designed from the ground up for specific missions. The mission type and goals determine what size the cubesat has to be, what capabilities and what scientific instruments to fit in the system. All these aspects of the cubesat can be autonomic individually and collectively, and can collaborate in a constellation.

Table I below summarises completed work on the draft CACM. The model consists of 5 autonomic levels derived from the IBM 2001 autonomic maturity model and the automotive automation models [34][35][36][37]. The proposed model shows how each level implements MAPE [1] of commands, and the tenets of Self-CHOP [1]. It also shows how cubesat functions and capabilities in the various incremental autonomic levels get more sophisticated as the level increases towards AC level 5.

Based on the literature review [5][13][38][39] conducted in this study, autonomicity is not common in the cubesat platform, especially as it relates to space debris clean-up. It was therefore deemed necessary to develop a roadmap model to help educate cubesat designers of the advantages of autonomic computing. The model will be a systematic implementation guide to autonomicity in the cubesat platform.

The CACM is inspired by CMMI [17][18][19], the Automotive Automation Model (AAM) [36][37], the IBM 2001 Autonomic Computing Model [1] and the ALFUS Model [11][12]. It derives from the structures and formulation of these models to create a capability model specifically designed to be implemented on cubesats by engineers, cubesat designers and mission architects. The model's purpose is to outline, draw up a roadmap for future cubesat autonomic designs and provides means to measure autonomic capabilities of cubesats against a standardized set of tiered self-management autonomic capabilities.

Another model that inspired CACM is the car industry AAM as described by SAE International [36]. It serves as a common taxonomy and descriptions for driving automation and attempts to simplify coordination and communication in the autonomous car industry [36]. This model comprises 6 levels ranging from full human driving with no automation to fully automated driving with no human intervention [36][37].

Since a cubesat is designed from the ground up for a specific scientific mission, whether it be monitoring

TABLE I. SUMMARY OF THE CACM.

CUBESAT AUTONOMIC CAPABILITY MODEL (CACM)	
Autonomic Capability Level	Autonomic Cubesat Level Description
AC1 **Incorporate Specific Capabilities**	Mission is fixed Limited on-board capability to transmit data and health signals Constellation: Information only. No propulsion
AC2 **Standardize Capabilities**	Mission is pre-scheduled, mission operations on-board. Transmits data to ground station on a schedule. Constellation: Information only. No propulsion
AC3 **Human & Machine Shared Capabilities**	Mission is pre-scheduled, mission operations on-board. Transmits data to ground station on a schedule. Some internal systems are autonomous Kill switch autonomously executed and by ground station. Mission goals can be adapted mid-mission
AC4 **Machine Delegated Capabilities**	Execution of goal-oriented mission operations on-board. Autonomic internal systems operations. Send health status to ground station and constellation. Mission goals can be adapted mid-mission Allows ground station to veto kill-switch execution. Propulsion Autonomic Avionics and collision avoidance – human instructions are optional
AC5 **Full Autonomic Capabilities**	Goal-oriented mission operations on-board. Can self-re-initialize OS and internal systems – no human intervention Sends health status to ground stations. Only receives new mission from ground station. Kill switch notification with error details

missions, exploration missions, defence / offence missions, and environmental study missions, cubesat functional specifications are therefore always mission specific. The CACM is product (cubesat) specific, and therefore, it would not follow the CMMI process areas, which are organisation specific [17]. However, it is envisaged that cubesat development can benefit from adopting this model because the CACM will form a basis for a systematic process of designing and developing cubesats incorporating autonomic behaviour from the ground up depending on mission specifics. Also, the CACM will be useful in setting the validation criteria for cubesat autonomic capabilities.

The drive to reduce space missions' costs is a strong catalyst in the development of safer, cheaper, smart, self-deorbiting cubesats and successful missions by implementing autonomic behaviour in cubesats. This will result in cubesats that will reduce space debris by deorbiting themselves and burn-up upon entry into the earth's atmosphere or any other planet's atmosphere. Part of the CACM capability definitions will be safe cubesats in that they can self-protect against potential dangers, e.g., change course if a cubesat is on a collision course with another object or if solar storms are predicted to be heading towards the satellite, the cubesat can self-shutdown. Self-protection helps to extend cubesat life-span, thereby allowing more successful missions on first take, resulting in low-cost missions.

Currently, there are no standard practices followed by all cubesat developers in reference to automation, autonomy and autonomicity. Every manufacturer seems to follow their own standards based on mission requirements and in CMMI terms, this would be similar to project management that is not standardized throughout an organisation.

B. *CACM Functional Areas*

Every cubesat contains the following components and functional areas, which form the core elements of a cubesat. Every cubesat implementation of the core components will vary depending on mission objectives. Their level of sophistication will be determined by the science mission objectives and the level of autonomicity the designers will want to implement. The main tasks and specific goals of each functional area are listed under each component. These tasks are high level, more details will be included as the model is further developed.

1) *Mission Control (MC)*
   - Hardcode mission objectives.
   - Mission tasks run on fixed schedules.
   - Software controlled mission objectives.
   - Change mission objectives mid-flight.
   - End / Terminate mission.
2) *Communication and Data Transmission (C&DT)*
   - Send science and internal systems data to ground stations.
   - Receive constellation communications and data.
   - Receive ground stations commands – including new mission plans and commands.
3) *Health Monitoring (HM)*
   - Monitor internal sensors.
   - Monitor internal modules (collection of sensors).
   - Send health status to ground stations and constellation.
4) *Ground Station (GS)*
   - Receive and analyse satellite data.
   - Plan new missions.
   - Change current missions.
   - Upload new missions.
5) *Management*
   - Monitor all systems on the spacecraft.
   - Manage and coordinate all sub-systems.
   - Collaborate with all spacecraft modules.
6) *Launch and Deployment (L&D)*
   - Power-up cubesat 2 hours after deployment.
   - De-tumble and stabilise cubesat after power up.
   - Deploy antennas and solar panels.
   - Collaborate with internal control systems.
7) *Electric Power Supply (EPS)*
   - Monitor available battery power.
   - Monitor power drainage rate.
   - Collaborate with Planning about schedules.
   - Regulate available power for components.
8) *Attitude Determination and Control System (ADCS)*
   - Use various methods to determine attitude.
   - Collaborate attitude determination in constellation.
   - Use available mechanism to alter attitude to meet mission goals.
9) *Orbit Determination and Control (ODC)*
   - Use various instruments and algorithms to determine orbit length, and inclination angle.
   - Collaborate orbit determination with constellation.
   - Use available propulsion mechanism to change orbit.
10) *Position Control (PC)*
   - Monitor spacecraft position relative to mission specification.
   - Use propulsion to manoeuvre the cubesat to various pre-planned and ad-hoc positions.
   - Move cubesat to specific positions in constellation.
11) *Scientific Instrumentation*
   - Monitor all scientific experiment instruments.
   - Validate instrument data.
   - Collaborate with Data Transmission.
12) *Kill Switch*
   - Enable provisional kill switch.
   - Override ground station kill switch commands.
   - Collaborate with Self-CHOP, De-Orbit Control and Management.
13) *De-Orbit Control*
   - Monitor Kill Switch status.
   - Collaborate with Orbit Determination and Control, Attitude Determination and Control, to quickly degrade the craft's orbit.
   - Collaborate with Constellation Management.
14) *Constellation*
   - Monitor individual members' health status.
   - Collaborate and coordinate flying formation through individual members' Attitude Determination and Control, Orbit Determination and Control, Position Control, and Data Transmission.

V. KILL SWITCH – EXEMPLAR APPLICATION

The kill switch functional area is designed to address the space debris problem of defunct satellites remaining in active orbit for many years after their missions have ended. We propose that all cubesats should implement a kill switch feature / function, which will shut down all onboard equipment, and deorbit the cubesat into the graveyard orbit, or cause it to deorbit towards the earth and burn up in the earth's atmosphere.

The highest level of autonomicity for single cubesat missions is level 3. This level, corresponds to the IBM autonomic level 5 [1], whereby the cubesat is "self-sufficient". Levels 4 and 5, only apply in constellations configurations. In all levels of autonomicity in the CACM, ground station has full access to the cubesat, but as the levels increase there is less need for human / ground station intervention. The sophistication of one CACM level, is built on the previous level's capabilities, features and functions. Each level adds more features and functions to the previous level's defining capabilities, and functions that are performed by the cubesat, thereby, reducing human intervention in the cubesat mission management process.

In level 1, the cubesat's monitoring subsystem polls sensors for heartbeats at fixed intervals and if no heartbeats are detected, it alerts the ground station. If ground station does not respond after 1 full orbital time, the cubesat restarts the faulty sensors. The restarts of the sensors are performed up to a maximum number of times, if the errors are not cleared. After the restart threshold is reached, then the cubesat executes the kill switch. All data validation processes are performed on the ground station systems. At this level, the only autonomic feature of the cubesat is this apoptotic function, which means if the cubesat loses contact with the ground station, it will, by default, deorbit.

Level 2 adds the ability for sensors to send their heartbeats and data at parameterised intervals to the monitoring subsystem of the cubesat. A high-level data validation, is performed by the monitoring subsystem. If, and when sensors become faulty, with errors that cannot be cleared, the cubesat can turns off those faulty sensors and continues the mission until all sensors are defunct. The cubesat will reboot itself to try and clear faults if all of its sensors have become faulty. If errors are not cleared after a maximum number of reboots, the kill switch will be executed.

Since level 3 is the highest CACM level for single cubesat missions, the cubesat implements all possible autonomic features within the limits of its processing power, and electrical power resources. As in previous CACM level, the features in this level are a cumulative addition to the above-mentioned levels 1 and 2. At this level, a cubesat can reload mission tasks from storage and recalibrate sensors. If the reload attempt threshold is reached and errors persist, the kill switch is executed. If the cubesat detects an imminent collision, it navigates around the obstacle without waiting for ground station instructions.

CACM level 4, introduces constellation configurations for cubesats i.e., a level 4 cubesat, is self-aware and constellation aware. It can announce itself with its functions and capabilities, it can join and leave the constellation, as and when required. It communicates with the constellation via the constellation coordinator / manager. A constellation member, as an individual device, implements the CACM level 3 of autonomicity. The science data and health status information, in a level 4 cubesat, is sent to the ground station via the constellation manager. If the cubesat's sensors all fail, the cubesat removes itself from the constellation – it notifies the constellation coordinator - and follow the CACM level 3 recovery process. If, and when the cubesat's sensors are working again, it re-joins the constellation.

At level 5, in addition to level 4 capabilities and features, cubesats are grouped according to features and capabilities in order to form redundancy groups. Cubesats at this level, can request to delegate some or all of their tasks to other members via the constellation manager. The constellation manager delegates other members' tasks to individual members of the same redundancy group. Cubesats at this level will take over other members' tasks in the same redundancy group at the request of the constellation manager. Members must be environment aware, i.e., be able to move in formation with others, and keep appropriate distances among themselves and avoid collisions.

The constellation manager can remove members with faulty statuses or corrupt data from the constellation, in order to protect the constellation's integrity. Constellation management delegation is performed by vote, i.e., if the primary manager and the initial backup manager go offline or fail, other members take a vote to elect the next constellation manager.

Similarly, CACM level 5 cubesats implement and operate at CACM level 3, at the individual level. The kill switch is executed if errors persist even after going through the recovery process as defined in CACM level 3.

VI. Conclusion and Future Work

This paper has presented the background literature review on autonomic computing as used in normal computing platforms, in the auto-industry, in unmanned systems, in monolithic satellites and cubesats. A review of the autonomic models used in the automotive industry and other unmanned systems has shown that autonomy is still in its infant stages, and therefore, more work still needs to be done.

An autonomic capability model geared towards advancing cubesats and their functionality has been proposed and is under development. A brief summary of the model has been presented in Table I, and it is a very high level view of the model. The model development has drawn inspiration from other models, e.g., the IBM Autonomic Maturity Model, CMMI, ALFUS and others. These models will continue to be used to fine-tune the CACM and through domain experts feedback collected through surveys in conferences.

The current CACM is in early stages of development, it is still a high-level work-in-progress document. Further development will be carried out as per the listed steps in both hypotheses. When the model has the details in each task and autonomic level, an exemplar application will be developed to illustrate practical applicability of the model. Challenges encountered during the application development phase will be used to modify and fine-tune the model. This process will be on-going until the end of the study.

The model will require cubesat developers to create components that are manageable through application software in order to implement full autonomic features. This will require an increase in the number of device sensors to enable the cubesats to monitor more of their internal systems and their surrounding environment.

References

[1] IBM, "Autonomic Computing White Paper: An Architectural Blueprint for Autonomic Computing," *IBM White Paper*, no. June, p. 34, 2005.

[2] T. O. Eze, R. J. Anthony, A. Soper, C. Walshaw, A. Computing, and U. Kingdom, "A Technique for Measuring the Level of Autonomicity of Self-Managing Systems," no. c, pp. 8–13, 2012.

[3] H.-M. Huang, E. Messina, and J. Albus, "Autonomy Levels For Unmanned Systems (ALFUS) Volume II : Framework Models," *Framework*, vol. II, no. December, 2007.

[4] A. Toorian, E. Blundell, J. Puig-Suari, and R. Twiggs, "CubeSats as Responsive Satellites," *Space 2005*, no. September, pp. 1–14, 2005.

[5] P. Marks, "CubeSat craze could create space debris catastrophe," *New Scientist*, Sep-2014.

[6] S. Sadeghi and M. R. Emami, "Multi-spacecraft Studies of the Auroral Acceleration Region: From Cluster to

Nanosatellites," *Advances in Space Research*, vol. 59, no. 5, pp. 1173–1188, 2016.

[7] K. Woellert, P. Ehrenfreund, A. J. Ricco, and H. Hertzfeld, "Cubesats: Cost-effective science and technology platforms for emerging and developing nations," *Advances in Space Research*, vol. 47, no. 4, pp. 663–684, 2011.

[8] E. P. Caillibot, C. C. Grant, and D. D. Kekez, "Formation Flying Demonstration Missions Enabled by CanX Nanosatellite Technology," *Small Satellite Conference*, 2005.

[9] IBM, "Autonomic Computing Toolkit," *User's Guide*, 2004. [Online]. Available: https://www.ibm.com/developerworks/autonomic/books/fpu0mst.htm#ToC_16. [Accessed: 15-Jan-2018].

[10] M. C. Huebscher and J. a McCann, "A survey of autonomic computing—degrees, models, and applications," *ACM Computing Surveys*, vol. 40, no. 3, pp. 1–28, 2008.

[11] H.-M. Huang, K. Pavek, J. Albus, and E. Messina, "Autonomy Levels for Unmanned Systems (ALFUS) Framework: Safety and Application Issues," *Proc. SPIE*, vol. 5804, pp. 439–448, 2005.

[12] G. T. McWilliams *et al.*, "Evaluation of autonomy in recent ground vehicles using the autonomy levels for unmanned systems (ALFUS) framework," *Proceedings of the 2007 Workshop on Performance Metrics for Intelligent Systems - PerMIS '07*, pp. 54–61, 2007.

[13] E. Levin, J. Pearson, and J. Carroll, "Wholesale debris removal from LEO," *Acta Astronautica*, vol. 73, pp. 100–108, 2012.

[14] P. Gao, R. Hensley, and A. Zielke, "A Road Map to the Future for the Auto Industry," *McKinsey & Company*, no. 4, pp. 42–53, 2014.

[15] M. Harris, "The 2,578 Problems With Self-Driving Cars - IEEE Spectrum," *Spectrum IEEE*. 2017.

[16] T. S. Kim, J. C. Na, and K. J. Kim, "Optimization of an Autonomous Car Controller Using a Self-Adaptive Evolutionary Strategy," *International Journal of Advanced Robotic Systems*, vol. 9, 2012.

[17] CMMI Product Team, "CMMI for Development, Version 1.3 (CMU/SEI-2010-TR-033). Software Engineering Institute.," 2010.

[18] CMMI Product Team, "CMMI for Services, Version 1.3 (CMU/SEI-2010-TR-034). Software Engineering Institute," 2010.

[19] M. Phillips, "CMMI for Acquisition (CMMI-ACQ) Primer, Version 1.3," 2011.

[20] L. Greiner, "Capability Maturity Model Integration (CMMI) Definition and Solutions | CIO," *Tutorial Capability Maturity Model Integration (CMMI) Definition and Solutions*, 2007. [Online]. Available: http://www.cio.com/article/2437864/process-improvement/capability-maturity-model-integration--cmmi--definition-and-solutions.html. [Accessed: 15-Jan-2018].

[21] E. Gibney, "CubeSats Set for Deep Space - If They Can Hitch a Ride.," *Nature*, vol. 535, no. 7610, pp. 19–20, Jul. 2016.

[22] Team Compass, "File:COMPASS-1 PR-Bild.jpg - Wikimedia Commons," *Wikimedia Commons*. [Online]. Available: https://commons.wikimedia.org/wiki/File%3ACOMPASS-1_PR-Bild.jpg. [Accessed: 15-Jan-2018].

[23] A. Chin, R. Coelho, L. Brooks, R. Nugent, and J. Puig-Suari, "Standardization Promotes Flexibility: A Review of CubeSats' Success," *Aerospace Engineering*, vol. 805, pp. 756--5087, 2008.

[24] W. Truszkowski, L. Hallock, J. Karlin, J. Rash, and G. Michael, "Autonomous and Autonomic Systems," p. 289, 2010.

[25] A. Heiney, "About ELaNa," 2015. [Online]. Available: https://www.nasa.gov/content/about-elana. [Accessed: 15-Jan-2018].

[26] A. Babuscia, K.-M. Cheung, D. Divsalar, and C. Lee, "Development of cooperative communication techniques for a network of small satellites and CubeSats in deep space: The SOLARA/SARA test case," *Acta Astronautica*, vol. 115, pp. 349–355, 2015.

[27] N. Cheeks, "From the Chief," *NASA Goddard Tech Transfer News*, vol. 11, no. 2, pp. 1–24, 2013.

[28] R. Walker, "Technology CubeSats," 2016. [Online]. Available: http://www.esa.int/Our_Activities/Space_Engineering_Technology/Technology_CubeSats. [Accessed: 15-Jan-2018].

[29] E. Gottzein *et al.*, "Challenges in the control and autonomy of communications satellites," *Control Engineering Practice*, vol. 8, no. 4, pp. 409–427, 2000.

[30] M. A. Viscio *et al.*, "Interplanetary CubeSats system for space weather evaluations and technology demonstration," *Acta Astronautica*, vol. 104, no. 2, pp. 516–525, 2014.

[31] M. Noca *et al.*, "Lessons Learned from the First Swiss Pico-Satellite: SwissCube," *23rd Annual AIAA/USU Conference on Small SatellitesConference on Small Satellites*, 2009.

[32] S. Zieba, P. Polet, F. Vanderhaegen, and S. Debernard, "Principles of adjustable autonomy: A framework for resilient human-machine cooperation," *Cognition, Technology and Work*, vol. 12, no. 3, pp. 193–203, 2010.

[33] I. Kronhaus, K. Schilling, S. Jayakumar, A. Kramer, M. Pietzka, and J. Schein, "Design of the UWE-4 Picosatellite Orbit Control System using Vacuum-Arc-Thrusters," no. Eit 1, pp. 1–11, 2013.

[34] R. W. Proud and J. J. Hart, "The Function-Specific Level of Autonomy and Automation Tool," *Engineering*.

[35] C. D. Wickens, A. S. Mavor, R. Parasuraman, and J. P. Mcgee, *The Future of Air Traffic Control: Human Operators and Automation*. 1998.

[36] SAE International, "Automated Driving: Levels Of Driving Automation Are Defined In New SAE International Standard J3016," *Global Ground Vehicle Standards*, 2016.

[37] M. Blanco *et al.*, "Human Factors Evaluation of Level 2 and Level 3 Automated Driving Concepts," *(Report No. DOT HS 812 182)*, no. August, p. 300, 2015.

[38] J. Su and Z. Lixin, "The European Union draft Code of Conduct for outer space activities: An appraisal," *Space Policy*, vol. 30, no. 1, pp. 34–39, 2014.

[39] F. Alby *et al.*, "The European space debris safety and mitigation standard," *Advances in Space Research*, vol. 34, no. 5, pp. 1260–1263, 2004.

Improvement of Self-optimizing in Selection and Composition of Services Using Reinforcement Learning Algorithm Based on Convex Hull

Hadis khorasaniNasab Abbasi
Faculty of Science& Computer Engineering
Shahid Beheshti University
Tehran, Iran
Email:Hadis.khorasani@gmail.com

Eslam Nazemi
Faculty of Science& Computer Engineering
Shahid Beheshti University
Tehran, Iran
Email:nazemi@sbu.ac.ir

***Abstract*—Web services are implemented by using many atomic or composite services. In a dynamic environment, some Web services require to select a service with defined Quality of Services(QoS) through runtime adaptation in changeable environments. In alignment with user satisfaction requirements, in selection of services a tradeoff between QoS should be considered, especially at runtime adaptation in dynamic environments. There are many methods for service selection and composite services with priority of QoS, but they do not predict optimizing service composition in the large scale environment. A self-optimizing method just continually adjusts the control service's parameters that pass to other services. In this paper, in a self-optimizing method, the goal and the procedure for selection and composition of optimal services are proposed. It includes three parts, services are limited in a defined scope by convex hull algorithm and then the optimal services are chosen by the divide-and-conquer algorithm. The optimal service selection is as input parameter goes to service composition algorithm. The QoS metrics taken into account and measured for the optimal service include response time, availability, throughput and reliability. The simulation results show that the system user satisfaction gradually increases by about 10% compared with the results of previous methods and show that the execution time is comparatively decreased by half.**

Keywords-text*; *self-adaption; self-optimizing; service composition; Reinforcement Learning; convex hull.

I. INTRODUCTION

Service-oriented environments have become more and more important in recent years, where various kinds of Web services and service-based processes are gathered within a certain domain or across domains [1][2]. They give people the ability to make, manage and share their own services, and make it possible to compose them based on a user's needs, providing them with extra value [1]. As reported in some previous studies on service selection, QoS attributes of atomic services are gathered for calculating the QoS of composite services in service composition environments [2][3].

Self-optimizing is considered a QoS optimization problem, choosing atomic services generating the highest QoS overall value as optimized solution [4][5]. It is presumed by most existing methods that QoS attributes pre-exist and QoS information of atomic services does not change. So, the ranking of declared QoS values is what determines the selection of a self-optimizing service. These approaches, however, have various constraints when the following problems are considered in the real environment. Firstly, service-oriented systems have various possible services because of the way they operate in distributed heterogeneous environments. Furthermore, existing services are ever-changing, so the selector should have the ability to adapt automatically to the dynamic environment. Finally, system should select optimal services based on QoS in reasonable time to meet user requirements.

In this paper, we propose a method for selecting and composition of services based on the self-optimizing. This is very important in service selection, because this kind of method can autonomously react to dynamic environments during its life cycle and adapt to them. This feature is very useful, and the reason is that nowadays, all services are distributed in large scale environment and they are always changing, so the system needs the method which can adapt to them. The self-optimizing method is also able to automatically improve behaviors by itself continually. It is considered as one of its features because one of the concerns for service composition in previous methods is selecting optimal services based on QoS.

The rest of the paper is organized as follows: In Section II, related works are discussed. Section III introduces a self-optimizing Method and process variability. Section IV demonstrates the validity of the proposed method by a series of simulation experiments. Finally, Section V draws some conclusions.

II. RELATED WORK

In this section, some related work from the perspectives of the self-optimizing service selection and composition based on QoS is introduced.

With the growth of Cloud Computing, Service Oriented Architecture (SOA) and Software as a service, possible services with similar functions but different QoS increase in numbers, which has made it far more difficult to select and compose services [5]. This has led to growing research in composition of QoS-aware Web service in SOA and Service-Oriented Computing (SOC) fields [6][7][8]. Yet, service composition is currently done mostly via approaches that utilize a semi-optimal approach relying on a single goal, instead of using Pareto optimal solutions that take into account the balance between various QoS objectives [9].

One sophistication that may arise is when a user quickly requires a service with a specific cost and certain performance, yet with increased availability. In real world usage, however, distinct dimensional attributes may not be compatible with one another.

Availability pair and the time it takes to respond are two of these contrasting characteristics. This means that QoS of optimal service composition has low response time and high Availability. Thus, reaching the optimal solutions given the different rules on the measured QoS and the competing goals is an NP-hard challenge. QoS weighting is used by some algorithms to dynamically adjust to these tradeoffs via a feedback controller [5]. However, the QoS weight sum method, has some constraints as follow: 1) weight vector directly influences the solutions, for which awareness of the problem in advance is needed; 2) there is a limited selection of solutions, which are not well-distributed; 3) as the scale of problem rises, so does the complexity and the time executed is dramatically increase; 4) if solutions are in out of reach areas of the Pareto front, Pareto optimal solutions may not be found; and 5) Clients may actually want to see a list of possible services, while only one, i.e., the Pareto optimal, is offered. Another field of work concerns utilizing the skyline operator to measure the real Pareto front [10][11]. The first one, the Bottom Up Algorithm, measures the biggest sections' workflow in order to boost the effectiveness of the process. The second Algorithm, consecutively provides the Pareto optimal services. But having temporal complexity in these algorithms is not possible, as the Pareto front might exponentially become larger with more tasks in the workflow. Also, the way the search area is pruned by the skyline operator means some possible services could be put aside even before selection occurs to meet the tradeoffs between multi QoS objectives, Pareto optimal workflows were set by Mostafa and Zhang [9]. It is provided tradeoff in linear domains with convex hall as well as the optimal Pareto front solution. Also Quick hull operator used to prune the search space may have polynomial time complexity because in the large number of workflow tasks, it has execution time at O(n2). Reinforcement Learning algorithm [12] has been introduced for solving sequential decision-making issue and makes learner optimal policy of Markov Decision Process (MDP) for services composition at runtime. This system can adapt to the dynamic environment by calculated reward function. It is supposed to receive reward value, which is equivalent to the cumulative reward of all the executed services [12]. However, there can be challenges as to how existing multi-goal service composition methods can work in dynamic environments. For example, to determine QoS value mathematical methods are used that presume a static environment. Once there are changes in the environment, there are no strategies for the system to deal with the emerging QoS. Also, some of these methods make use of explicit models so as to determine which services are chosen. No Rue is present in this model for addressing a new QoS parameter. Furthermore, in multi-object method, services are chosen by the weight which is defined in a static environment. Hence, the weight of a new service or an obsolete service in static environment cannot be dealt with changing environment. Finally, a near-optimal runtime policy is used by adaptive service Composition, meaning that in each of the system's lifecycles service composition is not optimal and the system cannot self-optimize.

In this paper, a new self-optimizing method is proposed. This method is based on Reinforcement Learning for calculated user satisfaction by reward function. A self-optimizing system is one that dynamically optimizes the operation of its service composition while it is running. The optimizer just continuously adjusts the control service which is selected based on QoS to compose with other services. In this system two main goals are followed, service composition can adapt with changing environment and system can optimize service composition based on QoS automatically and also multi-objective service composition approach is considered. In order to achieve those targets, this paper follows these steps: First, new search algorithm in convex hull is introduced for selecting multi-objective optimal services. Then, use Reinforcement Learning algorithm for compute services user satisfaction. This algorithm will obtain initial knowledge of the service selection from the divide-and-conquer algorithm and it will be optimized when service composition is based on optimal service.

III. PROPOSED METHOD FOR COMPOSITION OF SERVECES

In this section, the self-optimizing method is introduced for selection and composition of services in order to improve Reinforcement Learning method for service composition. In previous method, proposed service composition is not optimized in each life-cycle system. In this paper is proposed service composition that is optimized continuously. A self-optimizing composite service is one that dynamically own optimizes the service composition while it is running, so it needs to have some kind of rules that can follow in the system. The goal of the self-optimizing method is to maximize service composition based on QoS at all times. This method has ability to implement in the Large scale services and follows the goals like user satisfaction, being self-adaptive to the changeable environment, and presenting an automatic optimum service composition based on QoS. Before main algorithm is proposed, the schema of the self-optimizing method is mapped in MAPE_K loops, and the self-optimizing cycle in order to define the issue's scope should be explained.

A. *Adaption Loop*

Self-adaptive software is based on a closed-loop mechanism which is called the MAPE-K loop for autonomic computing, and includes the Monitoring, Analyzing, Planning and Executing functions. Self-optimizing is one of the most remarkable properties of self-adaptive systems. Therefore, my recommended plan for the self-optimizing is mapped in the MAPE-K loop in order to shows the workflow of the method.

Accordingly Figure 1, the QoS values are defined. In this paper response time, availability, throughput and reliability are as QoS parameters which are collected in "monitoring" step. Then, the collected data are analyzed in the "analysis" step. In this step, the value of those parameters is normalized. Then especial selected algorithm is executed in "Planning" stage. Optimal selected service as input parameter goes to the "execution" stage. In this stage, by Reinforcement Learning algorithm the best services are predicted for the user. MAPE-K loop is based on learning so there is one stage to share Knowledge with each part for predicting the system's behavior. In this case, the system needs to predict service composition to achieve high user satisfaction. Using reward function in Reinforcement Learning algorithm, the learning process is defined.

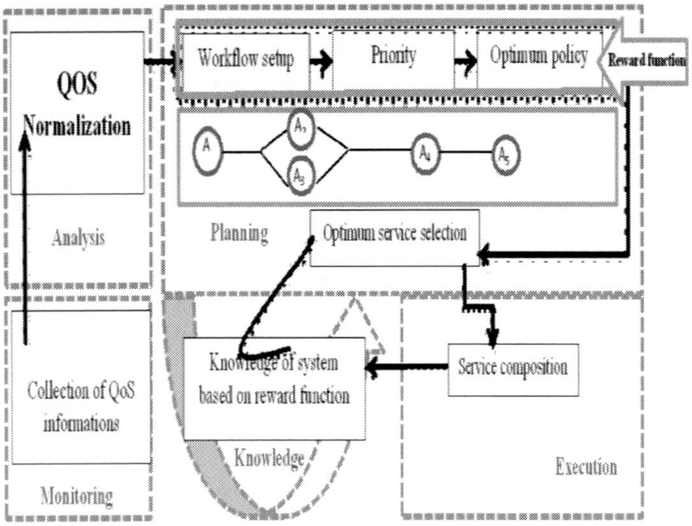

Figure 1. Abstract schema of the proposed method based on MAPE-K architecture.

B. *Self-optimizing cycle mapping*

The scope of service selection and composition is mapped on the cycle of the self-optimizing, which is depicted in Figure2.

The first step is "analyzing the current state". It is defining some QoS parameters which are normalized in a certain data range. The second step is "determining the goal of system". In this step the main goal of the system is defined. In this paper, the main target is selecting optimal services among distributed services, according to (1).

$$\pi := S \to A. \quad (1)$$

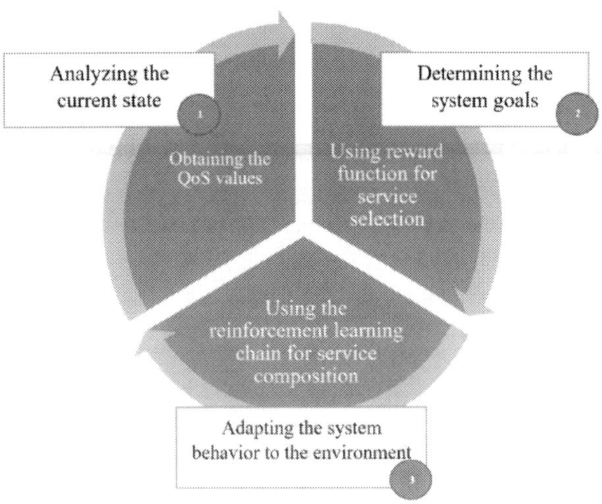

Figure 2. Self-optimizing cycle mapping for the selection and composition of service.

Geometric convex hull operator is used in order to reduce number of services. The convex hull is the smallest convex polygon that encloses all points in specific space. Here, points are services which should locate in defined geometric place. The service is limited as (2).

$$CH(S) = \{s_{i_1}.s_{i_2}.\dots.s_{i_m}\}.m \leq n.s_{i_j} \in S.j = 1.2.\dots.m. \quad (2)$$

Equation (2) shows that the convex hull of services includes "m" is members and "n" is the number of available services. So the number of services, which are known as members, are smaller than the number of available services. New services are adding in specific space by incremental convex hull algorithm. This process is implemented in three steps: first, place the visible facets for the services; the boundary of the visible faces is the set of horizon ridges for the services. Second, construct a cone of new facets from the service to its horizon ridges. Third, eliminate the visible facets. Therefore, the convex hull of the new service and the previous services is formed. Moreover, Convex hull is clustering services and categorizes them in a finite-dimensional space to set services in. In (3), "d" is number of dimensions in convex hull. In this paper, two dimensions are used. So, this algorithm translates the interior service to half spaces by dividing offsets into coefficients. Dimensions are allocated two QoS parameters, which are analyzed in first step, it shows (3).

$$Q = \{Q_i \in R^d | \forall Q_i \in Q. \exists s_i \in S\}. \quad (3)$$

According to Figure 3, the response time and throughput are determined with two-dimension space. Services are divided into four zones by the clustering of convex hull. It determines services' suitable zones according to the value of their QoS. For example, the optimal service placed in (b, c) zone which has highest throughput and lowest response time.

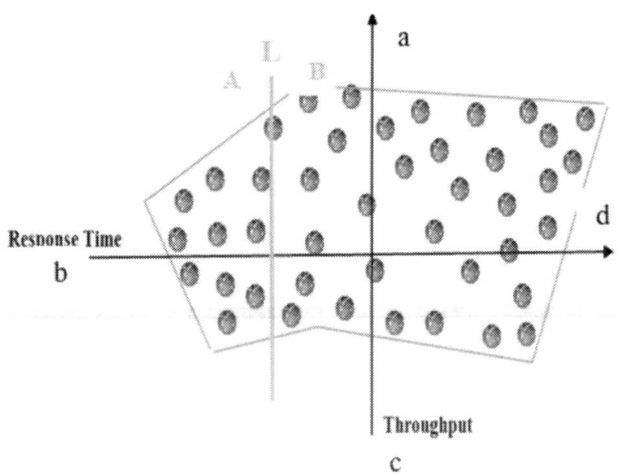

Figure 3. Selecting optimal services by clustering and divide-and-conquer.

After optimal services are determined in a defined zone, optimal service is selected by divide-and-conquer algorithm. This algorithm has O[$n \log n$] execution time in all cases. This algorithm operates as follows. In the first step, vertical line L divides services into two subsets A and B, each containing N/2 services (seen Figure 3). Since every service in A and B cluster has an x-value and y-value, in next step, x-value and y-value of each service in A and B cluster are compared together. In the last step, rank of each axes for any services is defined. As an example, when x-value of B dominates x-value of A but the y-value of B is not greater than the y-value of A. Comparing services based two QoS parameters are continued until the optimal service is selected; this is a recursive algorithm (4) and (see Figure4).

$$\pi^* := Dhull_\pi(s_t).(\forall s_t \in S) \quad (4)$$

Algorithm 1: selected optimal services based on convex hull and divide-and-conquer algorithm

```
initialize S, Q
/* clustering service in convex hull
For all atomic service s_i ∈ S do
    For all QOS attribute q_j (s_i) ∈ Q_si do
        Get convex hull  H(s_i)= (q_j (s_i)..., q_j (s_i))
    End for
End for
    Get divide-and-conquer on{H(s_i)} for i step
        If get an optimal service
            Return s
        End if
```

Figure 4. Selected optimal services based on convex hull and divide-and-conquer algorithm.

The third step of self-optimizing cycling is composing optimal services. In this section, reinforcement learning algorithm schema to orchestrate service composition is introduced. In this algorithm, the task of the learner or decision-maker is to learn a policy based on reward function. The complete learning process is depicted in the algorithm in Figure 5[12]. In this algorithm, the task of the learner or decision-maker is to learn a policy based on reward function [12].

Algorithm 2: Baseline Reinforcement Learning Algorithm for Service Composition

```
1: initialize Q (s, a)
2: for each episode do
3:     s← s0
4:     for each step of episode do
5:         Choose a ∈A(s) based on €-greedy policy
6:         Execute a, observe reward r and new state s'
7:  Q (s, a) ← Q (s, a) + α [ r+ γ max_a' Q (s', a') - Q (s, a)]
8:         s ←s'
9:     End for
10: End for
```

Figure 5. The Baseline Reinforcement Learning for Service Composition [12].

In this algorithm, initial state s_0, terminal state s and Q(s ,a) are defined. Q (s, a) is simulation of observed reward. In each episode (round), the learner starts from the initial state s_0, and takes a sequence of actions by following the ϵ-greedy policy (which is introduced subsequently). As line 7 shows, optimal service is chosen based on ϵ-greedy policy and old Q (s, a) value is completely replaced with the new value of reward function. Rate of learning is α, which is quantity between 0 and 1. The discount factor is γ that reflects the learning policy. Both value of α and γ are different in differ issue. The value of €-greedy is (€ < 1). The most significant part of this algorithm is computing the reward function which calculates user satisfaction. In this paper reward function is used as well as this algorithm [12] to predict service composition and observe user satisfaction. The policy of reward function is determined according to (5).

$$R(s) = \sum w_i \times \frac{Att_i^s - Att_i^{min}}{Att_i^{max} - Att_i^{min}} \quad (5)$$

where Att_i^s shows current value of the ith attribute of service s, and Att_i^{max} and Att_i^{min} show maximum and minimum value of Att_i for all services. W_i is the weighting factor of Att_i. This value is positive if users prefer Att_i to be high value (e.g. throughput). W_i is negative if users prefer Att_i to be low value (e.g. response time).

C. *Self-optimizing method for service composition*

In this selection, a self-optimizing method is proposed. According the self-optimizing cycle, the main goal is selecting optimal services based on QoS through distributed services. Response time, reliability, availability and throughput are the QoS parameters which analyze and compute the value of them for the self-optimizing method. This method has been shown in Figure6. According to the self-optimizing algorithm, Services and QoS parameters are initialized. Also, Q (s, a) as seen in Reinforcement Learning algorithm at the start of this algorithm is initialized. Line 3 to line 5, clustering convex hull based on QoS is calculated. All services in the convex hull are shown with H(si). The main purpose is selecting optimal services which is done with divide-and-conquer algorithm of convex hull. The optimal service selected is imported as an initial service parameter to composition algorithm. Then new action and next state (s') are defined in line 16. Reward function is calculated to compute user satisfaction in line 17. In order to predict services composition in next step, this algorithm needs to update the value of reward function for service selected according to calculate quantity of γ , α and new reward value of next optimal service is selected according line 18. In this line, new optimal service is selected

Algorithm 3: Self-Optimizing Algorithm for Select and Composition Service

```
1: initialize S,Q and  Q (s, a) arbitrarily ∀s,a
2: /* clustering service in convex hull
3: For all atomic service s_i ∈ S do
4:   For all QOS attribute q_j (s_i) ∈ Q_si do
5:       Get convex hull  H(s_i)= (q_j (s_i)..., q_j (s_i))
6:   End for
7: End for
8: /* compute composition service
9: For each episode do
10:  For each step of episode do
11:     Choose action a ∈ A(H (s_i))
12:     Get divide-and-conquer on{H(s_i)} for each step
13:        If get an optimal service, then
14:          Return s and DAC (s, a)
15:        End if
16:     Take action a and observe next state s' ∈ DAC(s)
17:    Observe reward vector r⃗ ∈ R⃗
18:   Q (s, a) ← Q (s, a) + α [ r + γ DAC Q (s', a') - Q (s, a)]
19:   s← s'
20: End for
21: End for
```

Figure 6. The self-optimizing for service composition.

based on divide-and-conquer algorithm of convex hull, it shows with DAC (s', a').

In this way, the self-optimizing strategy provides maximum user satisfaction. In each cycle of system, the services that have maximum user satisfaction are suggested to the user. Also, this algorithm can adapt itself to the dynamic environment. Service selection accuracy provides full potential of each service. In order to compare the result of this method with previous methods, consider to calculated average value of reward function. If the system gets higher score in reward function than other methods, it is optimal behavior in service selection and composition.

IV. EVALUATION OF THE PROPOSED METHOD

One of the vita factors in tourism website produces Web service with high QoS which are available and can respond to user requirements in reasonable time. Customers on the Web want to do anything conveniently and simply, such as booking hotels and flights with one service, which is called a tourist package, or take the best service offer from the system. The significant concern in a self-optimizing tourist website is how to increase user satisfaction gradually. So, the propose method is implemented on a tourist website, which is composed of services and adjusts to dynamic environment in order to meet user requirements.

In this paper, the self-optimizing occurs at the source code level as done by the program. The tourist website was implemented by C#.net and Asp.net. The website is based on MVC Architecture and SQL Server 2016 database. The database was designed based on the normal equation in such a way that it does not have redundancy at updating time. Web services are provided from valid dataset [13] which has 356 real Web services. Those Web services have nine Quality of Web Service (QWS) attributes, which are measured with a commercial benchmark tool. The advantage of this dataset is that Web services are collected from public source discovery, integration, registration, search engines and service portals. It is remarkable that each service was tested over a ten-minute period for three consecutive days. Therefore, calculation of QoS was ignored. But before using the value for each QoSs, they should be normalized because they are distributed over a wide range. Equation (6) was used for normalization, as introduced in [14].

$$Q_i' = \frac{Q_i - \min_i Q_i}{\max_i Q_i - \min_i Q_i}. \quad (6)$$

The main goal of the tourist website is that users choose a travelling destination. The website is based on two scenarios, both of which incorporate selection and composition of services to answer user requirements.

The first scenario is that the user fills a form in order to access a weather service. Then the user submits the information to the website in order to get a list of weather services for their destination. The website finds a list of weather services and presents the best ones as the result of the queries to the user. The second scenario consists of two possible ways. In the first way, flight and hotel services are chosen same as weather services. But the second way is definitely deferent, because service of hotels and flights is represented in one service, which is called tour package. User requests especial tour package which includes defined flight and hotel. The tourist agent requests to choose defined flight services. Then, it is receiving ID of flight services to send hotel service selector. At the end, it is receiving ID composition service which consists of flight and hotel services. The system can predict the best tour package service for users who enter the same information. The last scenario is payment services just like the first scenario. In Figure 6, each state is shown.

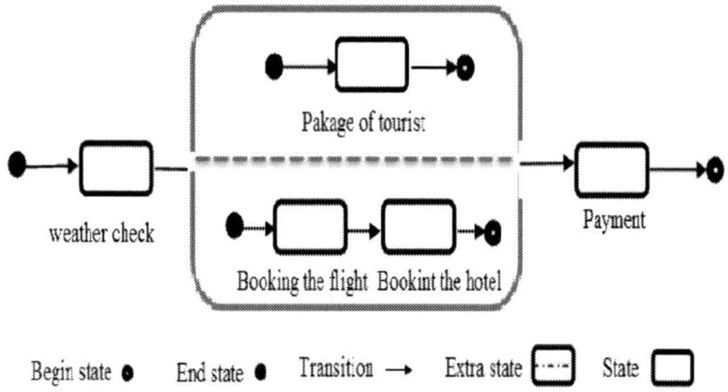

Figure 6. The work flow of tourist scenario.

The second scenario is the main scenario in order to obtain comparison between this method and the previous one. The previous method is Reinforcement Learning algorithm which is developed in the tourist website as well as the self-optimizing method. The reward function is calculated with deferent QoS parameters. In the experiment results, the discount factor ϵ is set at 0.9 and as the amount of α is set to 0.2 (Figure 7). Also according to Figure 8 , the value of γ is set to 0.5. All of the experiments were conducted on a Sony laptop with Core i5 3.1GHz processors and 12GB RAM, running Windows 7. All proposed services are observed on the tourist website after 2 minutes.

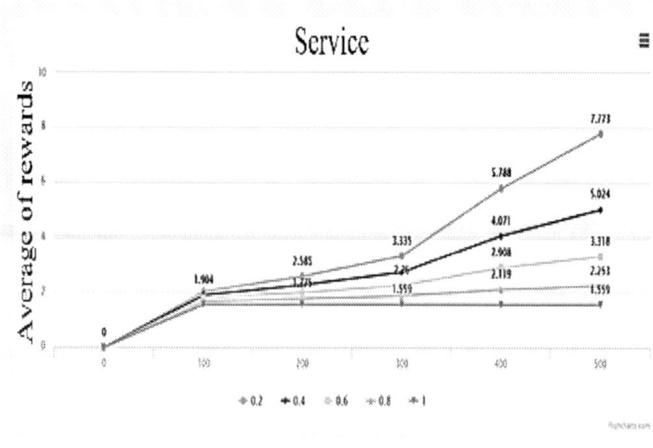

Figure 7. Choosing bestα.

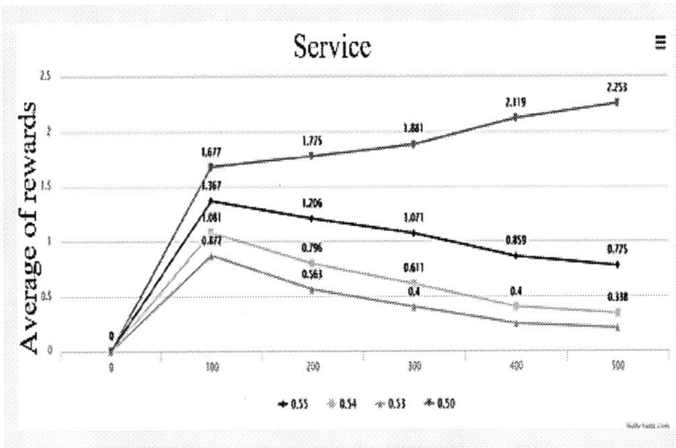

Figure 8. Choosing the probability γ.

In the first stage of evaluation, it is shown how Reinforcement Learning policy can be improved with the self-optimizing method. Reinforcement Learning algorithm is executed with zero knowledge about the QoS of the component of service composition and in some episodes the value of reward function is not better than the last stage and shows uniform behavior (see Figure 9). Proposed method is improved by adding a new policy about service selection for service composition, it has the ability to self-behavior and increase user satisfaction by achieving higher values of reward function. This simulation fixed six episodes; the number of services in each episode is increased in order to show the proposed method in large scale of services has the same self-optimizing attitude.

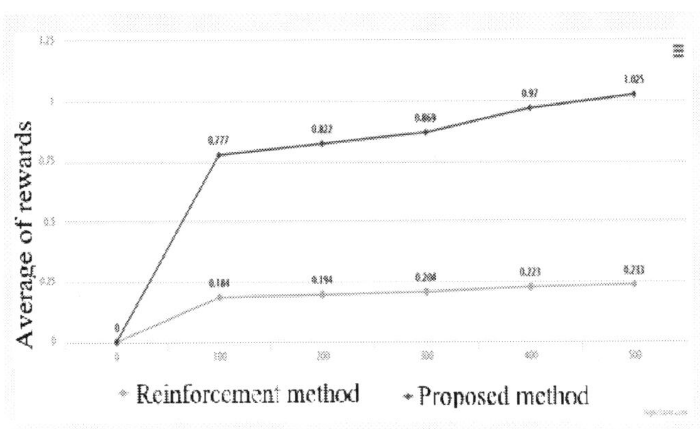

Figure 9. Comparing the proposed method with the Reinforcement learning method for increased user satisfaction.

In the second stage of our evaluation, it can be seen how a self-optimizing service composition adapts to the changes of the environment and value of the reward function, which represents user satisfaction, is steadily increased. Changing environments are simulated by periodically changing the QoS attributes of the services. At first environment is changed by 5%. It means, 5% of basic services are added to the environment with the uniform probability distribution formula. Then Reinforcement learning algorithm and the purpose algorithm are executed. Figure 10 shows the growth of the cumulative reward during the self-optimizing process. In comparison, increasing the change rate in Reinforcement learning algorithm has delay because it has to identify QoS and needs to learn optimal execution policy. Conversely, the reward value of the self-optimizing method is comparatively higher and changes do not stop the optimizing process. In second simulation, the environment is changing by 10% and the third simulation based on 15% .When the environment changes more and more, growth rate satisfaction of the self-optimizing method is more visible. In the third stage of our evaluation, Figure 11 shows how the self-optimizing service composition outperforms the reinforced algorithm in a large scale environment. In this evaluation, environment scale is represented by the number of services used in every tourist workflow. At first, hotel and flight services are increased up to 300, then reward function of the proposed approach is measured. The reward value depicts the user satisfaction. In the second and third picture reward functions are measured based on 400 and 500 services respectively. Comparing the proposed method with the Reinforcement learning method in the Large scale environment, self-optimizng method shows more satisfaction than the Reinforcement learning method. The fourth experimental results include test 1, test 2 and test 3. In this experiment, optimal services with low response time, high availability, high throughput and high reliability are selected. The results of test 1, as depicted in Figure 12, clearly show that the optimal tourist workflows have achieved high throughput, and high reliability among 50 services or lower response time and high availability. The outcomes of test 2 are represented in Figure 13, they support test1 statement, regardless of the bigger number of concrete Web services assigned to each task (100 services), as the optimal workflows obviously continue representing the same trend with lower response time and high availability, high reliability and high throughput. Finally test 3, as represented in Figure 14, has the same trends as test 1 and test 2 with large number of services (150 services). As a result, the size of environment does not affect selecting optimal services based on QoSs for each task in tourist website.

In Figure 15, the proposed method executed composed services in half the time of Multi-Object Service Composition algorithm which was introduced by Mostafa and Zhang [9], the reason is clearly observed; the previous algorithm used fast convex hull, whose execution time in the worst-case is $O[n^2]$ in contrast execution time of the self-optimizing method in all cases is $O[n \log n]$. Therefore, by this chart, different levels of execution time of the two algorithms in large scale are more distinguished

V. CONCLUSION

The main purpose of this paper is to introduce a self-optimizing method in order to select and compose services. Optimal services are selected based on QoS and composed with other services to answer user requirements. The significant algorithm in the self-optimizing method is the Divide-and-conquer algorithm used for selection. The reason is that the execution time of this algorithm is $O[n \log n]$ in all cases. So the self-optimizing method behaves similarly on the large scale, with shorter execution times. This time is half that of pervious method [9]. Therefore, when the tourist wants to take travel services, it can get optimal services in a reasonable time. Moreover, the Reinforcement Learning policy [12] has zero knowledge about the QoS of the component services, it takes some time to know services in large environment and predict user behavior.

Therefore, the rate of rewards value remains in consistent level when making comparison between

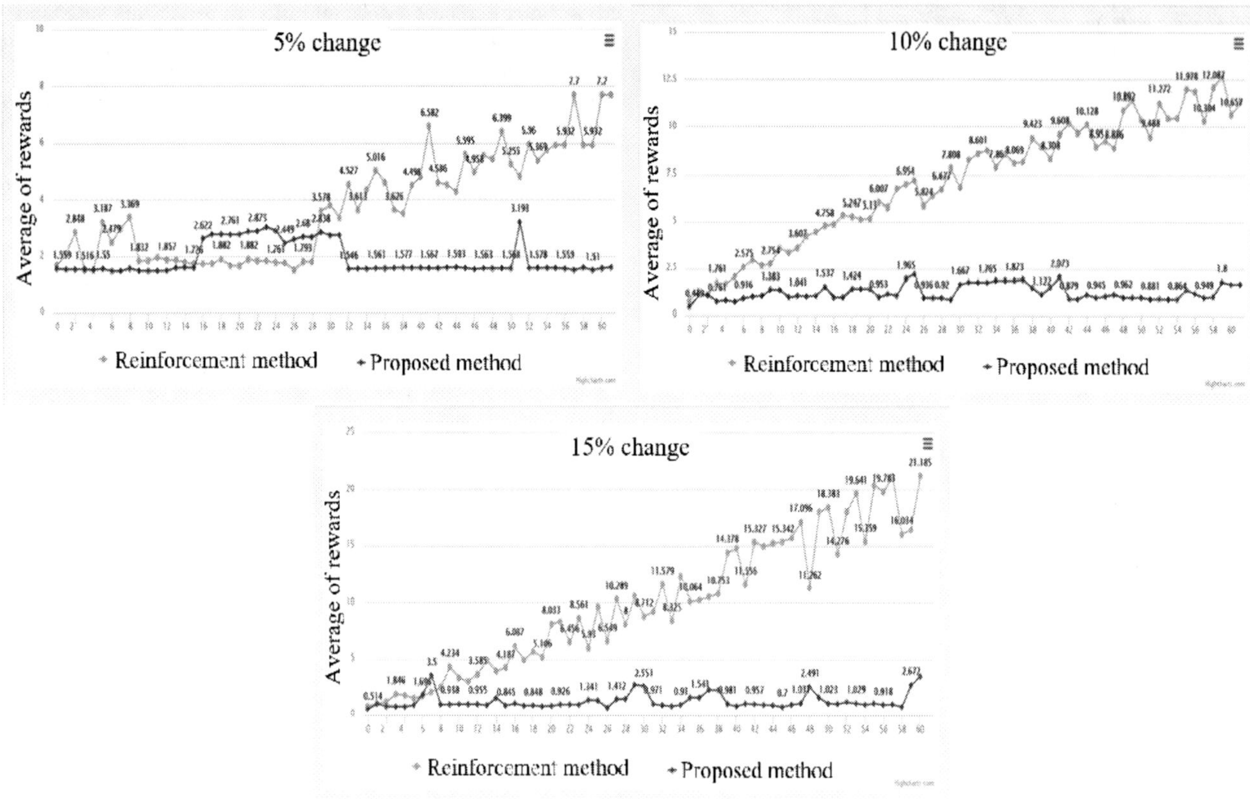

Figure 10. Comparing the self-optimizing method with the Reinforcement Learning method in dynamic environments.

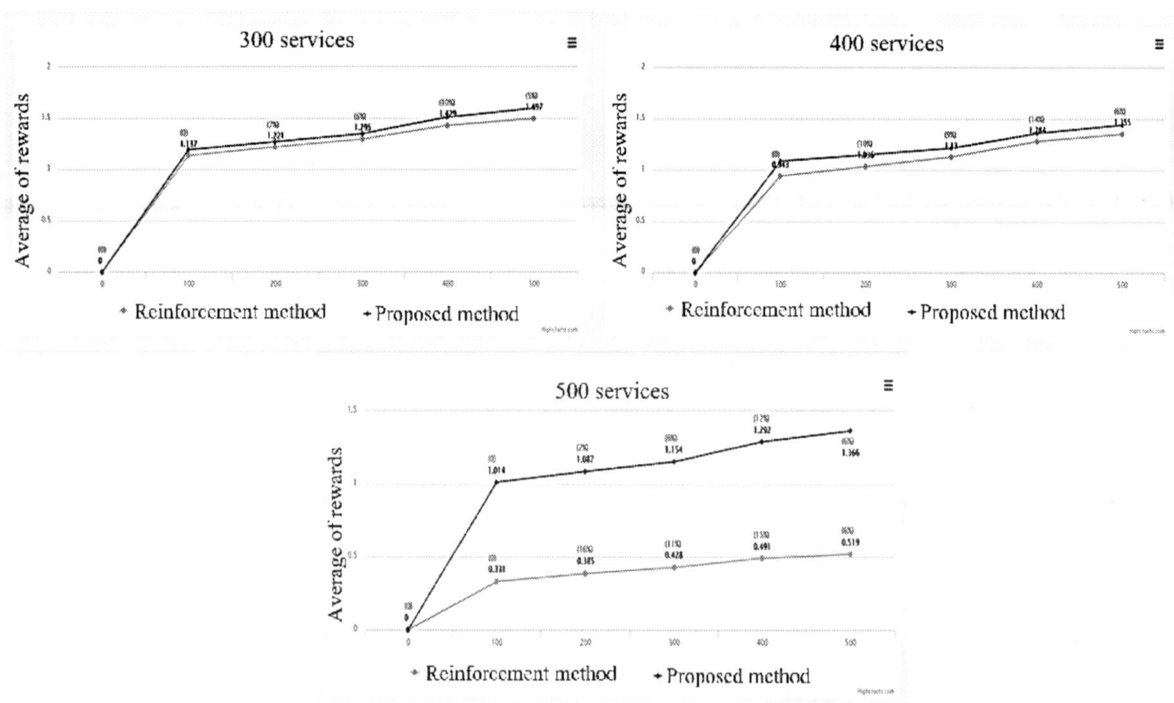

Figure 11. Comparing the performance of the proposed method with the base method.

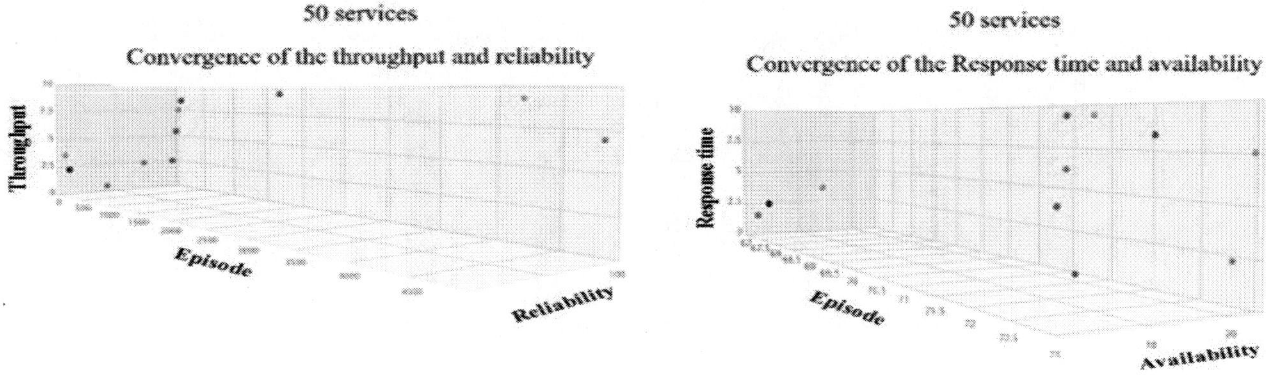

Figure 12. Optimal service based on QoS is Selected among 50services.

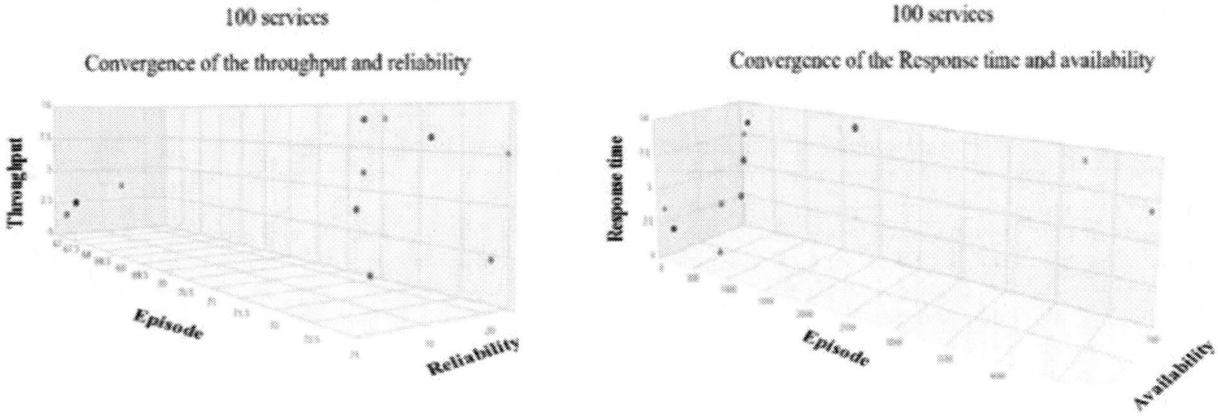

Figure 13. Optimal service based on QoS is Selected among 100services.

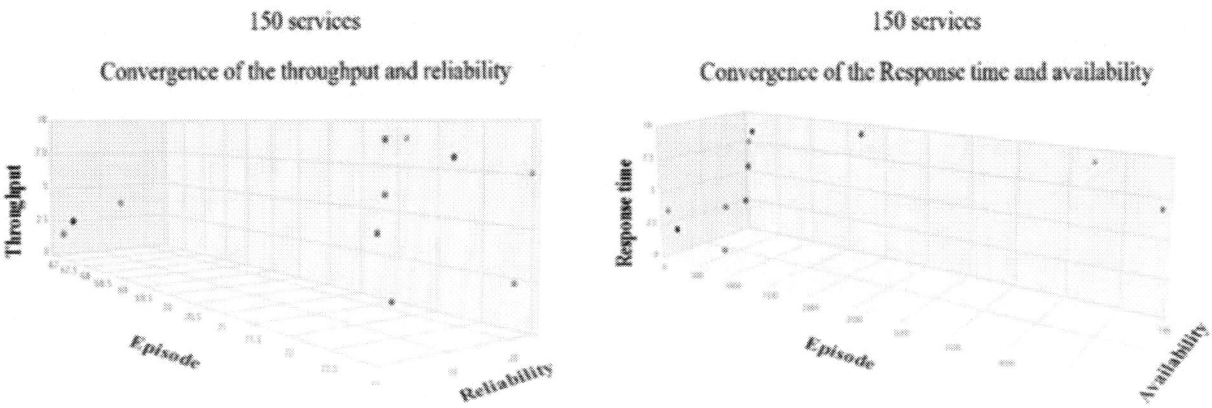

Figure 14. Optimal service based on QoS is Selected among 150services.

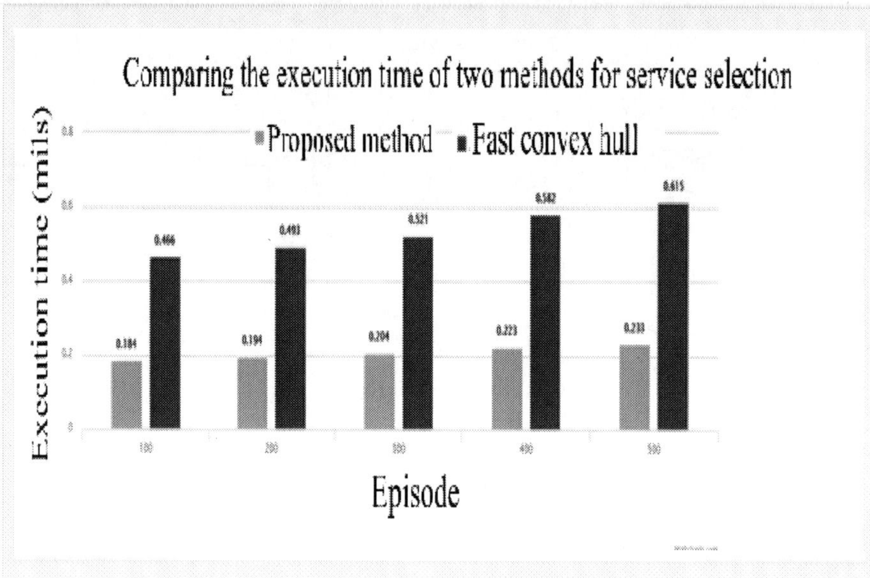

Figure 15. Comparing the proposed method with the method of selection service by fast convex hull.

two steps of this algorithm. It has near optimal execution policies efficiently. In this paper, Reinforce Learning algorithm is modified with new policy to selected optimal services. This policy optimizes service composition in each cycle-life. On the other hand, some QoSs is differing in best value. For example, response time is lower and availability is high in optimal services, so convex hull algorithm provides clustering in two diamonds which can choose optimal services with different values. The experiments show the efficiency of this algorithm is optimized in each steps.

Dynamic environment is one of the issues this day for websites like tourist website because services are always changing with improved performance or replaced with new services. The Self-optimizing method is a good solution to use here; it can optimize itself in large scale and adapt to a dynamic environment.

The proposed method takes about 2 ms to compute QoS. Therefore, it is useful for non-real-time systems like tourist systems. But it is not useful for real-time systems where time is very critical.

The future work is set to study the self-optimizing and self-reconfiguring method together. Therefore, when the service selection and composition fail, there are methods to help the system to reconfigure itself automatically. The self-optimizing and self-reconfiguring are implemented in many systems simultaneously but up to now, they are not implemented in service-oriented systems. Using this feature can also improve the proposed method.

REFERENCES

[1] Donghui Lin, Chunqi Shi, and Toru Ishida," Dynamic Service Selection Based on Context-Aware QoS ", In 2012 IEEE Ninth International Conference on services Computing.

[2] A. Moustafa and M. Zhang, "Learning efficient compositions for QoS-aware service provisioning," in 2014 IEEE International Conference on Web services, ICWS, 2014, Anchorage, AK, USA, June 27 - July 2, 2014. IEEE Computer Society, 2014, pp. 185–192.

[3] A. F. M. Huang, c.-w. Lan, and S. J. H. Yang, "An optimal QoS-based Web service selection scheme," Inf. Sci., vol.179, pp. 3309- 3322, September 2009.

[4] G. F. Franklin, J. D. Powell, and A. E. Naeini, Feedback control of dynamic systems. Prentice Hall, pp. 928, 2008.

[5] B. Chen, X. Peng, Y. Yu, and W. Zhao, "Requirements-driven self-optimization of composite services using feedback control," IEEE Transactions on Services Computing, vol. 8, pp.107-12, January, 2014.

[6] L. Z. Zeng, B. Boualem, D. Marlon, J. Kalagnanam, and Q. Z. Sheng, "Quality driven Web services composition," in Proc. of the 12th International Conference on World Wide Web, pp. 411-421, 2003.

[7] C. W. Zhang, S. Su, and J. L. Chen, "Genetic algorithm on Web services selection supporting QoS," Chinese Journal of Computer, vol. 29, pp. 1029-1037, 2006.

[8] R. L. Graham, "An efficient algorithm for determining the convex hull of a finite planar set," Elsevier, vol.1, pp. 132-133, 1972.

[9] A. Mostafa and M. Zhang, "Multi-objective service composition in uncertain environments," IEEE Transactions on Services Computing, vol. 99, pp.1-1, June2015.

[10] Q. Yu and A. Bouguettaya." efficient service skyline computation for composite service selection". *IEEE Trans. Knowledge and Data Engineering*, volume 25(4), pages 776–789, 2013.

[11] Q. Yu and A. Bouguettaya." computing service skyline from uncertain qows". *IEEE Trans. Services Computing*, volume3(1), pages 16–29, 2010

[12] H. Wang, X. Zhou, W. Liu, W. Li, and A. Bouguettaya, "Adaptive service composition based on Reinforcement Learning," 8th International Conference ICSOC, pp. .92-107, 2010.

[13] Available from: https://github.com/wsdream/wsdream-dataset.

[14] Y. Chen, L. Jiang, J. Zhang, and X. Dong," A Robust Service Selection Method Based on Uncertain os", Mathematical Problems in Engineering, vol2016, p. p10, January 2016.

Conception of a Type-based Pub/Sub Mechanism with Hierarchical Channels for a Dynamic Adaptive Component Model

Mohamad Ibrahim, Karina Rehfeldt, Andreas Rausch

Technische Universität Clausthal
38678 Clausthal-Zellerfeld, Germany
email: {mohamad.ibrahim, karina.rehfeldt, andreas.rausch}@tu-clausthal.de

***Abstract*—When attacking the problem of live information dissemination, then publish/subscribe technology plays a key role in crafting an efficient solution. Especially in safety-critical domains like automotive embedded systems a key factor for an efficient publish/subscribe mechanisms is type-safety. We introduce a solution for type-based and semantic publish/subscribe which allows to create hierarchical channels tailored to the needs of an embedded system with physical entities communicating. Our concept builds up on our dynamic adaptive middleware called Dynamic Adaptive System Infrastructure (DAiSI), which allows component configuration at runtime. As a technical medium, we use the industrial standard Extensible Lightweight Asynchronous Protocol (Exlap). Regardless of the fact that our implementation and example pertain to DAiSI and Exlap, our concept is introduced in an integrated framework, which allows the reusability of this model in other application domains.**

***Keywords*–Component Model; Publish/Subscribe; Channels; Dynamic Adaptive Systems; Embedded Industrial Systems.**

I. INTRODUCTION

Many application domains require data dissemination, like stock market data updates, online advertising, asynchronous events in graphical user interface (GUI) and many others [1]. Our focus lies on signals and live data dissemination in embedded and industrial systems. This domain implies certain requirements and restrictions the concept has to commit to. These environments require strict distinctions between data without the possibility of mistaking one for another (type safety). Also, the performance is critical in industrial environments where compared to content-based, ontology or internet wide pub/sub systems [2], [3] scalability and usability plays a more crucial role due to resource limitations. Type-based pub/sub also gives us several advantages that suit the embedded industrial systems environment like encapsulation, application-defined events, open content filters [4], and event semantics which we exploit here to provide the physical diversity of the same type or component.

This work is not intended to address the problem of providing a uniform interface for heterogeneous information sources, but to provide a light-weight system that satisfies specific industrial needs and yet flexible enough for wide-range of applications in the domain of Internet of Things. Examples of such domains can be equipping a car, a house, a factory or any entity of many components with a scheme that can ease information discovery and access from inside and outside the entity. Imagine for example a car, where you have a variety of distance sensors observing the distances around the car. One or more observe the front, some the back and so on. Our goal was to find a concept that presents to the subscriber a scheme that matches a physical entity and describes its components functional relationships, so that the subscriber would seamlessly subscribe to a group of components that share a common function or purpose regardless of their number, position or semantics. In other words, a subscriber should be able to subscribe to all distance sensors at once. But also, the subscriber should be able to subscribe to a specific sub-group or individual, like all distance sensors in the front.

The intention here is to discuss a flavour of pub/sub that is type-based, hierarchical and introduces a new dimension that allows extensibility, so we can represent many physical entities with the same type but different semantics. Figure 1 shows an example for a domain scheme. Engine represents the type (*IEngine*) with the data *speed*. Hierarchical structured, we have cylinders (*ICyclinder*) and a cooling system (*ICooling*). Notice, the domain scheme only states the structure of the data types for publishers, but does not state anything about instances of these publishers. We may have front and rear engine in a specific car domain. So if the domain scheme represents the class in object-oriented programming, then the object counterpart is the physical entity publishing. This arrangement creates two trees, the first is the types hierarchical scheme of the entity with its embedded components. The second represents the real components which has two dimensions: functional dimension which is depicted by the type, like *IEngirge*, and physical dimension which is depicted by the physical semantic, like front or rear engine.

In Section II we introduce some related works in the filed of publish/subscribe. The discussion of our concept begins with introducing the architectural model and system layers in Section III. Section IV focus on the software architecture of the proposed system with elements and APIs explained. We conclude with a disucssion of the proposed solution in Section V.

II. RELATED WORK

The main aim of this work is to introduce a pub/sub system for specific problem yet it can be applied in any other situation, that is why introducing it in an architecture or software stack is important.

Klus et al. [5] - which is the main related and direct previous work - introduce a component model and middleware for dynamic adaptive system that can adapt to different situations by supporting dynamic changing of pre-configured

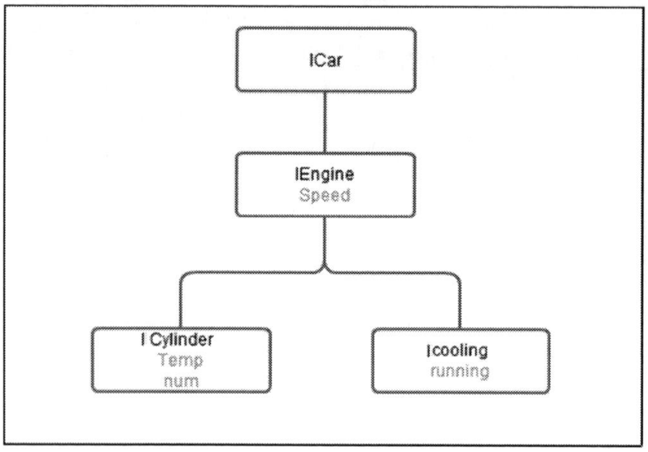

Figure 1. The ICar domain scheme

configurations. However, the proposed model, called DAiSI, is not able to support neither publish/subscribe communication paradigm nor asynchronous data exchanges. That deficiency led to our work that proposes a concept for pub/sub.

Eugster et al. [6] which sets the standards for pub/sub system solutions and gives the fundamentals and several aspects of designing such a system. Liu and Bale give an overview about general pub/sub system ins [7]. Another comprehensive survey of pub/sub systems is given by Filho and Redmiles in [8]. They define several dimensions of pub/sub system and add to them the versatility dimension which means for the concept to be able to adapt to different application requirements. However, what Baldoni et al. [9] are suggesting, is a general concrete system and introducing it in a specific architecture with giving alternatives to different types of applications. We are going to embody our system in this architectural model and make several justified design decisions.

The second category of papers we looked into, are concrete pub/sub systems that have been introduced to solve communication problems in several domains. The first is the semantic Toronto pub/sub system [10], [11], that discusses security on a domain-based infrastructure. Morales et al. [12] introduce a solution for scientific workflow management systems to monitor working processes using a pub/sub system. Bickson et al. [13] introduce a system that utilizes the IP unicast and multicast capabilities to save network resources. Demers et al. [14] take the content-based systems expressiveness to an advanced level depending on finite state automata to express subscription patterns. The given examples show the variety of pub/sub application domains and their different key concepts.

The third category are the type-based pub/sub systems [4], [15], [16], which all reach a consensus that the most prominent features of type-based pub/sub systems are: type-safety, encapsulation, application-defined events, open content filters and event semantics. Since our industrial use-case asks for those features, we decided to make use of type-based pub/sub in our concept.

III. System Overview

There have been a lot of architectural models that specify how to build pub/sub systems. One of the most famous is what Baldoni et al. [9] suggested. Their architecture is structured in the layers Network Protocol, Overlay Infrastructure, Event Routing and Matching. Those layers represent the logical functionality of the components of the pub/sub system. In the following, we will show how our concept is settled in these layers.

A. Network Protocol

The network protocols can vary depending on the environment of the deployment and the application. This layer connects the actual hardware infrastructure of the system [9]. Our realization uses TCP/IP conjugated with Exlap (Extensible Lightweight Asynchronous Protocol) [17]. The upper layers of the system should address all the shortcomings of this layer like security, reliability and unregulated delays. Those subjects are not in the scope of this paper.

Exlap on TCP/IP constitutes the lower layer in the implementation. It is a protocol that follows the client-server paradigm and provides basic interface for pub/sub communications between the client and the server identified by address, port and application-level ID that uniquely identifies any Exlap service. In addition, Exlap provides a discovery service that scans the network for public services. With Exlap, we have an interface for our system components to communicate over the physical layer.

B. Overlay Infrastructure

This layer addresses the organization of the components or nodes, the role of each node and the overall functionality on which the routing of the events rely on [9]. Here comes the role of DAiSI infrastructure, which we use to apply the broker pattern, thus components can act as subscriber, publisher or broker.

First, we take a quick overview on DAiSI before showing how DAiSI fits into the big picture. DAiSI is a dynamic adaptive system infrastructure that lets you create components which can offer certain kinds of services and uses other services in an environment where they dynamically activate the configuration that is of the highest priority or that best matches the existing required services.

For example, a cooling system in a car can be a component that needs to consistently read the temperature from the engine component, and it can provide the status of the cooling system to the car monitor to show it to the driver. This component can hold two configurations in order to dynamically adapt to what is provided. The first configuration can be to provide the status of the cooling system to the monitor, and the second can be to stream the temperature in real time from the engine, applying the logic and provide the status as a service to other components including the monitor, Figure 2 shows the component.

When there is an engine service available, *Conf 2* will be activated, otherwise *Conf 1* is activated. *Conf 1* needs no service in order to be resolved and then provide the *ICooling* service, but the *Conf 2* needs *IEngine* service in order to be resolved and then provide its *ICooling* service.

We employ this DAiSI component representation to provide the required roles in the pub/sub system. Where the broker is the service provided by the system that the publishers and subscribers will connect to. And the required services will take

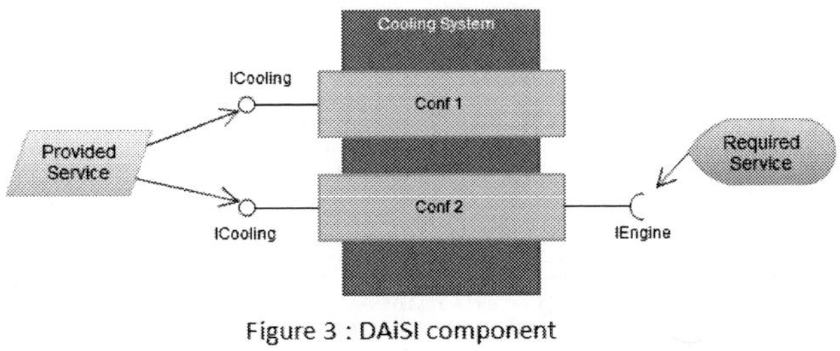

Figure 2. DAiSI Component

the role of the publishers and subscribers of a certain event type. We see in Figure 3 how the above Figure changed in the new context.

Now *Conf 2* will be activated not by the existence of *IEngine* service but when there is a broker service and this broker has *IEngine* being published to it. It is the same as before, but the old relationship is being mediated by the broker.

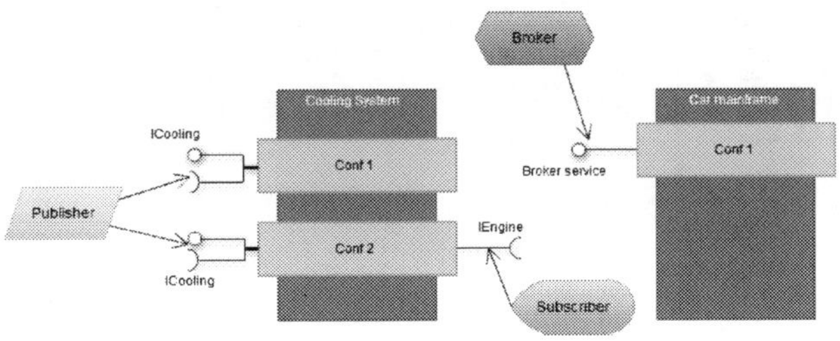

Figure 3. Pub/Sub components

C. Event Routing

In this layer lays the concept of domains. We divide the system space into domains, where every domain has a tree-structured types represent the events available in this domain (see Figure 1. This scheme represents the functional dimension we talked about earlier, and the head of the domain represent the type of the domain which can be conjugated with an ID to depict the physical dimension of the domain and uniquely distinguish the domains of the same type in the system space.

Now assigning an ID to the head of the domain - represented by broker(s) - makes the domain unique in the space with similar domains of the same type.

We will distinguish between two kinds of communications or event routing; inter-domain communication which is done on DAiSI overlay basis and it comprises the traffic between the broker and all the inner publishers and subscribers. The second is the intra-domain communication which is done on a star topology because Exlap can provide end-to-end communication between the brokers themselves. For a visualisation, see Figure 4.

So, the routing is done inside the domain by one-hub connection between the broker(s) and the clients (subscribers and publishers). The publishing is exclusive to the inter-domain components for security and encapsulation reasons, but subscribing can be internal in the same domain or external using the domain broker which in turn will subscribe to the broker in other domains to get the needed external data.

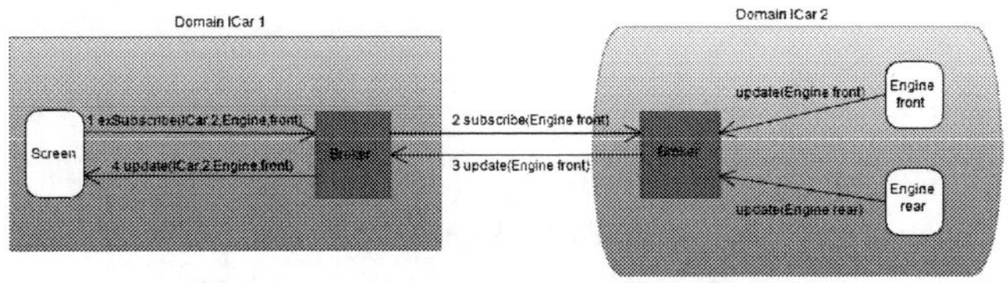

Figure 4. inter- and intra-domain communication

D. Matching

The matching mechanism depends entirely on the types defined in the tree, which describe the contents available in the domain, secure the type safety and provide encapsulation and hierarchical subscription. The type-based and hierarchical pub/sub is not new, as we discussed, but there is no system to our knowledge that addresses the problem of the multi-dimensional representation of the types inside the system. This model we are proposing gives a wide range of options to the designer and implementer.

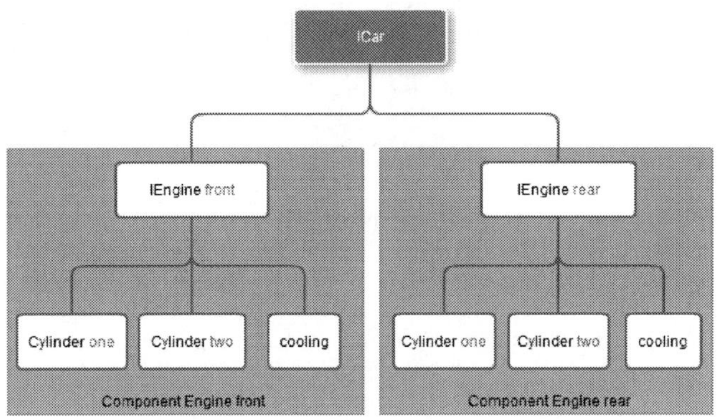

Figure 5. Physical scheme of the car

Specifying the physical dimension is optional and has several degrees, while declaring the type is mandatory. Suppose that we have the previous scheme for the car and the physical scheme in Figure 5, where we have two engines. Each engine has two cylinders and a cooling system. Here, we start with the publishing options; we can assign the cylinder an ID (give it a number) or not, then having two cylinders of the same ID or cylinders without IDs will publish the same content. Now assigning the parent is also optional, in case where no parent is assigned the component will be replicated in all engine components. On the other hand, specifying the parent will give the component unique place in the physical tree. Now subscribing is no less flexible, with the option of using the wild card; e.g., when subscribing to any engine without specifying IDs, it will return all components in the entity and all their children in case of using the wild card. But subscribing to it with ID, will return the corresponding component data only and, in case of using wild card, with its children. Now, if we are interested in just every cylinder, no matter from which engine, then that is also a possibility.

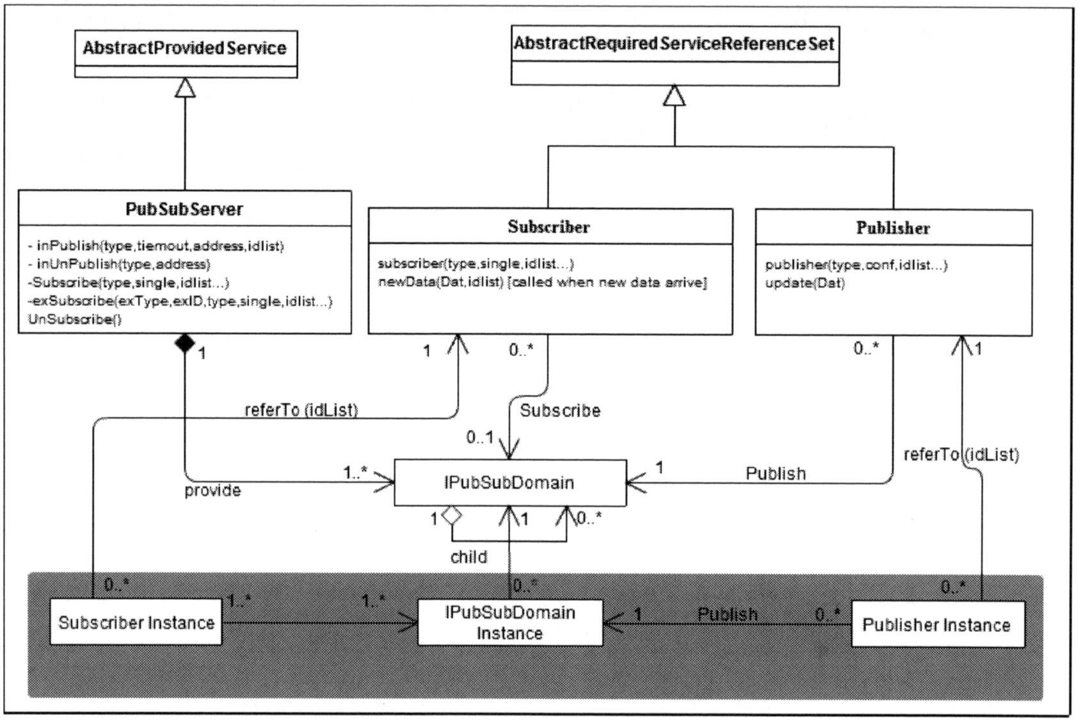

Figure 6. Core elements of the pub/sub system

We notice that once we specify the type there is no wrong answer when it comes to picking the physical dimension, including the use of wild card which implies the functional unity of the embedded components. The architectural details of this system will be discussed in the next section.

IV. System Details

In this section, we present the details of our concept's implementation and the core elements and concepts. For an overview of the core elements and architecture of our system, see Figure 6.

A. Architecture

Since this model is another layer added to DAiSI framework, it extends its framework classes. Review [5] for a complete overview of the used DAiSI frameworks elements. The *AbstractProvidedService* represents the abstract class of any provided service a component needs to offer, so is the *AbstractRequiredServiceReferenceSet* which indicates the services needed by the component. This pub/sub system also offer the broker service on the basis and using the infrastructure of DAiSI. The new element *PubSubServer* works with other normal services and provides the matching and brokering service only for Subscribers and Publishers elements, in other words it works with classic DAiSI. Also the system provides the elements Subscribers and Publishers as extended functionality from *AbstractRequiredServiceReferenceSet* in the same way as the broker.

1) PubSubServer: PubSubServer is a core element class of the framework, which provides the main functionality of pub/sub to the whole system. One instance of *PubSubServer* at least is required in every domain. *PubSubServer* depends on the types scheme to function and coin the required types and serve its clients. This service will provide two interfaces; external one for other brokers from other domains, and internal one to handle the internal subscription and publishing requests and real data streaming updates that are pushed to the subscribers.

This class extends the *AbstractProvidedService* and gives the developer the option to feed to this element the types' hierarchical scheme and define parameters like the maximum number of connected clients. The APIs provided by this element is the internal inPublish() and inUnPublish(). the parameters are timeout, which is the time before disconnecting, address is the address of the publisher and the idlist is what defines the physical dimension of the type which we want to publish to. For example, if one wants to publish to the second cylinder of the front engine then one starts with the lowest in the types' tree and makes his way up like that (second front). Subscribing is done automatically when the component in its environment activates a configuration which contains a subscriber. How to initialize the subscribers and publishers will be discussed in the next sections.

2) Publisher: The publisher in DAiSI is a normal *AbstractProvidedService* but with added functionality which are of two folds. The first is to provide a method that can be called to send new data to the broker once it is available. The second is to specify from the types' scheme a type to publish to with specifying the needed idlist. We can specify the idlist or leave it null which can be done on two levels. First, the idlist can be null on the target type itself which means that this hardware is the only one and has no physical semantics needed for further distinction. The second level is to leave the parents idlist unspecified which means that this component is replicated and embedded at every component that has its parent type no matter what id or physical semantics it holds. Here comes the type-safety to play its role, because it is not necessary to program the embedded systems with vague topic names or types which could lead to untraceable bugs.

3) Subscriber: The Subscriber extends the *AbstractProvidedService* also with added functionality which are: first to provide a method that will be called upon new data arrival, and the second is to specify from the types' scheme a type to subscribe to with specifying the needed idlist, or leave it null for general subscriptions as described before.

4) IPubSubDomain: IPubSubDomain represents the types coined in the implementation. This embody the structure of the types and their corresponding data object which will hold the idlist that represents the physical semantics. Many subscribers can refer to the same component with the same type and physical semantics. Also, publishers can publish to the same component, but this means they will form the same data stream without physical or other kind of distinctions. In this way, we can cover a great variety of use-cases in pub/sub systems.

B. Behavior

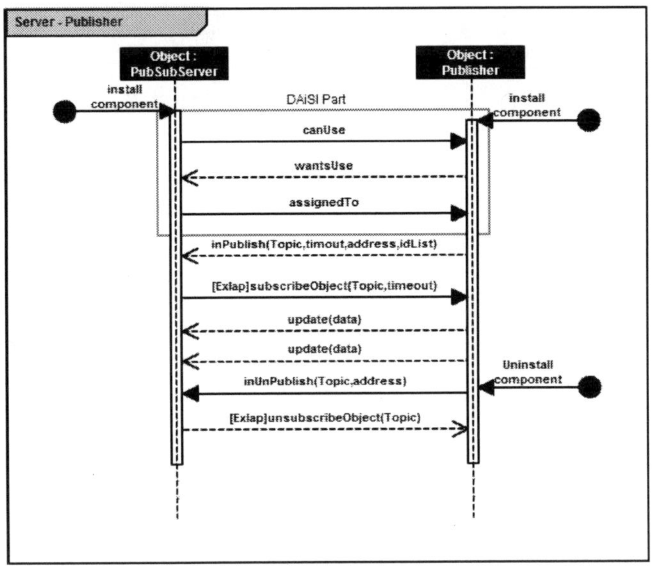

Figure 7. Broker-publisher interaction

The behavior of the system is based exactly on DAiSI components' behavior, where the publisher finds the broker, requests to use its service and when granted the publishing starts. For a visualisation of the data flow, refer to Figure 7. If the component is a subscriber, it will find the broker in the same way, asks for data, and, if granted, it will stream the data using the underlying communication protocol (Exlap in our implementation), see Figure 8. Both sequence diagrams shown are taken from the inter-domain communications.

C. Key Concepts

A key concept in this system is that it offers both pub/sub and the observer pattern communication architecture. Those distinctions can vary depending on the domain, but they include things like a one-to-many communication since the observed source has a high level of specificity, so it represents one entity and one only. Like subscribing to the first cylinder of the front engine, this is observing specific information presented by one authorized source. And because of this specificity there is no anonymity between the observer and the observee. On the contrary, we can deduce that when there is anonymity or generality is needed then the streamed data will be formed from several sources or maybe one and the communication will be many-to-many or pub/sub pattern. Figure 9 depicts the type channels and when they can be from single or multiple sources.

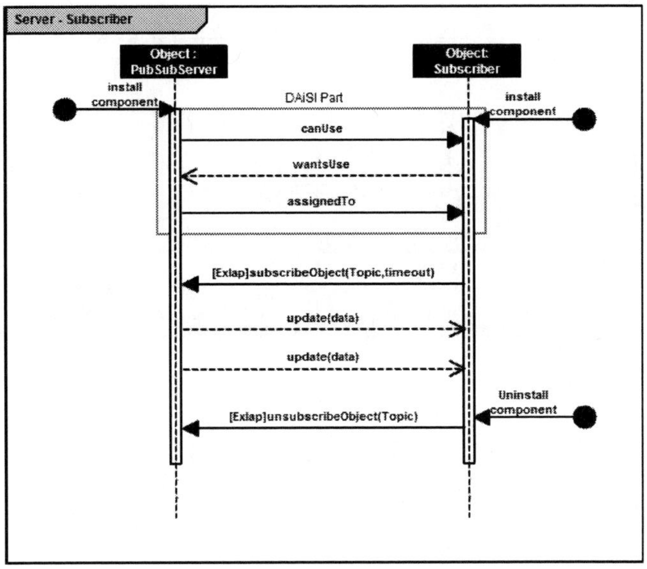

Figure 8. Broker-subscriber interaction

Another important concept is the degree of freedom given when using this framework altogether, in which we have the option to leave all the physical dimensions empty and not give the components any physical semantics (idlist). This is the case where we end up with identical types' scheme and real-world components' scheme.

Also, an important feature is that the broker should not need to know in advance the components participating, it only needs the types' scheme, so the components can join, leave or change the physical semantics or type at runtime without affecting the functionality of the whole system.

V. Conclusion

Our work is presented in a specific software architecture that allows for easy replacement of the layers or employing them else-where.

This model is intended for domain-based embedded systems infrastructure that needs to communicate live data asynchronously. We can mention cars, planes, smart houses, surveillance systems and information gathering systems and any autonomous system of which dynamicity depends on its internal data communication including the dynamic adaptive system infrastructure we originally aim to solve the asynchronous communication for.

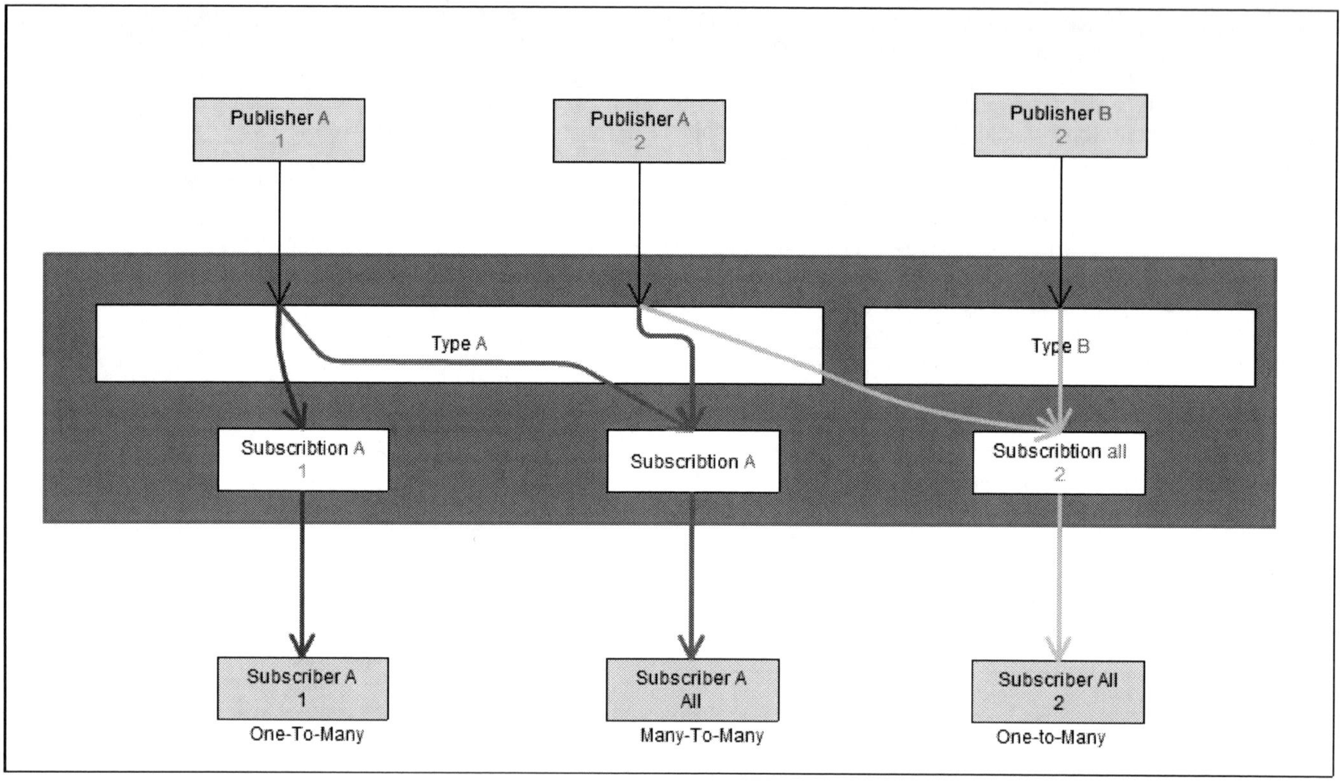

Figure 9. Type Channels

Those domains we talked about like a car for example, can have components of different computational capabilities, so it is critical to move some of the burden away from those components and equip them with an elegant and light-weight solution for their connectivity. Here emerged the idea of type-based pub/sub using a broker, not to mention that the broker provides the decoupling and removes the direct dependencies between the communicating parties in both space time and synchronization [6].

The disadvantage that can be taken on this model is the lack of clear policy that enhances the communication through content filtering mechanisms which can lessen the expressiveness of the model communications and increase the useful data exchanged, which can be a major enhancement in future works. Another great addition would be to extend the physical semantics from including only one feature to maybe group of features the component can be summoned according to.

It is evident in today's standards that the field of Internet of Things (IoT) will have a great share in the researching and industrial community. IoT where machine talks to a machine and exchanges information which helps in taking decisions that sometimes can be critical and need to be quick. Our work focuses on providing the right, scalable, easy to implement and flexible scheme for which these talks can depend on. And that is the key that will open the door for autonomous and smarter systems that exchange categorized data on both the functional and semantical dimensions.

REFERENCES

[1] S. Tarkoma, Publish/Subscribe Systems: Design and Principles, D. Hutchison, S. Fdida, and J. Sventek, Eds. John Wiley & Sons, Ltd, 2012.

[2] L. Zervakis, C. Tryfonopoulos, A. Papadakis-pesaresi, M. Koubarakis, and S. Skiadopoulos, "Full-text Support for Publish / Subscribe Ontology Systems," Proceedings of the 9th Extended Semantic Web Conference (ESWC), Crete, Greece, (postertrack), 2012, pp. 1–2. [Online]. Available: http://arxiv.org/abs/1307.2015

[3] J. Wang, B. Jin, and J. Li, "An Ontology-Based Publish / Subscribe System *," Ifip International Federation For Information Processing, no. 2002, 2004, pp. 232–253.

[4] P. Eugster, "Type-based publish/subscribe," ACM Transactions on Programming Languages and Systems, vol. 29, no. 1, 2007, pp. 6–es. [Online]. Available: http://portal.acm.org/citation.cfm?doid=1180475.1180481

[5] H. Klus and A. Rausch, "DAiSI A Component Model and Decentralized Configuration Mechanism for Dynamic Adaptive Systems," International Journal On Advances in Intelligent Systems, vol. 7, no. 3 and 4, 2014, pp. 27–36.

[6] P. T. Eugster, P. A. Felber, R. Guerraoui, and A.-M. Kermarrec, "The many faces of publish/subscribe," ACM Computing Surveys, vol. 35, no. 2, 2003, pp. 114–131. [Online]. Available: http://portal.acm.org/citation.cfm?doid=857076.857078

[7] Y. Liu and B. Plale, "Survey of publish subscribe event systems," Indiana University Department of Computer Science, no. TR574, 2003, pp. 1–19.

[8] R. S. S. Filho and D. F. Redmiles, "A Survey of Versatility for Publish / Subscribe Infrastructures," Architecture, no. May, 2005, pp. 1–77.

[9] R. Baldoni, L. Querzoni, and A. Virgillito, "Distributed Event Routing in Publish / Subscribe Communication Systems : a Survey," Technical Report, 2005, pp. 1–27.

[10] M. Petrovic, I. Burcea, and H.-A. Jacobsen, "S-ToPSS: Semantic

Toronto Publish/Subscribe System," Proceedings of the 29th international conference on Very large data basesVolume 29, 2003, p. 4. [Online]. Available: http://arxiv.org/abs/cs/0311041

[11] L. I. Pesonen, D. M. Eyers, and J. Bacon, "Access control in decentralised publish/subscribe systems," Journal of Networks, vol. 2, no. 2, 2007, pp. 57–67.

[12] A. Morales, T. Robles, R. Alcarria, and E. Cedeño, "On the support of scientific workflows over Pub/Sub brokers," Sensors, vol. 13, no. 8, 2013, pp. 10 954–10 980.

[13] D. Bickson, E. N. Hoch, N. Naaman, and Y. Tock, "A Hybrid Multicast-Unicast Infrastructure for Efficient Publish-Subscribe in Enterprise Networks," 2009. [Online]. Available: http://arxiv.org/abs/0901.2687

[14] A. Demers, J. Gehrke, M. Hong, and M. Riedewald, "Towards Expressive Publish / Subcribe Systems," Advances in Database Technology - EDBT 2006, 10th International Conference on Extending Database Technology, Munich, Germany, March 26-31, 2006, Proceedings, vol. 3896, 2006, pp. 1–18.

[15] J. Dayal, D. Bratcher, G. Eisenhauer, K. Schwan, M. Wolf, X. Zhang, H. Abbasi, S. Klasky, and N. Podhorszki, "Flexpath: Type-based publish/subscribe system for large-scale science analytics," Proceedings - 14th IEEE/ACM International Symposium on Cluster, Cloud, and Grid Computing, CCGrid 2014, 2014, pp. 246–255.

[16] P. Eugster, R. Guerraoui, and J. Sventek, "Type-Based Publish / Subscribe ."

[17] "EXLAP - Extensible Lightweight Asynchronous Protocol Specification," Tech. Rep. [Online]. Available: https://de.scribd.com/document/158754515/EXLAP-Specification-V1-3-Creative-Commons-BY-SA-3-0-Volkswagen-pdf

Distributed Simulation for Evolutionary Design of Swarms of Cyber-Physical Systems

Micha Rappaport,
Melanie Schranz

Lakeside Labs GmbH
Klagenfurt, Austria
Email: *lastname*@lakeside-labs.com

Davide Conzon,
Enrico Ferrera

Pervasive Technologies
Istituto Superiore Mario Boella
Torino, Italy
Email: *lastname*@ismb.it

Midhat Jdeed,
Wilfried Elmenreich

Institue of Networked and Embedded Systems
Alpen-Adria-Universität Klagenfurt
Klagenfurt, Austria
Email: *firstname.lastname*@aau.at

***Abstract*—Swarms of Cyber-Physical Systems (CPSs) can be used to tackle many challenges that traditional multi-robot systems fail to address. In particular, the self-organizing nature of swarms ensures they are both scalable and adaptable. Such benefits come at the cost of having a complex system that is extremely hard to design manually. Therefore, an automated process is required for designing the local interactions between the agents that lead to the desired swarm behavior. In this work, the authors employ evolutionary design methodologies to generate the local controllers of the agents. This requires many simulation runs and, as a consequence, distributed simulation. The paper first proposes a network-based Application Programming Interface (API) that employs a publish / subscribe broker architecture to distribute simulations among multiple Simulation Servers (SSs). Following this, a file-based API is proposed, which exports the agent controller to the simulator enabling deployment of the evolved solution on CPSs. Both approaches are compared in terms of time needed for the evolutionary optimization process with the support of simulations. A proof of concept demonstrates the portability to CPSs using TurtleBot robots. The results suggest that for most scenarios it is beneficial to export the agent controller to the simulator to avoid the vast communication overhead. The presented network-based approach currently lacks this feature but is well suited to offload computation-heavy simulations to a cluster of SSs.**

Keywords–Swarms; Evolution; Optimization; Cyber-Physical Systems (CPSs); Simulation; Architecture; Robot Operating System (ROS).

I. Introduction

Over the last decade, the phenomenon of self-organizing systems has gained significant traction in the research community, being observed in disciplines as diverse as physics and biology. Inspired by nature, swarm robotics is also seeing increased interest. On the one hand, coordinating multi-robot systems using swarm approaches offers many opportunities, such as self-organization, self-learning and self-reassembly [1]. On the other hand, it necessitates the difficult process of designing the individual agents to achieve the desired swarm behavior.

Designing swarms of Cyber-Physical Systems (CPSs) poses two main challenges. First, selecting the hardware that best suits the requirements of the swarm (see [2]–[5] for a further examination of this problem), and second, designing the control algorithm defining the behavior of the individual swarm agents. This paper focuses on the latter problem because many platforms for swarm research already exist, e.g., Spiderino [6] and Colias [7].

Approaches for designing local controllers of swarm agents, or more generally self-organizing systems [8], can be categorized into two approaches. First, hierarchical top-down design starting from the desired global behavior of the swarm and second, bottom-up design by defining the swarm agents and observing the resulting global behavior [9]. The design using either approach is still a difficult process as neither can predict the resulting swarm behavior based on the complex interactions between the agents [10]. This is especially true in dynamic environments. Evolutionary methods can be used to tackle such design challenges.

In this paper, we employ the bottom-up design process based on evolutionary algorithms. Generally, evolutionary algorithms aim to mimic the process of natural selection by recombining the most successful solutions to a defined problem [11]. In the context of swarm robotics, a solution refers to a control algorithm of individual agents that is gradually improved during the optimization process. As experiments with real robots require an extensive amout of time, such methods typically employ accurate and fast simulation to evaluate the performance of candidate solutions in the evolutionary process [12]. The evaluation of algorithms in evolutionary optimzation can be easily executed in parallel, which is for example supported in the FRamework for EVOlutionary design (FREVO) [13] by using multiple cores on the same machine. A further step would be the distribution of evolutionary optimization with a client-server-protocol, as exemplified by Kriesel [14]. This work introduces an architecture for parallel distributed simulations on remote Simulation Servers (SSs) and shows how the resulting agent controllers can be deployed on actual Robot Operating System (ROS)-based hardware platforms using TurtleBots [15]. Finally, the paper describes a performance analysis of the presented implementation.

The paper is organized as follows: In Section II, the evolutionary approach for designing swarms is reviewed. Section III introduces the proposed architecture and two implementations are described in Section IV. The performance of the different approaches is analyzed in Section V. Section VI provides a discussion and concludes the paper.

II. Designing Swarms by Evolution

As described in the previous section, design by evolution can be used to tackle challenges such as scalability and generality [16], as well as adaptive self-organization [17]. Both issues are not easy to handle, especially in changing environments and with dynamic interactions among individual agents of a system or a swarm.

Designing a swarm by using evolution is an automatic design method that creates an intended swarm behavior in a bottom up process starting form very small interacting components. This process modifies potential solutions until a satisfying result is achieved. Such an evolutionary design approach is based on evolutionary computation techniques [18] [19] and mimics the Darwinian principle [20]. It describes the process of natural selection by recombining the most proper solutions to a defined problem. Evolution can be done either on individual or on swarm level. Typically, the process of evolving a behavior starts with the generation of a random population of individual behaviors. Each of these individual swarm-level behaviors is evaluated, typically through simulations. This evaluation is performed by a fitness function that allows to rank the behavior's performance. The higher a behavior is ranked, the higher is the chance for the behavior to be modified with genetic operators, like cross-over or mutation, to form a next generation of agent behaviors. These serve as input for the next iteration. Finally, through multiple iterations an agent behavior is evolved that exhibits the desired global swarm behavior.

Nevertheless, designing by evolution poses several challenges, including no guaranteed, predictable convergence, complex data structures, and the high costs of evolutionary computation itself.

Design by evolution asks for several tasks a designer must face during designing a system model. Adapted from Fehervari and Elmenreich [21], we distinguish six tasks: (i) The *problem description* gives a high abstracted vision of the problem. This includes constraints and the desired objectives for such a problem. (ii) The *simulation setup* transfers the problem description into an abstracted problem model. This model specifies the system components, i.e., details about the agents and the environment. (iii) The *interaction interface* defines the interactions among agents and their interactions with the environment. For instance, the agents sensors and actuators as well as the communication protocols should be specified here. (iv) The *evolvable decision unit* represents the agent controller and is responsible for achieving the desired objectives, i.e., the global behavior of a swarm to achieve a common goal. Such a decision unit must be evolvable to allow genetic operations as cross over or mutation. It is most commonly represented by an Artificial Neural Network (ANN). There are different types of ANNs, e.g., fully-meshed ANNs, feed-forward ANNs, HebbNets, or Neuroevolution of Augmenting Topologies (NEAT) ANNs [22]. (v) The *search algorithm* performs the optimization using evolutionary algorithms by applying the results from the above steps. During this task, an iterative mathematical model will be used to find the optimal solution. The optimization result is dependent on the fitness function of the problem. (vi) The *fitness function* represents the quality of the optimization result in a numerical way. There is no specific way or rule to design such a function as it highly depends on the problem description. The main purpose of this function is to guide the search algorithm to find the best solution.

This paper describes how the evolutionary design process is performed using the architecture proposed in the EU H2020 CPSwarm project [23]. In this architecture, the Algorithm Optimization Environment (AOE) is responsible for generating the individual agent controllers that lead to the desired global swarm behavior. This architecture is described in detail in the next section.

III. Architecture

The following requirements exist for the design of the AOE:

- Multiple SSs, even remotely located, offer simulation capabilities to the Optimization Tool (OT) through a broker.

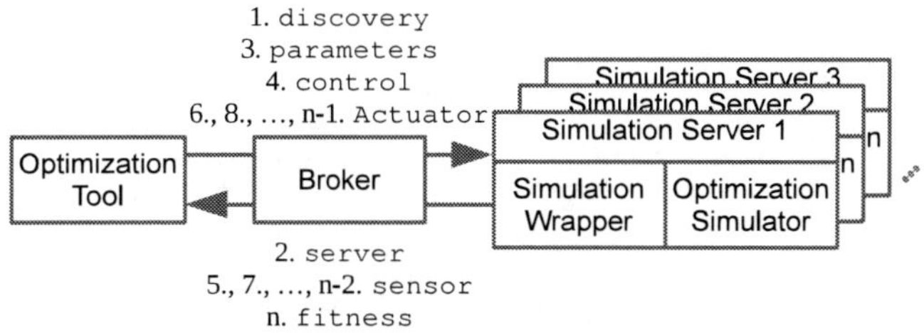

Figure 1. Network-based API.

- Each SS offers one or more Optimization Simulators (OSs).
- An OS exhibits certain characteristics but is also configurable to some extent by the OT.
- Candidate controllers of one generation can be evaluated in parallel.
- The OT can respond to requests from the OS at any point in time.

To fulfill these requirements, the AOE consists of two components: The OT, which is responsible for evolving candidate controllers using the mechanisms explained in Section II and the OS, which evaluates the behavior of each candidate through simulation. These two components are interconnected to each other through a set of interfaces called the Simulator Application Programming Interface (API), which allows them to communicate during the optimization process. Employing an OS as opposed to OT internal simulations gives the opportunity to build on well established simulators that support accurate simulation of swarms of CPSs with different levels of detail.

This section introduces two different approaches for the Simulator API. The first one leverages network socket-based inter-process communication to allow multiple simulations to be remotely run in parallel OSs. Since executing such a large number of simulation runs requires a significant amount of time, parallel distributed execution enhances the scalability and performance of the optimization process. The second approach is a file system-based inter-process communication technique which hands over full control to the OS. This approach requires no further communication between the tools and is therefore well-suited for deploying the generated candidate controllers on CPSs.

A. Network-based Approach

The network-based approach aims to improve scalability and performance through parallelization of simulations during the optimization process. This is achieved from two sides: on OT side, the candidates belonging to the same generation are evaluated in parallel using multi-threading. Each thread uses a different OS to perform the required simulation. The OSs are run in parallel, possibly on different, remote SSs.

The network communication is managed by a broker that offers a publish / subscribe infrastructure to the subscribing clients: OT and SS. Figure 1 gives an overview of the functional architecture of this approach, indicating the messages exchanged, numbered by the order in which they are sent (see Section IV for more details). The SS is decoupled from the OT via the broker. In this way, every SS can be on a dedicated machine with the hardware requirements needed to execute the simulations.

Every SS offers one or more OSs that communicate with the broker through a Simulation Wrapper (SW). The SW is a

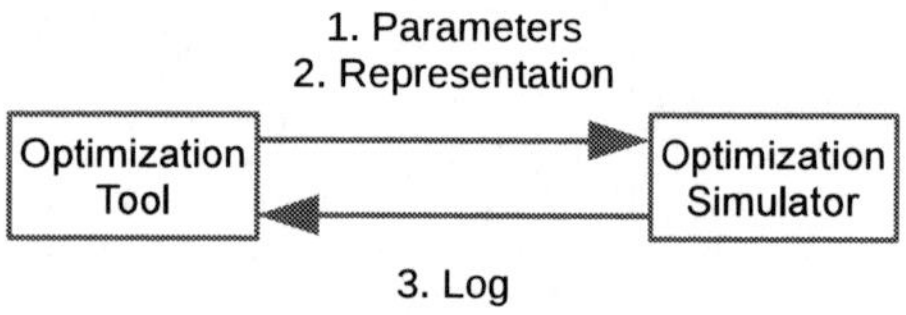

Figure 2. File-based approachAPI.

software layer installed on the SS that implements the Simulator API and acts as a client connecting to the broker. This allows the OT to communicate with the SS without knowing what type of OS is actually used. After the OT has created one generation of controller candidates, it can send different candidates to different SSs, which perform the simulation and calculate the fitness. When the fitness is returned from every SS, the OT can perform the evolutionary steps to create the candidates for the next generation.

Several SSs can work in parallel to reduce the time required to complete the simulations in one generation of the evolutionary optimization. Through the SW, different OSs can be employed, also if the OSs are heterogeneous among each other. Importantly, a SS can be used by several OT instances, but only by one at a time.

B. File-based Approach

Figure 2 shows the file-based approach and the files exchanged, numbered by the order in which they are sent. This solution aims to reduce the communication between OT and OS by passing a generated candidate controller as a file from the OT to the OS. The following three files are passed between the tools:

- Parameters: The parameters that need to be transferred from the OT to the OS to setup the OS.
- Representation: The representation of the candidate controller exported by the OT. The OS implementation includes this source code file to enable the agents in the simulation making decisions by translating the sensor readings to actuator commands.
- Log: Every agent in the simulation generates a log file containing the metrics for measuring the performance of a candidate. The log files are used by the fitness function to calculate the fitness of a candidate controller.

IV. IMPLEMENTATION

A set of existing tools was extended to implement the architecture presented in the previous section. These tools are interconnected using the two approaches of the Simulator API, the network-based approach and the file-based approach. This section first introduces the concepts and tools used for the development of the proposed solutions and then details the specifics of the Simulator API.

FREVO is selected as the OT since it is a very modular optimization tool that satisfies the principles addressed in Section II [13].

The current implementation of FREVO relies on simulations implemented in the problem component. This implies that each problem needs an implementation of the simulation including models of the agents. This can be avoided by using state-of-the-art robotics simulators that build on standard models. The integration of these tool into the CPSwarm architecture requires the current implementation to be improved, enabling it to use multiple SSs, as addressed in the list of requirements in Section III.

A. Network-based Implementation

As mentioned in Section III-A, the network-based approach is implemented using a broker architecture. The broker employs the Message Queue Telemetry Transport (MQTT) protocol [24] which is based on the publish / subscribe paradigm. In recent times, this solution has been recognized as the defacto standard for event-driven architectures in the Internet of Things (IoT) domain. MQTT has been chosen because of its extreme simplicity. Its design principles attempt to minimize network bandwidth and device resource requirements whilst also ensuring reliability and some degree of assurance of delivery. Therefore, both FREVO and the SW implement a client for the MQTT protocol.

FREVO implements the client as a helper class called `simMQTT` that contains the MQTT callbacks for receiving messages from the broker. The class is instantiated by the problem component in FREVO that evaluates a candidate controller through simulation. The `simMQTT` class handles all the communication with the broker.

As described above, the SS consists of an OS and a SW. The OS evaluates a specific candidate controller in the optimization process. The SW serves as client that handles the connection to the MQTT broker. The SW is implemented as a Java library. It embeds the MQTT Paho client [25] for MQTT communication. The library exports an abstract class called `SimulationWrapper`, which implements the behavior that is common to all the simulators. It provides a set of API functions to be used by the SS to handle the messages received from and to sent to FREVO. To test the implementation, the `SimulationWrapper` has been integrated with a very basic Java simulator called *Minisim*, which is a command-line, multi-agent simulator simulating a capture-the-flag game with multiple robots on a two-dimensional grid. *Minisim* has been specifically developed for testing the network communication between FREVO and the SS [26].

The messages exchanged between FREVO and the SS through the Simulator API are explained in the following. When FREVO needs to evaluate a candidate, it queries for available SSs by sending a `discovery` message containing the requirements for the OS. Every SS that has an OS fulfilling these requirements and has enough resources available answers the request with a `server` message. The server message contains the OS capabilities and ID. FREVO selects a suitable SS and initiates the simulation by sending a `parameters` message to setup the OS followed by a `control` message to start the simulation. The `parameters` message contains the parameters that describe the models as well as the necessary configuration parameters for the simulation environment. As a direct reaction to the `control` message, the addressed OS starts the simulation with the model parameters received earlier and publishes the `sensor` messages of the first simulation time step. The `sensor` message transmits the sensor readings of one agent to FREVO, which uses this information to compute the next actuator commands for this agent and replies with an `actuator` message to transmit the corresponding actuator commands. The process continues until the end of the simulation is reached. The `fitness` message is the final message of a simulation run, calculated by the SS once the maximum number of simulation steps has been reached. Every message contains a server ID and a simulation hash that can be used to uniquely identifying the OS and the simulation it is running.

B. File-based Implementation

With the file-based approach, FREVO communicates with the OS through the file system. The OS is based on ROS, a middleware that can control CPSs in simulation and on physical hardware. Hence, all simulators that are compatible with ROS can be used with this implementation. Two very popular simulators, namely Stage [27], a low-fidelity two-dimensional robot simulator and Gazebo [28], a high-fidelity three-dimensional robot simulator have been tested successfully with this implementation.

To perform the ROS simulations, FREVO first exports the candidate representation of the agent controller and problem specific parameters into the ROS workspace. Then FREVO executes a script that compiles and runs the simulation. When the simulation terminates, FREVO reads the log files created by ROS to compute the fitness of the simulated candidate. The API is implemented in the helper class `simROS` of FREVO, allowing every problem component to access ROS.

The three files described in the previous section are implemented as follows:

- Parameters: The parameters that need to be transferred from FREVO are written into parameter files in the YAML Ain't Markup Language (YAML) [29] format that is used by ROS. These are problem specific parameters such as description of the agents in terms of hardware or positioning.
- Representation: The candidate controller is represented as a fully meshed ANN. It is exported by FREVO into a C source code file. ROS includes this file into the source code of the package that implements the agent behavior. Once this file is exported to ROS, a recompilation of the ROS package becomes necessary.
- Log: The performance of a candidate is measured by performance metrics defined in FREVO. The simulator measures the metrics and writes them to log files in text format. FREVO reads these log files and applies the fitness function to calculate the fitness of a candidate controller.

This implementation uses a simple multi agent simulation called *EmergencyExit* [26]. On one hand, this implementation enables the communication between FREVO and ROS for evolving a controller using ROS-based simulations. On the other hand it allows the evolved result, i.e. the ANN, to be exported from FREVO and run in ROS standalone on actual CPS. As a proof of concept, an evolved ANN is used to guide TurtleBot robots in Gazebo simulations and in real world experiments.

V. PERFORMANCE ANALYSIS

The previous sections presented two different approaches for distributed simulation during the optimization process. The main difference between the presented approaches is that with the network-based approach the agent controllers reside within the OT FREVO and communicate with the simulator by exchanging messages, whereas with the file-based approach the agent controller is exported to the simulator and communication takes place only at the beginning and the end of the simulation. This section compares both approaches in terms of scalability. The relevant parameters for this analysis are the number of parallel threads n_{threads}, the number of agents n_{agents}, and the length of a simulation in terms of steps n_{steps}. First, a theoretical comparison is performed that is complemented by simulation results using FREVO with the above mentioned *Minisim* and *EmergencyExit* simulations. The performance is measured in time to perform a complete optimization.

A. Theoretical Comparison

For the first part of this analysis the approaches are abstracted to represent the different locations where the agent controller can reside. This is either internal within the OT (network-based implementation) or external within the simulator (file-based implementation).

In the evolutionary optimization process, there is a population of n_{pop} candidate controllers that can be evaluated in parallel. They are evaluated through simulation consisting of n_{step} steps. When all candidates have been evaluated, a new generation is created using evolutionary operators. The total number of generations is n_{gen}. This results in a total number of simulations for a complete optimization of

$$n_{\text{sim}} = n_{\text{gen}} \cdot n_{\text{pop}} \cdot n_{\text{eval}} \quad (1)$$

where each candidate is evaluated in n_{eval} simulations. When simulations are parallelized on n_{threads}, the number of simulations that need to be performed sequentially results to

$$n_{\text{sim}} = \frac{n_{\text{gen}} \cdot n_{\text{pop}} \cdot n_{\text{eval}}}{n_{\text{threads}}} \quad (2)$$

given that n_{thread} is within the range $[1, n_{\text{pop}} \cdot n_{\text{eval}}]$.

In general, the time t_{opt} needed for one optimization run consists of the time needed for performing the evolutionary calculations t_{evo}, the time needed for performing the simulations t_{sim}, and the overhead t_{overhead}

$$t_{\text{opt}} = n_{\text{gen}} \cdot t_{\text{evo}} + n_{\text{sim}} \cdot (t_{\text{sim}} + t_{\text{overhead}}) \quad (3)$$

where $t_{\text{sim}} = n_{\text{step}} \cdot t_{\text{step}}$. The difference between both approaches lies in the overhead t_{overhead}.

With the OT internal controller, the number of messages that need to be exchanged between the OT and the simulator depends on the number of agents n_{agent} in the simulation. The `discovery`, `server`, `parameters`, `control`, and `fitness` messages are only transmitted once for every simulation. The `sensor` and `actuator` messages are transmitted in every simulation step for every agent. Therefore, the number of messages exchanged in each simulation is

$$n_{\text{msg}} = 5 + 2 \cdot n_{\text{step}} \cdot n_{\text{agent}} \quad (4)$$

which gives us an overhead based on the communication time between the OT and the simulator:

$$t_{\text{overhead,int}} = (5 + 2 \cdot n_{\text{step}} \cdot n_{\text{agent}}) \cdot t_{\text{msg}}. \quad (5)$$

For the external controller, the overhead is

$$t_{\text{overhead,ext}} = t_{\text{export}} + t_{\text{compile}} + t_{\text{fitness}} \quad (6)$$

based on the time needed for exporting representation and simulation parameters t_{export}, the time needed for recompiling the simulator t_{compile}, and the time for reading the log files and computing the fitness t_{fitness}.

The total optimization time of both approaches is therefore

$$t_{\text{opt,int}} = n_{\text{gen}} \cdot t_{\text{evo}} + \frac{n_{\text{gen}} \cdot n_{\text{pop}} \cdot n_{\text{eval}}}{n_{\text{threads}}} \cdot (n_{\text{step}} \cdot t_{\text{step}} + (5 + 2 \cdot n_{\text{step}} \cdot n_{\text{agent}}) \cdot t_{\text{msg}}) \quad (7)$$

$$t_{\text{opt,ext}} = n_{\text{gen}} \cdot t_{\text{evo}} + \frac{n_{\text{gen}} \cdot n_{\text{pop}} \cdot n_{\text{eval}}}{n_{\text{threads}}} \cdot (n_{\text{step}} \cdot t_{\text{step}} + t_{\text{export}} + t_{\text{compile}} + t_{\text{fitness}}). \quad (8)$$

TABLE I. Optimization parameters measured through simulations.

parameter	value
n_{gen}	200
n_{pop}	50
n_{eval}	1
t_{evo}	12 ms
t_{msg}	30 ms
t_{export}	5.35 ms
$t_{compile}$	8833 ms
$t_{fitness}$	0.69 ms
t_{step}	100 ms

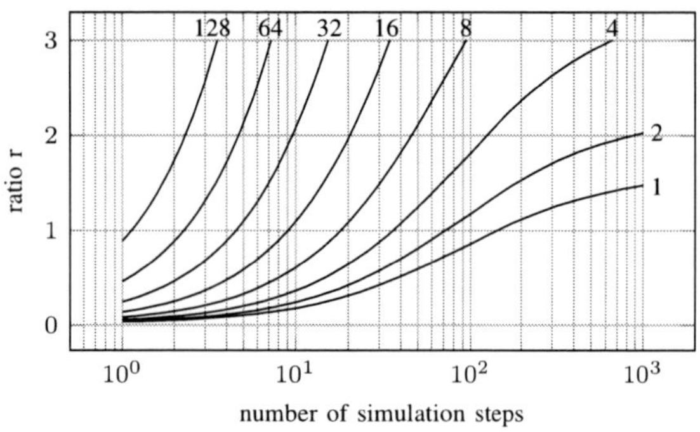

Figure 3. Ratio of optimization times between OT internal agent controller and OT external controller for different numbers of agents.

Table I shows specific parameters and execution times measured on a dual Intel Xeon X5675 3.07 GHz system with 16 GB memory and 12 cores in total, supporting up to 24 threads with hyper-threading. The operating system is Debian 9. The evolutionary parameters were chosen to yield good results. The times are measurements of the MQTT broker implementation and the ROS-based implementation.

Using these values with (7) and (8) the specific optimization times are

$$t_{\text{opt,int}} = 2.4\,\text{s}\left(1 + \frac{250}{n_{\text{thread}}}\left(2.5 + n_{\text{step}}\left(1.67 + n_{\text{agent}}\right)\right)\right) \quad (9)$$

$$t_{\text{opt,ext}} = 2.4\,\text{s}\left(1 + \frac{416.67}{n_{\text{thread}}}\left(88.39 + n_{\text{step}}\right)\right). \quad (10)$$

To decide whether to run optimization with internal or external agent controller, the ratio between both optimization times is a suitable metric.

Figure 3 shows the ratio $r = \frac{t_{\text{op,int}}}{t_{\text{opt,ext}}}$. A value of $r > 1$ means that the external approach performs better whereas a value of $r < 1$ means that the internal approach is favorable. As both approaches can use parallelization, the resultant ratio is independent of the number of parallel threads used. It can be seen that for most cases the controller should reside externally within the simulator. This is due to the fact that if all agent controllers are executed in a single tool it creates a bottleneck situation. This is not so crucial for small swarms but already for a swarm size of eight agents, the optimization with internal control takes longer when simulations last more than 18 steps.

B. Scalability of the network-based approach

This study analyzes the scalability of the network-based approach where the agent controller resides locally within FREVO. The optimization is performed with a population size of $n_{\text{pop}} = 4$ and $n_{\text{gen}} = 4$ generations. Figure 4 shows the time needed for optimization with $n_{\text{agent}} = 8$ agents. As expected, the time needed for a complete optimization run scales linearly with the length of a single simulation. Only for extremely short simulations the overhead introduced from discovering available SSs renders the parallelism pointless. In fact, the discovery process limits the scalability of the proposed implementation. As the broker is the central point that enables the discovery, the optimization time does not scale for more than two SSs, because the `discovery` and `server` messages already account for most of the traffic. Therefore, the discovery procedure needs improvements as described in Section VI. Nevertheless, using two SSs rather than one speeds up the optimization significantly. The speed-up continues to increase as the number of simulation steps increases as longer simulations decrease the relative time spent in the discovery phase.

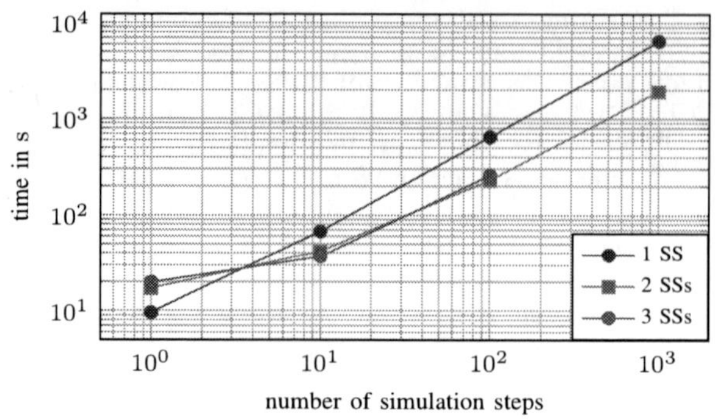

Figure 4. Optimization time using the network-based approach for varying number of SSs and 8 agents.

VI. Conclusion and Future Work

This paper presents a solution for the evolutionary design of swarms of CPSs based on remote simulation tools. The architecture designed for this solution is composed of three main components: The OT that is responsible for evolving candidate controllers, the OS evaluating the behavior of each candidate through simulation, and the Simulator API that connects the OT and the OS. For the latter component, two different approaches and related implementations are presented: A broker-based approach, which parallelizes the simulations of the optimization process to improve scalability and performance, and a file-based approach, which is used to prove the compatibility with CPSs.

A performance analysis shows that the broker-based approach does not scale well for more than two SSs because of network congestion at the OT when it discovers the SSs. Therefore, the current implementation cannot exploit the full potential of this approach. Furthermore, in this approach all agent controllers are executed in a single OT which creates a bottleneck. Hence, this implementation of the broker-based approach is suitable for simple simulations. This could be either short simulations with few time steps or simulations with only a small number of agents, e.g., swarms of up to eight agents and up to 18 time steps. The file-based approach is a viable alternative where the agent controller is exported to the OS and is especially suited for large swarms of robots as the messaging overhead is drastically reduced. In any case, the broker-based solution is the better choice if simulations are performed where OT and OS are not located on the same machine.

Considering this, further improvements could be made to increase the performance of the broker-based approach. First, the optimization process could be split into two phases. In the first phase, a handshake between OT and SS would take place, where the OT would discover the SSs fulfilling the requirements and would select one of them for simulations. In the second phase, the OT would perform the optimization and would execute the simulations using the selected SSs. This approach is expected to reduce the number of `discovery` and `server` messages and to avoid the congestions that inhibit the scalability with more than two SSs. Second, the controller candidate represented as ANN could be exported to the SS as done in the file-based approach. In this way, it would be possible to avoid the use of `sensor` and `actuator` messages, reducing the overall number of messages exchanged and the time required to complete the optimization drastically. The drawback of the file-based implementation of this approach is the time required for recompiling the simulator code to include the ANN source code. This could be avoided by creating a generic ANN wrapper that would only read the ANN parameters from a configuration file avoiding the need for recompilation. Hence, a combination of both the presented approaches is needed for a distributed and scalable network architecture that can support the large amount of simulations during the optimization process.

ACKNOWLEDGMENT

We thank Robotnik Automation S.L.L. for porting the implementation to TurtleBot robots and the Gazebo simulator. We also thank Arthur Pitman for proofreading the text. The research leading to these results has received funding from the European Union Horizon 2020 research and innovation program under grant agreement no. 731946.

REFERENCES

[1] M. Patil, T. Abukhalil, S. Patel, and T. Sobh, "UB robot swarm – design, implementation, and power management," in Proc. 12th IEEE International Conference on Control and Automation (ICCA), Jun. 2016, pp. 577–582, ISBN: 978-1-5090-1738-6.

[2] I. Fehérvári, V. Trianni, and W. Elmenreich, "On the effects of the robot configuration on evolving coordinated motion behaviors," in Proc. IEEE Congress on Evolutionary Computation, Jun. 2013, pp. 1209–1216, ISBN: 978-1-4799-0452-5.

[3] R. Goldsmith, "Real world hardware evolution: A mobile platform for sensor evolution," in Proc. 5th International Conference on Evolvable Systems: From Biology to Hardware (ICES), Mar. 2003, pp. 355–364, ISBN: 978-3-540-36553-2.

[4] J. Bongard, "Exploiting multiple robots to accelerate self-modeling," in Proc. 9th Annual Conference on Genetic and Evolutionary Computation (GECCO), Jul. 2007, pp. 214–221, ISBN: 978-1-59593-697-4.

[5] D. Floreano and F. Mondada, "Hardware solutions for evolutionary robotics," in Proc. European Workshop on Evolutionary Robotics (EvoRobot), 1998, pp. 137–151, ISBN: 978-3-540-49902-2.

[6] M. Jdeed, S. Zhevzhyk, F. Steinkellner, and W. Elmenreich, "Spiderino – A low-cost robot for swarm research and educational purposes," in 13th Workshop on Intelligent Solutions in Embedded Systems (WISES), Jun. 2017, pp. 35–39, ISBN: 978-1-5386-1157-9.

[7] F. Arvin, J. Murray, C. Zhang, and S. Yue, "Colias: An autonomous micro robot for swarm robotic applications," International Journal of Advanced Robotic Systems, vol. 11, no. 7, Jul. 2014, pp. 1–10, DOI: 10.5772/58730.

[8] W. Elmenreich, R. D'Souza, C. Bettstetter, and H. de Meer, "A survey of models and design methods for self-organizing networked systems," in Proc. 4th International Workshop on Self-Organizing Systems (IWSOS), Dec. 2009, pp. 37–49, ISBN: 978-3-642-10865-5.

[9] V. Crespi, A. Galstyan, and K. Lerman, "Top-down vs bottom-up methodologies in multi-agent system design," Autonomous Robots, vol. 24, no. 3, Apr. 2008, pp. 303–313, ISSN: 1573-7527.

[10] I. Fehérvári and W. Elmenreich, "Evolving neural network controllers for a team of self-organizing robots," Journal of Robotics, vol. 2010, 2010, pp. 1–10, DOI: 10.1155/2010/841286.

[11] C. M. Fernandes and A. C. Rosa, "Evolutionary algorithms with dissortative mating on static and dynamic environments," in Advances in Evolutionary Algorithms. InTech, Nov. 2008, pp. 181–206, ISBN: 978-953-7619-11-4.

[12] L. Winkler and H. Wörn, "Symbricator3D – A distributed simulation environment for modular robots," in Proc. 2nd International Conference on Intelligent Robotics and Applications (ICIRA), Dec. 2009, pp. 1266–1277, ISBN: 978-3-642-10817-4.

[13] A. Sobe, I. Fehervari, and W. Elmenreich, "FREVO: A tool for evolving and evaluating self-organizing systems," in Proc. 1st International Workshop on Evaluation for Self-Adaptive and Self-Organizing Systems (Eval4SASO), Sep. 2012, pp. 105–110, ISBN: 978-0-7695-4895-1.

[14] D. Kriesel, "Verteilte, evolutionäre Optimierung von Schwärmen [Distributed, evolutionary optimization of swarms]," Diplomarbeit, Rheinische Friedrich-Wilhelm-Universität Bonn, Mar. 2009.

[15] Open Source Robotics Foundation, Inc., "Turtlebot," http://www.turtlebot.com/, accessed: 2017-12-07.

[16] M. Dorigo et al., "Evolving self-organizing behaviors for a swarm-bot," Autonomous Robots, vol. 17, no. 2, Sep. 2004, pp. 223–245, ISSN: 1573-7527.

[17] Y. Yao, K. Marchal, and Y. Van de Peer, "Improving the adaptability of simulated evolutionary swarm robots in dynamically changing environments," PLOS ONE, vol. 9, no. 3, Mar. 2014, pp. 1–9, DOI: 10.1371/journal.pone.0090695.

[18] J. H. Holland, Adaptation in Natural and Artificial Systems. Cambridge, MA, USA: MIT Press, Mar. 1992, ISBN: 9780262082136.

[19] I. Rechenberg, Evolutionsstrategie – Optimierung technischer Systeme nach Prinzipien der biologischen Evolution [Evolution strategy – Optimization of technical systems according to the principles of biological evolution]. Stuttgart, Germany: Fromman-Holzboog, 1973, ISBN: 978-3772803734.

[20] M. Brambilla, E. Ferrante, M. Birattari, and M. Dorigo, "Swarm robotics: a review from the swarm engineering perspective," Swarm Intelligence, vol. 7, no. 1, Mar. 2013, pp. 1–41, ISSN: 1935-3820.

[21] I. Fehervari and W. Elmenreich, "Evolution as a tool to design self-organizing systems," in Revised Selected Papers from 7th IFIP TC 6 International Workshop on Self-Organizing Systems (IWSOS), Jan. 2014, pp. 139–144, ISBN: 978-3-642-54140-7.

[22] I. Fehervari, "On evolving self-organizing technical systems," Ph.D. dissertation, Alpen-Adria-Universität Klagenfurt, Nov. 2013.

[23] J. Liang et al., "D3.1 – initial system architecture & design specification," EU H2020 CPSwarm Consortium, Public deliverable, Aug. 2017.

[24] "Information technology – Message Queuing Telemetry Transport (MQTT) v3.1.1," Geneva, Switzerland, Standard ISO/IEC 20922:2016, Jun. 2006.

[25] "Eclipse paho," https://www.eclipse.org/paho/, accessed: 2017-12-07.

[26] M. Rappaport, D. Conzon, and E. Ferrera, "D6.1 – initial simulation environment," EU H2020 CPSwarm Consortium, Public deliverable, Oct. 2017.

[27] R. Vaughan, "Massively multiple robot simulations in stage," Swarm Intelligence, vol. 2, no. 2-4, Dec. 2008, pp. 189–208, ISSN: 1935-3820.

[28] N. Koenig and A. Howard, "Design and use paradigms for Gazebo, an open-source multi-robot simulator," in Proc. IEEE/RSJ International Conference on Intelligent Robots and Systems (IROS), Sep. 2004, pp. 2149–2154, ISBN: 0-7803-8463-6.

[29] "YAML Ain't Markup Language (YAML)," http://www.yaml.org/spec/, Specification Version 1.2, Sep. 2009.

Automated and Connected Driving in Urban Scenarios

Maximilian Flormann, M.Sc.*, Adrian Sonka, M.Sc.*, Priv. Doz. Dr.-Ing. Roman Henze*
*Institute of Automotive Engineering
TU Braunschweig
Braunschweig, Germany 38106
Email: m.flormann@tu-braunschweig.de
Telephone: +49 531 391-2619

***Abstract*—Scenarios for automated driving in inner-city applications differ heavily from highway or rural road scenarios. Various challenges like obstacles in the sensors field of view and actions beyond the vehicles sensory reach can be overcome by using wireless communication. This paper focuses on current developments in Car2X communication standards. Therefore, the various communication protocols and standards are described and their applications are detailed. The described wireless technologies involve basic communication standards like Bluetooth and Wi-Fi, as well as advanced implementations, such as cellular data and the IEEE standard 802.11p WAVE. The approach presented here focuses on the evaluation of these wireless technologies for various vehicle applications in urban scenarios. The advantages, as well as the challenges of the different protocols are determined and their suitability for different use-cases is described and validated. Concluding, the implementations are described exemplary by detailing the developed applications at the Institute of Automotive Engineering, TU Braunschweig.**

Keywords–Car2X communication, 802.11p, WAVE, wireless vehicular systems, automated , cooperative driving

I. Introduction

Automated vehicles, as well as human drivers have to deal with similar issues when it comes to inner-city driving. Sharp corners and obstacles like buildings, plants and city infrastructure limit the automated vehicle's sensory field of view. Furthermore, objects out of the vehicle sensors' reach are not detectable, yielding a potential hazard. Other than the human driver, the vehicle can overcome this issue by connecting to other vehicles and surrounding infrastructure. This connected vehicular systems compensate the potential drawbacks mentioned beforehand by exchanging relevant dates with other traffic participants. Especially the need for cooperative driving, i.e., driving in cooperation with not connected and automated road users, in urban scenarios yields this Car2X communication to adapt to the ever changing scenarios.

Comprised in this communication can be, among others, informations each traffic participant sends about himself, such as speed, planned trajectory and position [1]. Furthermore, the communication partners can send object lists and other information regarding their surroundings.

Equipping automated vehicles with advanced communication units massively increases the adaptability of these vehicles and vehicular networks.

This paper focuses on the communication protocols for connected vehicles as implemented at the Institute of Automotive Engineering (IAE), TU Braunschweig. Therefore, the used communication protocols are described and their usage is detailed. The introduced standards include Bluetooth, WiFi, cellular data and the dedicated IEEE standard for Car2X-communication, 802.11p.

After detailing these protocols and giving a short overview of current exemplary applications at the IAE, the assets and drawbacks of each standard are stated. Concluding, a lookout on potential challenges and future developments is presented.

II. Hardware Base and used Communication Standards

The introduced communication systems are all implemented on two test vehicles at the Institute of Automotive Engineering. The first vehicle is called *Testing and Engioneering of Automated driving SYstems* (TEASY III), the second vehicle *Testing of Integrated Automation and MOnitoring Systems* (TIAMO). Both vehicles are equipped with various sensors and controllers in order to develop automated driving functions. These sensors include mono and stereo cameras, radars and 360° laserscanners for advanced object detection. This sensor and controller setup enables these vehicles to drive automatically in various scenarios, such as highways, rural roads and urban environments.

Especially automated driving in urban environments has a much higher amount of relevant data compared to other driving environments. Since the ego-vehicles sensors have a limited reach and their line of sight can be blocked by various obstacles, vehicles in urban scenarios have to constantly adapt their trajectory planning to the ever changing boundary conditions. This yields the need for connected vehicular systems as described in the following sections.

A. Bluetooth

The IEEE standard 802.15.1 Bluetooth is a dedicated short range wireless communication protocol [2]. Since most modern mobile devices support Bluetooth connections, this standard is very suitable to transfer real time vehicle data quickly and to control various vehicle functions remotely [3]. Since the range of Bluetooth connections is fairly short, the applications at the IAE comprises mainly of quick and modular connections within the vehicle. Among these applications is the linkage between vehicle electronics and the passengers mobile devices, as well as a the communication between the vehicle's central controller and a test manager [4]. This makes it possible to control the vehicles automated driving functions remotely and comfortably from mobile devices.

Since Bluetooth has been developed as a wireless alternative to RS-232, connections can be set up fairly quick and with only a basic handshake between the participating systems. This makes it highly suitable for short and very sporadic data transmissions between vehicles and mobile devices or other vehicles over very short distances.

B. 802.11 b/g/n WLAN

Another widely spread wireless communication is the IEEE standard 802.11b/g/n for *Wireless Local Area Networking* [5], often abbreviated to *Wi-Fi* or *Wireless Fidelity*. This communication standard combines high data rates with intermediate range. Due to this features, this protocol is highly suitable for transferring large amounts of data between vehicle and infrastructure. Since WLAN requires the participants to register in the network before the beginning of the communication, it takes relatively long until actual payload can be transferred. This network protocol is used at the IAE to update the vehicles' software modules remotely, to transfer measured data and to establish a communication between to vehicles. This enables applications like platooning. Hereby, two cars travelling in the same direction connect via such a local network in order to transfer vehicle data or join their trajectory planning.

C. Cellular Data

Cellular Data (i.e., LTE as state of the art and 5G as a future developmen) enables the test vehicles to communicate over very long distances [6]. Since every vehicle dials into the closest cellular radio cell and changes the cells dynamically when driving, cellular data allows the connected vehicles to establish a stable long-term connection over long distances. A downside of this dynamic changing of cells is that the connection can be disturbed for a short time while driving.
Thus, the test vehicles can connect to distant city-infrastructure via cellular data and communicate less time-critical data. The IAE's vehicles use this communication standard to transmit their positions and planned trajectory to other traffic participants and the involved infrastructure. This enables the test vehicles to adapt their track planning to potentially occurring obstacles or traffic peaks.

D. 802.11p WAVE

The most advanced standard in Car2X communication is the on the IEEE Norm 802.11p based WAVE protocol (**W**ireless **A**ccess in **V**ehicular **E**nvironments) [7]. This version of the WLAN-Norm utilizes a special frequency band at 5.9 GHz and forgoes the process of registering to the network. Every traffic participant broadcasts their messages to all other participants in reach.
In order to enable the messages to reach targets further away, the WAVE protocol uses knot-hopping similar to delay tolerant networks (DTN) [8]. Hereby, messages are configured to be forwarded a defined number of times. The first test vehicle sends a message, which is then received and forwarded by all other participants in reach. These participants can be other test vehicles or infrastructure units. The messages can be divided into two main types for different applications [9]:

- CAM: Cooperative Awareness Message:
  This message contains cyclic status information send by every participant continuously
  Examples: Ego vehicle's position, personal identification, sensory information
- DENM: Decentralized Environmental Notificantion Message:
  This message contains non-cyclic information on special events
  Examples: Position of obstacles or potential hazards, incoming emergency vehicles

This communication concept makes 802.11p WAVE very suitable for dynamic applications, such as connected driving in urban scenarios. Traffic participants can communicate quickly and without the need to conduct a registration to the network. While this speeds up the communication establishment, it also can lead to messages not reaching their destination because of missing links. The absence of such registration process yields the use of other methods for securing the communication, this is specified in the corresponding security norm IEEE 1609.2 [9].
At the IAE, this communication protocol is exclusively used for urban scenarios. The test vehicles exchange their driving intentions with each other quickly. Since this information is broadcasted, the test vehicles can communicate with each other or city infrastructure even when crossing each other or passing by quickly.

III. Conclusion and Lookout

Automated driving in urban scenarios demands for special communication standards. This Car2X communication increases the automated vehicles' performance by extending the on-board sensors with infrastructure information and the sensory data of other traffic participants. By equipping automated vehicles with these communication modules, the adaptability on the ever changing urban driving environment is increased heavily. However, when increasing the amount of connectivity and adaptability it has to be taken care of not to impair the security and safety of such systems.
This paper describes the Car2X communication standards used at the Institute of Automotive Engineering and details on the current applications in the context of urban automated driving. The described variants cover Bluetooth, 802.11b/g/n WLAN, Cellular Data and 802.11p WAVE. These four communication standards are detailed regarding their assets and drawbacks. This comparison yields various applications for which each described variant is variously suitable.
The focus of future work on this promising topic of Car2X communication is the combination of these different network interfaces in order to achieve a higher amount of adaptability by automated connected vehicular systems. Furthermore, it has to be made sure that while adding connectivity and adaptability, security is key to increase these systems safety.
In order to achieve this, the ongoing research described in this paper has to further investigate the potentials of Car2X communication with special regards to security issues. Particularly, 802.11p and its security norm IEEE 1609.2 [9] has to be evaluated further.

References

[1] H. Steubing, M. Bechler, D. Heussner, T. May, I. Radusch, H. Rechner, and P. Vogel, "simtd: a car-to-x system architecture for field operational tests [topics in automotive networking]," IEEE Communications Magazine, vol. 48, no. 5, May 2010, pp. 148–154.

[2] J. C. Haartsen, "The bluetooth radio system," IEEE Personal Communications, vol. 7, no. 1, February 2000, pp. 28–36.

[3] J. r. Lin, T. Talty, and O. K. Tonguz, "On the potential of bluetooth low energy technology for vehicular applications," IEEE Communications Magazine, vol. 53, no. 1, January 2015, pp. 267–275.

[4] H. Znamiec, B. Reuber, R. Henze, and F. Kücükay, "A Method for the Efficient Testing of new Automated Driving Functions," Fast Zero, 2017.

[5] "Ieee standard for information technology–telecommunications and information exchange between systems local and metropolitan area networks–specific requirements - part 11: Wireless lan medium access control (mac) and physical layer (phy) specifications," IEEE Std 802.11-2016 (Revision of IEEE Std 802.11-2012), Dec 2016, pp. 1–3534.

[6] E. Hossain, M. Rasti, H. Tabassum, and A. Abdelnasser, "Evolution toward 5g multi-tier cellular wireless networks: An interference management perspective," IEEE Wireless Communications, vol. 21, no. 3, June 2014, pp. 118–127.

[7] D. Jiang and L. Delgrossi, "Ieee 802.11p: Towards an international standard for wireless access in vehicular environments," in VTC Spring 2008 - IEEE Vehicular Technology Conference, May 2008, pp. 2036–2040.

[8] M. Doering, S. Lahde, J. Morgenroth, and L.Wolf, "IBR-DTN: An Efficient Implementation for Embedded Systems," Chants '08, 2008, pp. 117–120.

[9] T. Schütze, "Automotive Security: Cryptography for Car2X Communication," Rohde + Schwarz, 2011.

Highly Accurate Map-based Path and Behavior Planning for Automated Urban Driving

Björn Reuber, Holger Znamiec, Dr. Roman Henze, Prof. Dr. Ferit Küçükay
TU Braunschweig - Institute of Automotive Engineering
Email: b.reuber@tu-braunschweig.de
Telephone: (+49) 531 391-66605

***Abstract*—To overcome challenges of automated driving in inner-city scenarios, this paper's approach is to realize a robust behavior and path planning based on highly accurate maps combined with localization and communication methods. The main idea is to build up the model based on an existing modular automated driving architecture which was initially developed for highway use cases. This should enable a possibility of implementation with an significantly reduced effort.**

Keywords–Automated Urban Driving; Behavior Planing; Connected Driving; Highly Accurate Maps; Localization.

I. Introduction

Automated driving is undoubtedly one of the most important technological development components for the automotive industry. For example, the first series applications of individual Society of Automotive Engineers (SAE) Level 3 systems are now almost ready for market launch [1]. However, their range of functions is still rather low and the scope is limited to the highway.

On the other hand, a number of complex challenges have to be overcome in order to realize automated driving in the inner-city area. Therefore, the high complexity of the static and dynamic environment within cities leads to increased requirements to the robustness of in-vehicle behavior planning.

This is where the following papers approach is focusing on. Based on a high-precision digital map, additional information about the static environment is provided to the vehicle's planning modules. This is complemented by additional information from communication infrastructure to the dynamic environment.

At first, in Section II, an exemplary use case is presented in which the concept can be applied. Section III is focusing on the key elements of the concept and their purpose as well as the connection among them. In Section IV an overview about the integration in an existing architecture is given. The paper is concluded by a summary of the current work status and the outlook for upcoming activities in Section V.

II. Motivational Use-Case

The problem given is the approach of an automated driving vehicle on a road with two lanes to an inner-city intersection with three lanes branching off into three direction - one lane for turning right and going straight, one lane for going straight and one lane for turning left. Regardless of other dynamic object vehicles, some really big challenges come up to the automated driving vehicle in such a complex scenario [2].

The correct localization on the approaching road and the high precise localization within the intersection area is difficult to handle. Based just on Global Positioning System (GPS), it is almost impossible to localize within a required tolerance for automated intersection crossings [3]. At this point, this paper's approach to use map and communication data combined with vehicle sensor data is set up. After the data fusion, it is possible to locate the ego vehicle with high precision within the right lane and on the right spot, e.g., the stop line of a traffic light on the lane for left turning.

The localization is followed by the behavior and path planning model, which provides the vehicle with the necessary intelligence to deal with for example complex intersection scenarios. Therefore, in addition to this, the planning model needs information about the traffic lights, other crossing object vehicles, e.g., the opposing traffic on the straight lane or pedestrians crossing the target road. This can be solved by different communication methods, e.g., road-side-units, backend-server communication and is work in progress.

III. Concept

The basic idea to overcome the challenges of the inner-city area is to expand the information sources of the behavior planning of the automated vehicle to high-precision map data and communication.

For this purpose, a tool chain is developed, which is initially dedicated to the processing of map data in the online vehicle application. In the first step of preprocessing, a map is parsed into the structure of the framework. Thus, in the next step, an interpretation can be made, which provides the logical and geometric information of the map.

The proposed architecture offers the possibility to integrate different map formats and extract specific information from them. Thus, on the one hand, behavior planning purposefully receives information about, e.g., the change in the road cross-section and the associated logical assignment of tracks, which then in turn lead to an adequate behavior decision.

On the other hand, geometric information of the lane course is used to support and optimize path planning. For example, complex lane courses at inner-city intersections can be taken into account in a timely and precise manner in the planning.

The extraction of the information can be done in two ways. On the one hand, a predefined route can be stored on the basis of which, in combination with the current vehicle position, specific information can be forwarded to the planning level. On the other hand, it is possible to provide information by means of a virtual horizon during free driving. The former, of course, offers the higher precision, since the route is known in advance.

The localization within this map is realized by a combination of different data. First, a rough assignment within the map is achieved via the GPS of the vehicle. This was done by comparing the current vehicle position and the global reference stored in the map. Next, a track accurate assignment of the vehicle is supplied. This is calculated by a model which processes information of the vehicle camera and matches these with the GPS data.

If a higher accuracy is required in individual situations, this is also anticipated in the model. A comparison between specific landmarks within the map and the scenario perceived by the vehicle provides additional potential for this. In particular, this can also be used to support the localization during a lack of GPS signal quality.

The model is also supplemented by external dynamic information. On the one hand, there is the possibility to provide data from a backend server. Here, individual events or specific information can be collected centrally and transmitted to the behavior model. Thus, a timely and targeted response of the automated vehicle can be realized on, for example, a construction site with a lane closure without a critical or uncomfortable situation arises. Situations of these types classified by the vehicle itself are correspondingly reported back via this interface and can in turn be made available to other vehicles.

IV. Integration in Existing Automated Driving Architecture

An important point for the design of the concept is the practical feasibility. In doing so, particular attention was paid to the modularity of the individual elements. This is particularly important with regard to the integration of the model in an existing vehicle architecture.

Figure 1 illustrates the relationship between the individual modules, as well as the general structure in the overall overview.

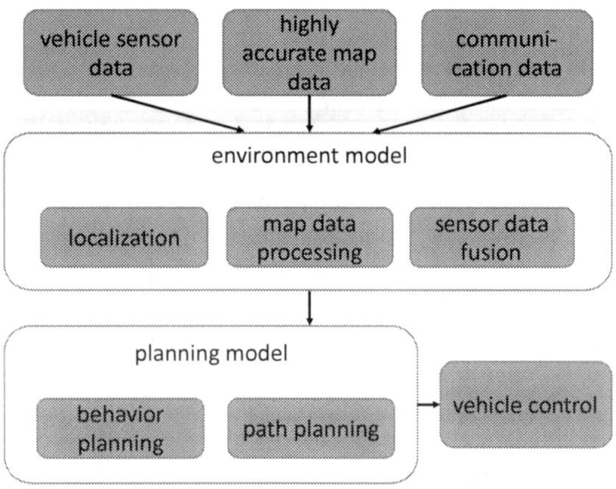

Figure 1. Relationship between the environmental model, the planning model, the vehicle control as well as the map and the communication data set on the same level as the vehicle sensor data.

The first level shows the provision of the most important input information for the model chain. Here, the existing vehicle sensors are extended by the highly accurate map data and the communication data. The latter are therefore considered in the overall context as an additional source of information at the sensor level. These data form the basis for the extended environment model. At this level, the processing of map data is integrated. In combination with the localization module, information is passed on to the planning level from there. The communication data are also processed and linked here.

At the planning level, this additional data can now be used directly to enhance the behavioral planning, as described in Section II, or as additional support in path planning.

For this purpose, the existing planning module is extended so that specific information can now be extracted. This can be done on the one hand in addition, in which, for example, information about speed limits can be adapted in advance. On the other hand, additional information which is not yet detected by the vehicle sensors, such as the distance to a stop line is taken into account.

Furthermore, the path planning model is edited, so that, in addition to the information of the existing vehicle sensors, now also information from the map are directly considered. These are for example the exact course of tracks within complex intersection scenarios.

The finally planned vehicle movement is then transferred to the vehicle control level. The advantage at this point is that the existing control algorithms do not have to be edited but can persist. This is possible because the existing interface can be adopted here unchanged.

V. Conclusion and Outlook

The paper proposes a new approach for a highly accurate map-based path and behavior planning for automated urban driving. In summary, the presented approach realizes a model that can contribute to overcoming the specific challenges of inner-city automated driving. One of the main advantages of the model is that the individual components can be integrated into the existing vehicle architecture due to the modular design. Consequently, on the one hand, the implementation effort is significantly reduced, and on the other hand, extensions can be added easily.

The next step is to complete the hole practical implementation. In particular, the communication data processing model and its complete integration into the planning level are currently still under development.

Following this, a comprehensive evaluation of the overall function is planned. For this purpose, specific test cases have to be carried out in simulation based on an existing test methodology [4]. This is followed by integration into a test vehicle and the execution of tests on a test site.

References

[1] "AUDI AG," 2017, URL: http://www.audi.com/en/innovation/piloteddriving/piloted_driving.html, [accessed: 2018-01-13].

[2] J. Abhau, "Challenges in Automated Driving," https://www.hightechzentrum.ch/, [accessed: 2018-01-12], 2014.

[3] H. Lategahn, M. Schreiber, J. Ziegler, and C. Stiller, "Urban Localization with Camera and Inertial Measurement Unit," IEE Intelligent Vehicles Symposium, 2013, p. 1.

[4] H. Znamiec, B. Reuber, and R. Henze, "Method for the efficent Testing of new Automated Driving Functions," FAST-zero Conference, 2017, pp. 1–2.

Vehicle Antenna Footprint Optimization for Efficient MIMO V2X Communications

Andreas Pfadler, Christian Ballesteros, Jordi Romeu, and Lluis Jofre

Antenna Laboratory
Signal Theory and Communications Department
Universitat Politecnica de Catalunya
Barcelona, Spain
Email: {andreas.pfadler, christian.ballesteros, romeu, jofre}@tsc.upc.edu

***Abstract*—Improving efficiency of upcoming vehicle communication networks is one of the main goals in near-future wireless systems. In addition, multi-antenna configurations are known as the main technique to improve the system performance with current constrains, such as the limited spectrum. They are an unlimited and non-lasting resource, but they imply a more complex implementation. In this context, the design of this type of geometries must be optimized considering the entire scenario and the final propagation conditions. Due to the relation between the propagation environment and the correlation between elements, the antenna inter-element spacing has to be adjusted to reach the maximum performance at the minimum possible footprint size. This work investigates the impact of correlation on channel capacity and also proposes a proper separation of the elements when they are mounted on a vehicle for two different urban scenarios: communication between two vehicles (V2V) and car connected to the cellular network (V2I).**

Keywords–MIMO systems, Urban propagation, Vehicles.

I. Introduction

Vehicle communications have become a recurring topic over the last years due to the increasing interest on creating an efficient and reliable network of connected cars, Vehicle to Everything (V2X). The goal ranges from providing driving aids to the user to self-driving cars. Then, energy efficiency and low latency are two main factors to consider.

In the following work, the focus will be put on the car antenna configuration in order to improve the whole performance of the system by means of numerical simulations for two main situations: Vehicle to Vehicle (V2V), in which two cars try to communicate, and Vehicle to Infrastructure (V2I), where a Base Station (BS) is introduced. For both cases, Multiple Input Multiple Output (MIMO) geometries will be compared with respect to the Single Input Single Output (SISO) case, especially focusing on the impact of the inter-element spacing on the system performance [1]. Conventional MIMO systems for automotive applications are already detailed in [2]. Otherwise, related work in [3] also analyzed the beamforming capabilities of such structures using monopole arrays.

In particular, the study is based in the experimental validation of the specified configurations in a simulated urban environment, in which the cars and the BS will be placed to emulate a realistic situation. A district of the city of Barcelona has been chosen to provide an approach close to reality. The operating frequency is located in the upper side of the S-band, from 3.4 GHz to 3.8 GHz, with better propagation properties as compared to higher bands, and which the automotive industry has also become interested in [4].

Next sections are organized as follows: Section II introduces some theoretical concepts that will be useful for the following discussion, Section III describes the environment and numerical tools, Section IV defines the methodology used to evaluate the results, Section V presents the results for the V2I simulations, whereas Section VI does the same for the case of V2V, and, finally, Section VII summarizes the previous work in some major statements deduced from the study.

II. Theoretical Background

A. Capacity in MIMO Channels

One of the most used figures of merit at physical layer in the analysis of communications systems is the channel capacity. For a MxN MIMO system, being M the number of transmitting units and N the receiving ones, capacity may be obtained as [5]:

$$C = \log_2\left(\det\left[\boldsymbol{I}_N + \frac{P_T \boldsymbol{H}\boldsymbol{H}^*}{P_N}\right]\right), \tag{1}$$

where I_N is the identity matrix, **H** is the channel matrix, whose entries correspond to the addition of all multipaths between each input and output port, P_T is the transmission power and P_N, the noise level. The operator (.)* denotes the conjugate transpose operator, i.e., Hermitian matrix.

$$\|\boldsymbol{H}\|_{\mathrm{F}} = \left(\sum_{i,j=1}^{N,M} |h_{ij}|^2\right)^{1/2} \tag{2}$$

$$\boldsymbol{H}_C = \frac{\boldsymbol{H}\boldsymbol{H}^*}{\|\boldsymbol{H}\|_F^2} \tag{3}$$

Otherwise, we can express the same equation as a function of the channel eigenvalues, $\lambda_i(\boldsymbol{H}_C)$. In this case, the channel matrix is normalized using the Frobenius norm, in (2), and the eigenvalues are those corresponding to the product between both **H** and its Hermitian, as in (3).

$$C = \sum_{i=1}^{N} \log_2\left(1 + \frac{P_R \lambda_i(\boldsymbol{H}_C)}{P_N}\right) \tag{4}$$

In (4), capacity is defined by means of two main concepts in multi-element cellular communications: the Signal to Noise Ratio (SNR) at the receiver, defined as the ratio between

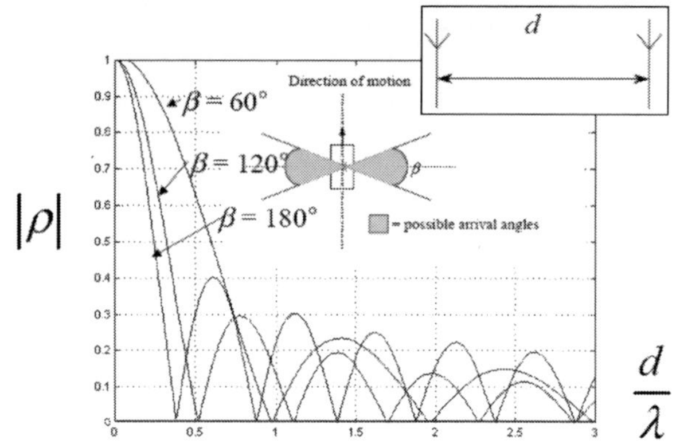

Figure 1. Correlation for two dipoles with changing inter-element spacing and three distinct angle of arrival [7].

received power and noise level ($SNR_{RX} = P_R/P_N$), and the channel richness, determined by the number of relevant eigenvalues. In this analysis, multi-user interference is not considered, but it would affect the noise term (if it is assumed uncorrelated with respect to desired signal), degrading the system performance.

B. Correlation and Spatial Diversity

In a MIMO system, the distance between antennas has a direct impact on the channel capacity through the correlation between the antenna elements. This fading correlation was researched by Shiu et al. [6]. The smaller the angle spread becomes, the higher is the correlation and the lower the responding channel capacity [5]. Therefore, a higher inter-element spacing is needed for small angle spreads.

Figure 1 shows the correlation for three different kind of possible arrival angles for two dipoles with varying inter-element spacing. Furthermore, mutual coupling between the antennas is another penalty on the channel capacity, which is not studied in this work.

III. Simulation Environment

The study of vehicle communications implies complex and large environments, which require the support of numerical tools to model the performance of the system in a realistic situation. This section is dedicated to detail the elements involved in the process of design and simulation of both the scenario and the antennas. The latter is considered to be the entire vehicle when mounted on the car due to its impact in the field distribution.

A. Software simulation

Initially, *FEKO* [8] is used to model the vehicle, as well as the BS for the V2I case, together with the antenna structure. It considers the effect of all the structure when calculating the field. The resulting radiation pattern is imported in a second tool, *WinProp* [9], that is used to simulate the propagation environment. It is possible to create the scenario for the case of study, with a geometrical approximation of buildings, trees and any other element and simulate using the ray tracing method the interaction of all them when one or more radiators are activated. In this case, a car (V2V) or a BS (V2I) are used as transmitting elements and several points over a virtual

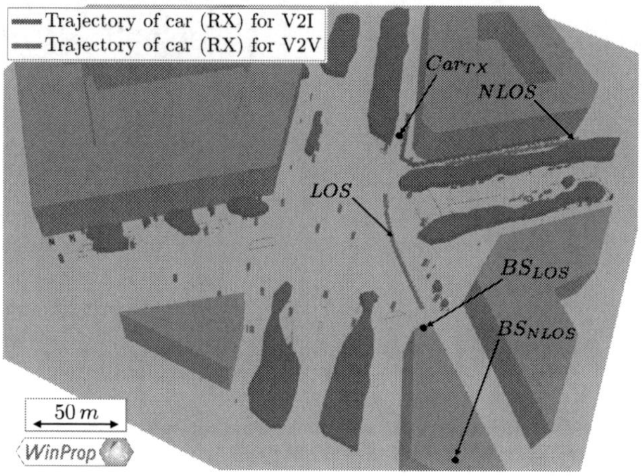

Figure 2. Scenario representation with the location of transmitting vehicle (V2V), transmitting BS (V2I) and trajectories used in the simulations.

trajectory are assumed to calculate the received fields. At the receiving points, the effect of the car is considered, as the radiation pattern calculation is including its structure. It is important to mention that all receiving points assume a still vehicle located on them, which is neglecting any Doppler effect.

B. Scenario

The chosen scenario is an urban area with medium-height buildings, some trees and streetlights. In particular, it is a model of an intersection in a district of Barcelona called as *L'Eixample*, which is known for its rectangular shape and corners close to $90\,\text{deg}$. In Figure 2, the 3-D view of the scenario is shown.

All buildings are made of concrete walls of $30\,\text{cm}$ thickness and $18\,\text{m}$ height, some of them including a courtyard. The ground is made of asphalt, streetlights are modelled as metallic cylinders and trees include a solid wooden trunk and the top is assumed to be a foliage semi-transparent to the rays (only a certain attenuation applied as they pass through).

C. Vehicle configuration

For the vehicle model, a prototype of a conventional car is used. It includes two types of materials: metal for the body and laminated glass for the windows. Wheels and internal elements are excluded to simplify the design and to reduce computational complexity and time consumption during the simulations.

As shown in Figure 3a, the antenna is mounted on the car rooftop. For V2V communications, both transmitter and receiver will have the same height and, for the case of V2I, if large distances are assumed, the angle of arrival is close to the horizontal plane. In consequence, the ideal radiation pattern should be maximum for angles close to the horizontal plane and minimum in the vertical axis. Thus, the chosen antenna is a monopole. In case of MIMO configurations, two or four antennas are placed in a straight line, appropriated to fit in a shark-fin footprint.

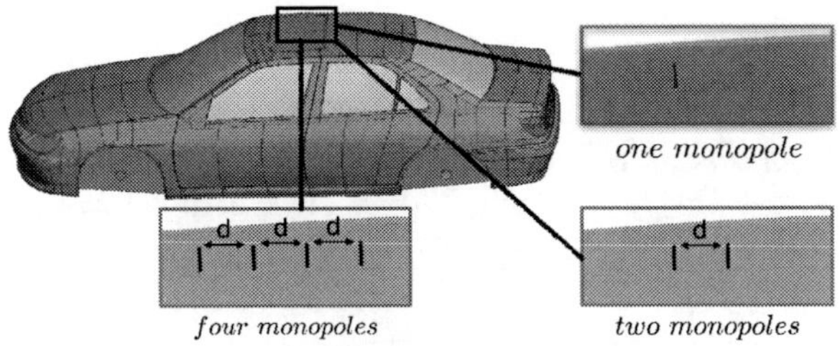

(a) Antenna configurations on the car.

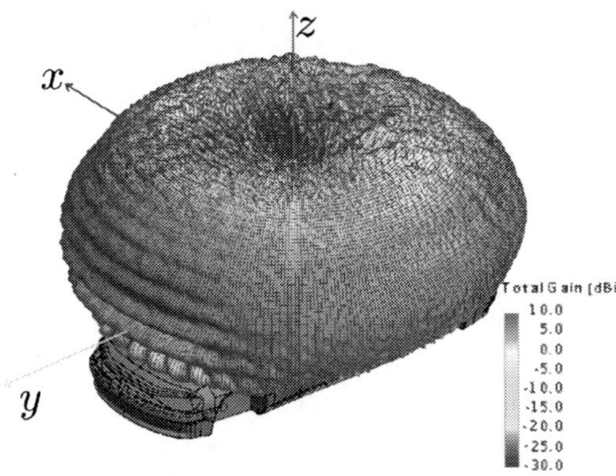

(b) Radiation pattern of a monopole mounted on the car rooftop.

Figure 3. Model of the vehicle and antennas.

D. Base Station

It consists of a set of omnidirectional elements placed on the top of a building as shown in Figure 2. The total height is 21 m over the ground, or 3 m over the rooftop. Depending on the case, one, two, or four antennas are used (for SISO and MIMO 2x2 or 4x4, respectively), with a constant spacing in all cases.

IV. Methodology

The figure of merit to estimate the system performance is the average capacity for the set of points used in each specific path. For each one, the capacity is calculated using (4), once the channel matrix is obtained by the numerical simulation. The noise level is not fixed in the calculation, but a mean SNR is assumed for the overall trajectory. Its value is set to 10 dB. In addition, in order to determine the achievable performance and validate the results, a theoretical maximum is calculated with ideal channel eigenvalues, i.e., $\sigma_i = 0.5$ (i=1,2) for MIMO 2x2 and $\sigma_j = 0.25$ (j=1,2,3,4), for MIMO 4x4.

The spacing between the antenna elements (monopoles) on top of the car is chosen to be in the range of 0.1 to 4 times the wavelength, in steps of 0.1λ. For each one, the average capacity over a given trajectory is calculated and then compared with respect to the SISO case.

V. Impact of the Inter-Element Spacing in V2I MIMO Communications

In this section, the performance in terms of capacity is studied for MIMO V2I systems. The analysis distinguishes between two different situations: Line of Sight (LOS) and Non Line of Sight (NLOS). In the first case, the BS is placed at the edge of the building, whereas, in the latter, the direct view is blocked by placing it some meters backwards (see Figure 2).

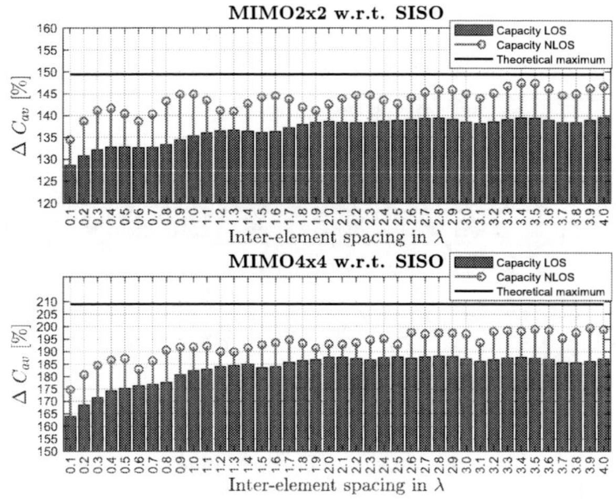

Figure 4. V2I channel capacity for different inter-element spacing for MIMO 2x2 and MIMO 4x4 with respect to the SISO channel capacity in percent and a fixed SNR of 10 dB.

Figure 4 shows the average channel capacity obtained for distinct inter-element spacing with respect to the SISO case in percentage. It illustrates the MIMO 2x2 case (upper figure) for the LOS in blue, the NLOS in red and the theoretical maximum in black. The same illustration is shown in the lower figure for MIMO 4x4.

First, if MIMO 2x2 is analyzed, it is observed a theoretical maximum channel capacity 149% respect to SISO. The minimum for LOS case is 129 % and, in NLOS, it is 135%, both obtained with an inter-element spacing of 0.1 wavelength. The maximum with 147% for NLOS is achieved with a spacing of 3.4 λ and is almost reaching the theoretical maximum of 149%. In the case of LOS, the maximum of 139% although the channel capacity is almost flat after inter-element distances of 1.9λ. The evolution for NLOS is expected as in the theoretical graph (see Figure 1). Regarding MIMO 4x4, the theoretical maximum channel capacity is now 209%. The lowest channel capacity is again obtained for both LOS and NLOS when inter-element spacing is 0.1 wavelengths (164% and 175%, respectively). On the other hand, the greatest capacity is achieved at the spacing of 2.8λ, with 188%, for LOS and 3.9λ, and 198% for NLOS.

From the previous results, it is deduced that MIMO 2x2 is almost reaching the theoretical maximum for NLOS communication, whereas MIMO 4x4 has a bigger step until its maximum. It can be determined that the channel is not rich enough, even increasing the inter-element spacing. Otherwise, it is also true that MIMO 4x4 provides a larger improvement with respect to SISO in terms of capacity although the channel rank is low.

Additionally, in MIMO 4x4 case, there is a more significant increment when the spacing is increased if the values are compared from the lowest distances to the largest. As stated in [10], "the specific behavior is also depending on the amount of elements in the car, which seems to indicate that higher is the number of elements, higher may be the necessary inter-element distance to obtain the optimal performance."

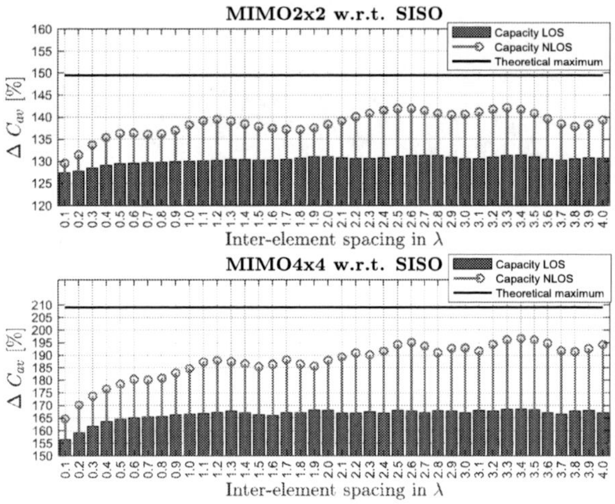

Figure 5. V2V channel capacity for different inter-element spacing for MIMO 2x2 and MIMO 4x4 with respect to the SISO channel capacity in percent and a fixed SNR of 10 dB.

VI. Impact of inter-element spacing in V2V MIMO communications

The goal now is to analyze the communication between two equal vehicles (V2V). This situation has some major differences as compared to previous case: both transmitter and receiver have the same height, their spacing is modified at the same time and both use monopole antennas.

The transmitting vehicle is fixed in a still position. Otherwise, two trajectories are considered for the receiver: one in LOS in which the car is driving along the same path as the transmitter and another in NLOS behind the building close to the corner (Figure 2).

Figure 5 compares both situations when MIMO 2x2 or 4x4 are used. In contrast with V2I model, the increment in capacity is much more evident for NLOS. It is necessary to remind at this point that the SNR is fixed to 10 dB and the performance is only affected by the eigenvalues distribution. Then, we can deduce that the rank of the channel matrix is clearly increasing when there is no direct path.

In NLOS, the average capacity is very similar to previous case. There is a maximum of 123% at 3.3λ for MIMO 2x2 and 194% at 3.4λ for MIMO 4x4. In any case, the oscillation is considerably stable above 2λ. Otherwise, for the LOS situation, capacity is much more reduced. This behavior indicates a very strong path, corresponding to the direct view, and low power reflections. Now, the behavior is almost stable after 0.5λ and maximum values are 132% and 168% for MIMO 2x2 and 4x4, respectively.

VII. Conclusions

Based on the realistic numerical modeling of a V2X urban environment, two main conclusions may be extracted. In terms of antenna footprint, it has been shown that higher the order of the MIMO system, larger has to be the inter-element distance to obtain optimal performance. Furthermore, the increment of the distance improves capacity in both LOS and NLOS for V2I; whereas, for V2V, a significant improvement is only obtained in NLOS.

Acknowledgment

This work was supported by the Spanish "*Comision Interministerial de Ciencia y Tecnologia*" (CICYT) under projects TEC2013-47360-C3-1-P, TEC2016-78028-C3-1-P, MDM2016-O6OO and Altair Engineering, Inc.

References

[1] C.-N. Chuah, D. N. C. Tse, J. M. Kahn, and R. A. Valenzuela, "Capacity scaling in mimo wireless systems under correlated fading," IEEE Transactions on Information Theory, vol. 48, no. 3, Mar 2002, pp. 637–650.

[2] A. Paier, L. Bernado, J. Karedal, O. Klemp, and A. Kwoczek, "Overview of vehicle-to-vehicle radio channel measurements for collision avoidance applications," in 2010 IEEE 71st Vehicular Technology Conference, May 2010, pp. 1–5.

[3] T. Kopacz, A. Narbudowicz, D. Heberling, and M. J. Ammann, "Evaluation of automotive mimo antennas for v2v communication in urban intersection scenarios," in Antennas and Propagation (EUCAP), 2017 11th European Conference on. IEEE, 2017, pp. 2907–2911.

[4] "Frequency bands for v2x," ACEA Position Paper, no. 8, 2016.

[5] G. J. Foschini and M. J. Gans, "On limits of wireless communications in a fading environment when using multiple antennas," Wireless personal communications, vol. 6, no. 3, 1998, pp. 311–335.

[6] D. S. Shiu, G. J. Foschini, M. J. Gans, and J. M. Kahn, "Fading correlation and its effect on the capacity of multielement antenna systems," IEEE Transactions on communications, vol. 48, no. 3, 2000, pp. 502–513.

[7] W. C. Jakes and D. C. Cox, Eds., Microwave Mobile Communications. Wiley-IEEE Press, 1994.

[8] Altair Hyperworks, FEKO User Manual 2017, Altair Hyperworks.

[9] Altair Engineering Inc., WinProp Software for Wave Propagation and Radio Planning, Altair Engineering Inc.

[10] A. Pfadler, C. Ballesteros, J. Romeu, and L. Jofre, "Multi-antenna configuration modeling for massive mimo v2i," in Antennas and Propagation (EUCAP), 2018 12th European Conference on. IEEE, 2018, pp. 215–219.

Improving Thermal Management of Electric Vehicles by Prediction of Thermal Disturbance Variables

Peter Engel
TU Clausthal
Department of Informatics,
Clausthal, Germany
e-mail: peter.engel@tu-clausthal.de

Sebastian Meise
TLK-Thermo GmbH,
Braunschweig, Germany
e-mail: s.meise@tlk-thermo.de

Andreas Rausch
TU Clausthal
Department of Informatics,
Clausthal, Germany
e-mail: arau@tu-clausthal.de

Wilhelm Tegethoff
TLK-Thermo GmbH,
Braunschweig, Germany
e-mail: w.tegethoff@tlk-thermo.de

Abstract— **In addition to the powertrain, heating and air-conditioning represents the second-largest energy consumer in electric vehicles. Optimization in this area can therefore contribute significantly to enhance the range of these vehicles. A new approach exploiting this optimization potential is the use of a model predictive controls. These controllers are based on a mathematical process model, which predicts the trajectories of the output variables. The predicted output variable trajectories are then evaluated by a non-linear cost function in order to find the corresponding optimal manipulated variable trajectory. Since external disturbances also affect the system in addition to manipulated variable, it is also necessary to predict these disturbances with sufficient precision. This is the core problem of this control approach and is not adequately addressed in previous approaches. For vehicle cabin heating and air-conditioning, the disturbances correspond to the thermal loads. These loads are mainly caused by the energy input of solar radiation, outside temperature, wind speed and humidity. In the following work, we will show how the coupling of methods of machine learning with Car2X technologies can lead to a high-precision prediction of thermal disturbances for an electric vehicle.**

Keywords- Model Predictive Control; BEV; Applied Machine Learning; HVAC; Mobile Data Mining

I. INTRODUCTION

The limited range of Battery Electric Vehicles (BEV) continues to be a major cause of the low market penetration of this technology. In addition to the drive train, the energy requirement for climate control is a key factor here. The energy requirement for heating, ventilation, and air-conditioning and (HVAC) can reduce the range by up to 50% [1] [2]. A recent promising approach reducing this additional energy demand is the replacement of conventional controls by Model-Predictive Controls (MPC). MPC are based on a linear or nonlinear model (NMPC) of the system to be controlled, which predicts future states for given input variables. The resultant states over a prediction horizon are then evaluated with a cost function. By means of an optimization method, the manipulated variables are then adjusted until an overall optimal state of the system is achieved. In various previous investigations [3] - [5], the potential of this method in the field of the vehicle thermal management was demonstrated. For example, an NMPC was used in [6] to simultaneously control the battery temperature and the vehicle cabin temperature. Compared to a conventional PI controller, it was shown that the set-point values were achieved considerably faster, nearly without overshoot while maintaining a high degree of overall energy efficiency. However, all these investigations showed a weak spot. The future disturbance variables were either assumed to be known in advance, were not taken into account or predicted by a very weak estimate. The disturbance variable over the current prediction range is most frequently estimated by the last measured value. This is unrealistic, since in the real world, however, the outside temperature, but also the solar radiation, fluctuate very dynamically over the course of the journey.

In this paper, we will first discuss the state of the art, discuss the impact of the prediction accuracy in Section III and then introduce our approach to a structure of the disturbance variable prognosis system in Section IV. Our approach is to train machine learning algorithms with data from weather forecasts for an upcoming vehicle ride and obtained vehicle sensor data of a subsequent measurement ride. The trained functions are then used to generate a forecast for the thermal disturbances of an upcoming trip using the current weather forecast. We will show in Section V how the data collection and processing is carried out with the help of an electric vehicle and the corresponding server structure. Finally, we will explain the applied machine learning techniques in Section VI and discuss the results of the test runs in Section VII.

II. STATE OF THE ART

As already mentioned, no precise prediction of the disturbance variables was used in any known work in the field of vehicle HVAC. In [6] and [7] the ambient temperature is kept constant over the prediction horizon, [8] analyzed HVAC power consumption for different given ambient temperatures, [9] estimates disturbance variables from measurement data, [4] and [10] use no ahead prediction at all. For vehicle cabin heating and air-conditioning, the disturbances correspond to the thermal loads. These loads are mainly caused by the energy input of solar radiation, outside temperature, wind speed and humidity. The prediction of these magnitudes is, however, a sub-area of the scientific discipline of atmospheric science and, in particular, of meteorology, which has a major focus on weather forecasting. The findings from this research are applied in various neighboring sciences such as agricultural meteorology, aviation meteorology, maritime and technical meteorology. The meteorological weather forecast is based on Synoptic Meteorology. Here, a network of ground-based atmospheric observing stations is used to perform measurements under a standardized procedure. These observations take place uniformly throughout the world at fixed time intervals. The information obtained is then supplemented by radiosonde ascents, satellite observations and aircraft measurements. The collected data is then mapped in weather maps and is used, on the one hand, for the shortest-term forecast (0-2h forecast), the so-called nowcasting and further as input for Numerical Weather Models (NWM). One of the most widespread NWM is the global GFS model (Global Forecast System) of the US National Oceanic and Atmospheric Administration (NOAA). Using the NWM, very short-term forecasts (2-12h), short-term forecasts (12-72h) and medium-term forecasts (3-10d) are then prepared by state and private weather services [11].

In recent years, dramatic progress has been made in the field of weather forecasting. The quality of the weather forecast fluctuates during the year. Thus, in the summer, more reliable forecasts can be drawn up in more stable weather conditions than in winter. For example, the average forecast error of the daily high temperature for a one to two-days forecast of the German weather service fell from 2.5 K in the year 1984 to 1.6 K in the year 2008 [12].

The use of weather forecasts for control engineering applications in combination with model predictive controllers has already been investigated in several scientific papers [13]-[19]. The main application area was the climate control of buildings. In [17], the impact of forecasting accuracy of different prediction models on the quality of a model-predictive control for climate control of buildings was investigated. Different methods based on historical data (TMY2 predictor, same-as-yesterday predictor, bin predictor) were compared with methods based on unbiased random walk and on seasonal autoregressive and moving average prediction model (SARIMA). It was observed that the bin predictor models, in particular the 30-days and 60-days bin models provide the best performance. Furthermore, it was found that in comparison to the model predictive control with perfect prediction, the quality of the methods with bin predictor were only slightly behind. In [18], an improved disturbance prediction method as well as an extended MPC method, the stochastic MPCs (SMPC), have been used. Stochastic MPCs take into account the uncertainties of the measuring system, the overall system and the state estimator. An overview of SMPC can be found in [19]. For the prediction of the weather, results of the numerical weather prediction model COSMO-7, locally measured weather by the SWISS Meteological Network and building measurements were used. Furthermore, a linear error model was generated, which then provided the forecast in combination with the weather data via a Kalman filter. The use of online weather predictions is discussed in [20] and [21]. In order to forecast the future temperature value, the predicted temperatures of various online accessible weather services were combined in [21] to an improved prediction. Furthermore, the prediction of the solar radiation, which is not part of the weather forecast, is discussed. In this case, a method is proposed, which calculates the theoretical global radiation as a function of location and time for a clear sky as well as a method for calculation reduction in the irradiation through the predicted cloudiness. By means of a linear regression model, these forecast data are then linked with actual measured data.

In summary, it can be said that the results obtained are a great advance for application to the regulation of building climate control, but can be transferred only partly to the area of electric vehicles HVAC. There are several reasons for that. Due to the size, design, the storage capacity and thermal insulation, the entire system responds much slowly to external disturbances. As a result, short-term fluctuations do not have a very strong effect on the overall system. Furthermore, the system is generally operated continuously and not as in the case of the vehicle from only a few minutes to a few hours. This requires for building climate control a rather long-term forecast, which tolerates a wider standard deviation in the sense of the distribution of the forecast error. Secondly, buildings do not rotate and do not change their positions either. As a result, the associated weather observation stations and also the distance to this stations do not change, which can lead to a different prediction quality. The relative position to the sun in the case of buildings depends only on astronomical laws. This, on the other hand, affects the maximum possible global solar radiation as well as the side of the system facing the sun. Similarly, the relative position to shadow-causing obstructions like neighboring buildings, plants and trees does not change. In addition, a moving object is obviously exposed to bigger weather fluctuations, since the weather can differ from place to place. In [22], a high resolution system for routes, which monitors not weather data but road infrastructure based on acquired vehicle sensor data and machine learning was introduced. In [20], a range prediction system was introduced, which considers continually updated and locally resolved GFS weather data. The finest resolution of this system is 1 km. This resolution is too low for our application since, e.g., shadow-causing obstructions are not taken into account. All this require a more elaborate prognosis technique than in the upper case, which will be presented in this study.

III. IMPACT AND EVALUATION OF THE PREDICTION ACCURACY

The quality of control of a model predictive control essentially depends on the accuracy of the predicted manipulated variables, the accuracy of the predicted variables of the constraints and the range of the prediction horizon. Since the control optimizes only within the range of the prediction horizon, the optimum found is locally limited to this horizon. If a manipulated variable is predicted incorrectly in this horizon, the control deviation is also predicted incorrectly, which is why the control cannot find the true optimum for the given boundary conditions. The prediction value of the future behavior of the manipulated variables is subject to two uncertainties. On the one hand, it is subject to the accuracy of the process model, which is not part of this work, and, on the other hand the consideration of the disturbance variables of the control. If a disturbance variable changes only slowly in relation to the range of the prediction horizon, then the prediction accuracy can be improved by integrating the current values of the measurable quantities into the control. Additionally, immeasurable state and disturbance variables can be estimated by using observers or Kalman filters [20]. Since in the case of vehicle air conditioning, the disturbance variables, such as temperature and solar radiation, are subject to strong fluctuations with respect to the forecast horizon, these measures are only limited sufficient.

The exact quantification of the impact of a tangible prediction error, e.g., in terms of energy saving is difficult, as this effect depends on the particular MPC model and the state of all system parameters and variables. The quality of the forecasting method is therefore evaluated below in relation to the quality of the existing methods and the measurement inaccuracy of the respective sensor. In the case of the outside temperature prediction, the temperature sensor has a resolution of 0.5 K. This equates to an RMSE of 0.5, which is used as reference value. Since in this study the forecast horizon is assumed to be the duration of a journey up to one hour, the best state of the art reference estimate of the temperature is used on the basis of historical data and a naive prognosis. The estimated value of the naive prognosis corresponds to the first measured value of the temperature. The historical data estimate is usually in 1 hour increments. So, here it is assumed that this can be represented by the mean value of the vehicle measurement. The evaluation of the radiation prognosis is carried out analogously, whereby in this case the measurement inaccuracy is in each case 10% of the measured value.

IV. STRUCTURE OF THE DISTURBANCE VARIABLE PROGNOSIS SYSTEM

The task of the disturbance variable prognosis system is to predict the thermal disturbances acting on the system precisely in terms of extent and, if applicable, effective direction for the period of an impending journey with an electric vehicle. The accuracy must be described with a rating system. Each predicted single value for a variable corresponds to the realization of an event. Since this realization of an event is subject to a certain probability, a good prediction method must also predict a whole probability distribution for each individual event to be predicted [24].

The reference system is thus the continuous time of travel in the vehicle. Since the disturbances are caused externally and locally, the reference system must be related to the local state. This is done by two successive predictions. First of all, the location, time and orientation of the vehicle are predicted for the course of the journey. For this purpose, the route is discretized in road sections. Secondly, a prediction of the local disturbances is made for each discretized road section at the predicted time, taking into account the direction of travel. The forecasting procedure is described below. In this case, it is assumed that the destination of the trip is known to the system in advance.

A. Location – Time Prediction

As already mentioned, the prediction for the upcoming journey takes place in the form of a series of predictions for the separate road sections of the route ahead. Every road section is referred to as a segment in the following. A segment always consists of 2 nodes. The nodes used here originate from the OpenStreetMap data model (OSM). A node consists of a single point in space defined by its latitude, longitude, altitude and node ID. Currently, as of June 2017, 3,900,000,000 points are defined in the OSM data model.

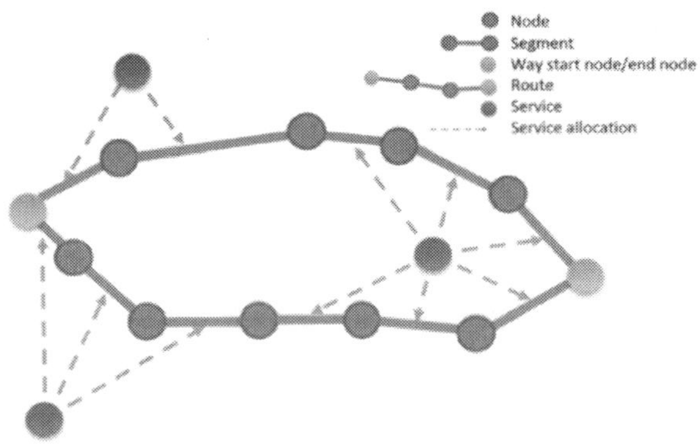

Figure 1. Definition of map elements

A journey is made on a defined way. The way is defined by its start and end nodes. Several routes are possible for each way. The allocation of ways and routes is done in a separate table of the database of the system. Each route is defined by a fixed sequence of segments. The definitions used here are shown graphically in Figure 1. For the first prediction, it is now necessary to predict the segment entry time and the dwell time of the vehicle in this segment. This must be done successively for all segments to be traversed on the entire route. For this purpose, it is necessary in a first step to find an optimal path between the start and the destination. This can be accomplished with the aid of a suitable route planning algorithm, e.g., the Dijkstra's algorithm. Since the finding of the optimal route is not subject of this investigation, the routing API of the open source routing library GraphHopper was used for this purpose. The GraphHopper API provides the optimal route for a given way in the form of individual waypoints of OSM-nodes and associated time points. From this, a predicted dwell time can be derived for each segment, and additionally, since the length of the segment can be calculated, a predicted velocity in the segment can also be derived. In the context of vehicle measurements, however, it was found that these prognosticated times are not suitable as a basis for the following predictions of the disturbance variables. Although on average the arrival time is predicted relatively well, there are strong deviations in the individual segments. This is based on the fact that depending on the type of road, a certain average speed is assumed and individual conditions such as the occurrence of traffic lights are not taken into account individually.

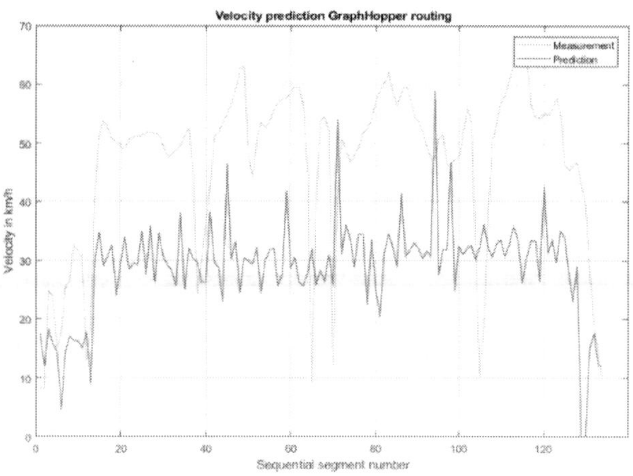

Figure 2. Predicted velocity by GraphHopper routing

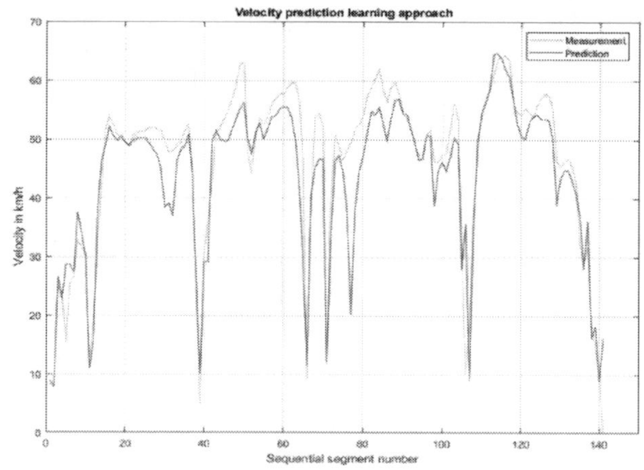

Figure 3. Predicted velocity by wknn-approach

Figure 2 shows the comparison of a velocity prediction made with the GraphHopper routing and a corresponding vehicle measurement. However, a more precise prognosis of the dwell time in the segment is necessary, since it is necessary to determine how long the vehicle will be subjected to the respective disturbance variable, e.g., of the solar radiation, in the individual segment. For this purpose, a forecast function based on machine learning was developed, which more accurately predicts both the time of arrival and segment dwell time. Figure 3 shows the comparison of the predicted velocity and the actual measured velocity. The prediction function is described in more detail in Section VI.A.

B. Prediction of Disturbances Variables

In the subsequent second prediction, the prediction of the disturbance variables must now be performed for each segment at the predicted arrival time. The measured values of local weather stations, local weather forecasts and the last known measured value of the vehicle are used as input for the prediction function. Various online weather services are available for querying weather data. These include, for example, YR (Norwegian Weather Service), DWD (German Weather Service), OpenWeatherMap (Extreme Electronics LTD), Weather Underground (IBM) and Here (Intel, Audi, BMW, Mercedes, etc.). These services provide current and historical weather data as well as weather forecasts to developers of web services and mobile applications. In this study, primarily OpenWeatherMap is used. However, further services will be integrated into the system in perspective. OpenWeatherMap uses, among other tools, the already mentioned GFS model of the NOAA as a NWM. An API can be used to access data on cloudiness, air temperature, air pressure, wind speed, wind direction, precipitation and humidity. These data also include the coordinates of the assigned weather station, the time of the last measurement as well as the projected time period for the forecast of the predicted weather events. The data of the weather services are referred to below as services. A number of specific services are assigned to each individual segment. The assignment of services to segments is determined by a request to the respective weather services and then registered in a separate table of the database. This is done once when creating a new route. The entities are in a many-to-many relationship. This means that each segment can be assigned to several services and each service can be valid for several segments. Since the segment sequence is fixed for each route based on the primary prediction, all associated services can now be determined for an upcoming journey. In advance to the disturbance variable prediction, the weather data for all services for all affected segments are queried and stored in the database. The weather data are supplemented by additional data to interpret their informative value. For example, the relative position of the affected weather station to the affected segment, as well as the time difference between the segment entrance time and the weather forecast time are stored. To predict the disturbance variables, all these data are entered into a mathematical algorithm, which outputs the desired variables. This algorithm is based on machine learning. Each segment is initially considered independent of other segments. The approach for the learning is so-called supervised learning. The algorithm learns a function from given pairs of inputs and outputs for each segment. The correct result of the function is available during the learning process as training data. The goal of supervised learning is to train the system until it can establish the correct associations.

In addition to the input data, the output data are also required for the learning process. In this case, this corresponds to the measured disturbance variables. The measurement and preparation of this data are subject of the next chapter.

V. DATA COLLECTION AND PROCESSING

For this investigation, an electric vehicle of the VW e-Golf type was used. This vehicle is equipped, as standard, with various sensors for recording vehicle and climate data. These are, for example, the ambient air temperature sensor, the fresh air intake duct temperature sensor, the humidity sensor, the sunlight penetration photo sensor, the brightness and rain sensor of the windscreen wiper. In addition, the current position can be determined via GPS and, of course, the speed can also be measured. The signals from the sensors can be tapped via the various CAN busses as well as via the onboard diagnostic interface (OBD). Since, in the case of the Can bus, the data can be recorded in finer time frames with cycle times of 20 ms to 200 ms, access was made to these data. For the vehicle measurement, the powertrain-CAN, infotainment-CAN and comfort-CAN were cut free and connected to a data logger. The data logger, on the other hand, can transfer the recorded data wirelessly to the central server via WiFi or 3G. These measurement data are organized in a first processing step in such a way that a vector of time stamp, geographical length, geographical latitude, outside temperature of the air, precipitation quantity, solar radiation, air humidity and vehicle speed are assigned to each measured time point in the 200 ms time grid. In a further processing step, each of these vectors is assigned to a known segment of the database. For this purpose, it has always been ensured that the segments have already been registered in the database as part of the prediction. Depending on the vehicle speed and time grid, the number of measuring points per segment varies in each case. Figure 4 shows the location of the measurement points (red dot) and the predicted segments (colored line with segment number) for a part of a trip.

The mapping of the vectors to the segments is carried out by means of a mapmatching algorithm, taking into account the distance from the measured point to the center of the segment as well as the segment length. In order to improve the route planning, the determined segments are compared with the predicted segments and, when appropriate, a new path is registered in the database. If no measured value is measured for a prognosticated segment, this segment is not subsequently learned.

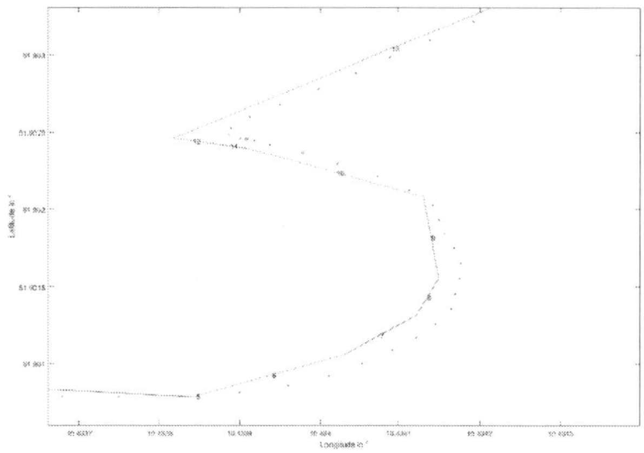

Figure 4. Predicted segments and measurement points

In the next processing step, all the values of assigned measuring points of a segment are aggregated to a single value x_s for each variable

$$x_S = \frac{\sum_{i=1}^{n} t_i * x_i}{\sum_i^n t_i} \quad (1)$$

After this step, the target data for the learning functions are ready for use.

VI. APPLIED MACHINE LEARNING TECHNIQUES

There is a wide range of different methods of machine learning for different tasks like classification, regression or clustering. For our underlying problem of regression, there are a number of methods that differ by calculation effort, ability to generalize, fast convergence or overfitting. Since we have a huge number of road segments, which we have to train separately, we choose the procedures with the least computational effort. These methods are based on k-nearest neighbor and linear regression algorithms.

A. *Vehicle Speed and Segment Dwell Time*

The vehicle speed in a segment is related to vehicle type, driving style, traffic situation, road type, road geometry, and possible obstacles, e.g., traffic lights or construction sites. In the first approach, it is assumed that these influencing variables are essentially related to the time of the trip and are subject to similar patterns. While the road type and road geometry hardly change, the other factors tend to vary more. Our approach is based on the assumption that, e.g., the overall situation on a Monday morning always behaves similarly and again different than on Saturday night. Therefore, a dwell time in the segment is to be predicted depending on the time and the day of the week.

$$
\begin{aligned}
&V: S \times T \times D \rightarrow R && (2)\\
&S \subseteq \mathbb{Z} && segment\ ID\\
&T = \{0 \dots 86400\}\\
&T \subseteq \mathbb{Z} && continuous\ second\ of\ the\ day\\
&D = \{1 \dots 7\}\ D \subseteq \mathbb{Z} && day\\
&R \subseteq \mathbb{R} && dwell\ time
\end{aligned}
$$

The non-parametric distance-weighted k-nearest-neighbor method, which has already been published in [25], was used for this purpose. The wkNN algorithm is one of the simplest machine learning algorithms and due to the multitude of segments to be learned well suited. The feature space (labeled examples) consists of all the aggregated measured data of the segment. The output consists of the property values of the k closest training examples in the feature space. The Euclidean distance is used as a distance metric. Since the feature space is circular in both dimension, e.g., the Monday (numerically represented as 1) beside the Sunday (numerically represented as 7), the feature space at the edges was expanded by copies of the opposite edge. For the k-property values, a weight w is calculated according to their distance.

$$w_n = \frac{\frac{1}{d_n}}{\sum_{i=1}^{k} \frac{1}{d_i}} \qquad (3)$$

With these weights of the individual neighbors, the resulting total value for the prediction r_{pred} is then calculated.

$$r_{pred} = \sum_{i=1}^{k} w_i * r_i \qquad (4)$$

As Figure 4 shows, the quality of the results is already significantly higher than that of the route planning. Figure 5 shows the distribution of the error for this measurement run.

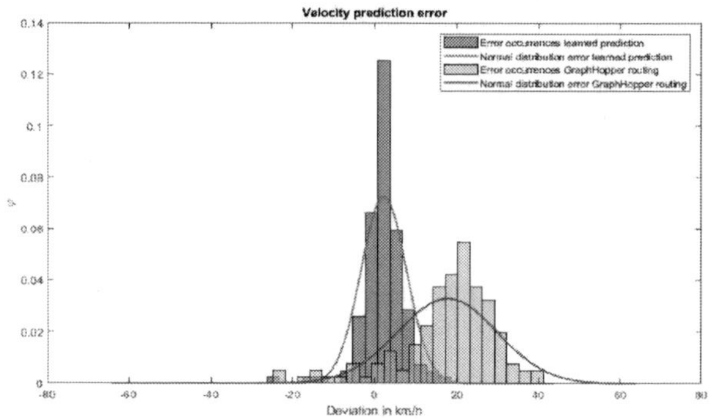

Figure 5. Velocity prediction error

As can be seen from this, it can be approximated with standard normal distribution. The dwell time for each segment can now also be determined from the vehicle speed. The prediction is performed sequentially one step ahead for all segments of an upcoming trip. To calculate the segment entry time of the following segment t_{k+1}, the predicted dwell time r_{pred} of the last segment is added to the segment entry time of the last segment.

$$t_{k+1} = t_k + r_{pred_k} \qquad (5)$$

B. *Temperature Prediction*

The prediction of the ambient temperature is based on the work described in Section II. and extended to routes. On the basis of data from online weather services the local temperature in a specific segment is to be predicted. As already mentioned, in the first instance only the OpenWeatherMap service was used for this purpose. Our following machine learning approach is based on the assumption that the temperature of two different places at the same time within a close area has a fixed offset. The second assumption is that the temperature changes by a constant slope over a limited period of time. This slope is assumed to be constant in a limited area for limited time span. The slope is calculated from the weather forecast for the next 3 hours. The input to the learning process is the last measured value and the predicted time slope of the 2 closest weather stations for every segment.

For temperature prediction, a learning method with a weighted multivariate regression is used. The weights w are used to represent the temporal change of the temperature of a segment and correspond to the time elapsed since the query of the respective weather date. Using the weights a multiple linear regression analysis using least squares algorithm is performed for the following equation:

$$y = b_0 + \sum_{i=1}^{2} b_i * T_i + \sum_{i=2}^{4} b_i * w_i * \Delta T \qquad (6)$$

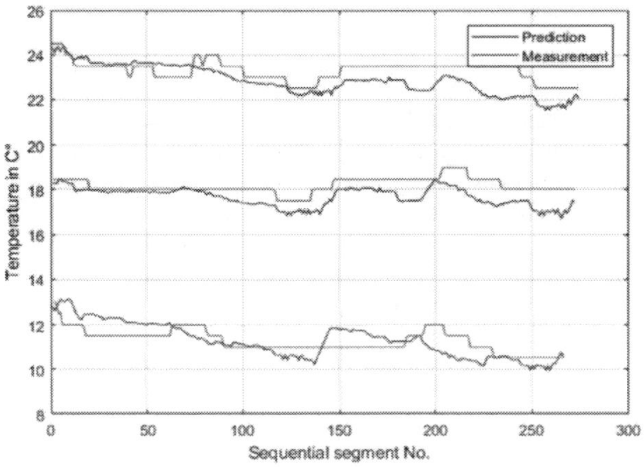

Figure 6. Temperature forecast and measurement

The system was trained by 30 test runs and tested in 3 further vehicle measurements to validate the learned function. The 3 test runs averaged a RMSE of 0.626. As can be seen in Figure 6 the predicted results were not very accurate. The reason for this was the strong deviation of the forecasted openweathermap weather data from the actual temperature value. Therefore, the openweathermap weather data for Clausthal was substituted by weather data retrieved from the control engineering institut weather station in Clausthal and applied in another test series. The system was subsequently trained and tested again.

Figure 7 shows the results of the prediction and measurement for a test run from Goslar to Clausthal and back. Both places have a height difference of 300 meters, which explains the strong temperature change. Two additional test runs were performed, which gave similar results. The quality of the prediction can be evaluated by calculating the root mean square error (RMSE).

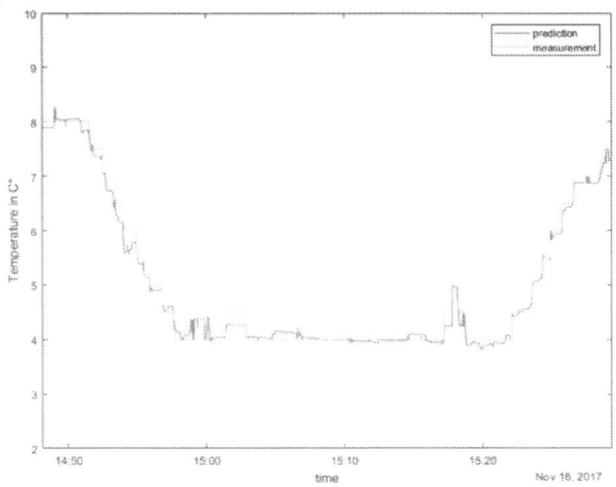

Figure 7. Temperature forecast and measurement

The test runs averaged a RMSE of 0.151, which is significantly lower than the naïve prognosis (RMSE 3.325), the historical data estimation (RMSE 1.3459) and resolution (RMSE 0.5K). The error probability can approximately be described with a standard normal distribution. The prognosis procedures for humidity and air pressure are carried out analogously to the temperature prognosis method. Therefore, a further explanation thereof will be omitted.

C. *Prediction of Solar Radiation*

The energy input to a vehicle by solar radiation is essentially dependent on the relatively constant radiation power of the sun, the angle of solar irradiation, the degree of atmospheric reflection and absorption, the cloudiness and the position of shadow-causing objects. The solar radiation consists of direct and indirect radiation. The prediction of solar radiation is more difficult, since weather services do not provide a direct forecast for radiation. The weather services provide only a description and prediction of the cloudiness in the form of a scalar valuation from 0 to 100. However, studies in the fields of agricultural meteorology [26] and regenerative energy systems [27] show that the proportion of direct radiation can be calculated very well when the position of the sun relative to the own location is known. However, if diffuse solar radiation occurs due to dispersion of the light through obstacles, fog or clouds, the irradiance can hardly be calculated. In our approach, it is assumed that if there is no cloud or mist, the energy input by solar radiation can be learned. The reason for this is that the reduction in the radiation caused by shadow causing obstacles (buildings, plants and trees) again depends only on the angle of the sun radiation. The shadow as a function of the sun position is thus learnable. The position of the sun can be described by the azimuth and the solar altitude. Azimuth and solar altitude can be calculated with the values predicted in Section IV.A. by using the astronomical formula referred to in [27]. If now additionally information about the weather, as the extent of the cloudiness, is added, this effect is also be learnable. The input variables for the prediction algorithm are therefore the position of the sun, described by azimuth and sunshine, as well as the predicted degree of cloudiness by the weather service. In analogy to the calculation of the temperature, normalized weights are calculated for the cloud values from the weather data in order to compensate the temporal offset between predicted segment entry time and measurement time. This initially predicts the degree of cloudiness. In the first approach, the recorded and aggregated signals of the brightness sensor of the windshield wiper control were used as training data. The distance-weighted k-nearest-neighbor approach from Section VI.A is again used as a learning method. The system was again trained by 30 vehicle measurements, then tested in 4 measurements in August and November.

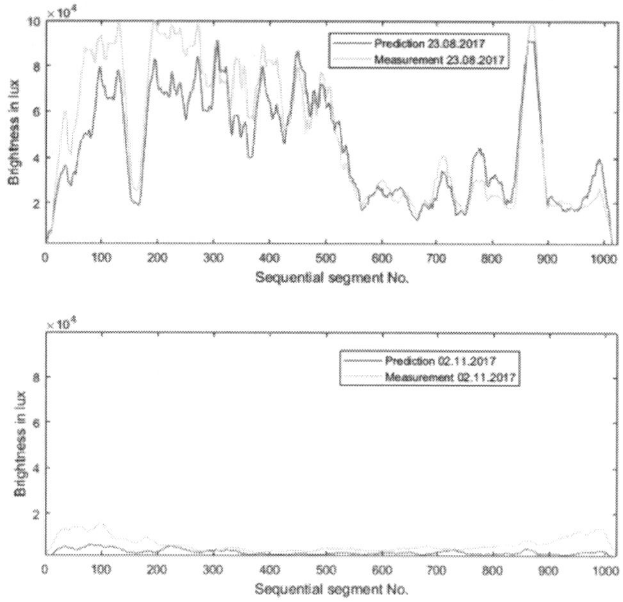

Figure 8. Results of the solar radiation prediction

Figure 8 shows the results of the experiment. In this case, it can be seen that the course of the radiation acting on the vehicle is relatively well predicted, but in absolute terms there are sometimes high deviations. This can be explained by the small number of measuring journeys, which did not adequately reflect the possible constellations of cloudiness in the training data. The prediction for the test runs averaged an RMSE of 1131.2, which is significantly lower than average RMSE for the naïve prognosis (RMSE 5499.4) and the historical data estimation (RMSE 3097.4). As can be seen in Figure 8, the predicted brightness is partly significantly lower than the later measured brightness. The reason for this is that the samples gained in the training had a lower degree of cloudiness compared to the test run. This error can be predicted by evaluating the aggregated mean distance from formula (3). The difference of the cloudiness of the k-similar samples to the expected cloudiness is represented by the distance weight w_n. To tackle this problem, the quality measure J of the prediction is determined in advance.

$$J = \frac{\frac{1}{k}\sum_{n=1}^{k} w_n}{\sqrt{3}} \qquad (7)$$

If the prediction is insufficient, due to insufficient learning data, an error handling routine must be integrated in the MPC algorithm. This could be realized, for example, by the temporary use of a conventional controller.

VII. CONCLUSION

The limited range of BEV is still a big challenge. To tackle this, we have shown an approach to improve the promising MPC-control strategy. We have trained machine learning algorithms with data from weather forecasts and vehicle sensor data to generate various prediction functions for the individual thermal disturbance variables. The quality of the thermal disturbance variable prediction strongly depends on the weather forecast quality and on the quality and quantity of the training data. Increasing this quality will be the subject of the upcoming work steps. In order to increase the quality of the input forecasts for the individual segments, further weather services are to be integrated into the system on one hand. On the other hand, the use of several vehicles in the course of a fleet test should result in a larger training data volume.

REFERENCES

[1] A. Wiebelt und M. Wawzyniak, „Thermal Management for Electrified Vehicles,“ *MTZ worldwide Volume 77,* p. 38–43, May 2016.

[2] E. Rahimzei, „How does data about energy consumption and range of electric vehicles come about?,“ VDE e. V., Frankfurt am Main, 2015.

[3] H. Esen, T. Tashiro, D. Bernardini and A. Bemporad, „Cabin heat thermal management in hybrid vehicles using model predictive control,“ in *22nd Mediterranean Conference on Control and Automation*, Palermo, Italy, 2014.

[4] M. Auer, Ein Beitrag zur Erhöhung der Reichweite durch prädiktives Thermomanagement, Stuttgart, Germany: Springer Vieweg, 2015.

[5] A. Karnik, A. Fuxman, P. Bonkoski, M. Jankovic and J. Pekar, „Vehicle Powertrain Thermal Management System Using Model Predictive Control,“ in *SAE International Journal of Materials and Manufacturing - V125-5*, Detroit, USA, 2016.

[6] J. Eckstein, C. Lueke, F. Brunsteina, P. Friedela, U. Koehler and A. Traechtler, „A Novel Approach Using Model Predictive Control to Enhance the Range of Electric Vehicles,“ in *3rd International Conference on System-integrated Intelligence: New Challenges for Product and Production Engineering, SysInt 2016*, Paderborn, Germany, 2016.

[7] J. Lopez-Sanz, C. Ocampo-Martinez, J. Alvarez-Florez, M. Moreno-Eguilaz, R. Ruiz-Mansilla, J. Kalmus, M. Graeber and G. Lux, „Nonlinear Model Predictive Control for Thermal Management in Plug-in Hybrid Electric Vehicles,“ in *IEEE Transactions on Vehicular Technology Volume 66*, 2017.

[8] M. A. Al Faruque and K. Vatanparvar, „Modeling, Analysis, and Optimization of Electric Vehicle HVAC Systems,“ in *Design Automation Conference (ASP-DAC), 2016 21st Asia and South Pacific*, Irvine, 2016.

[9] M. Graeber, C. Kirches, D. Scharff and W. Tegethoff, „Using Functional Mock-up Units for Nonlinear Model Predictive Control,“ in *Proceedings of the 9th International Modelica Conference*, Munich, Germany, 2012.

[10] T. Fischer, T. Kraus, C. Kirches and F. Gauterin, „Nonlinear Model Predictive Control of a Thermal Management,“ in *Proceedings of the 12th International Modelica Conference*, Prague, Czech Republic, 2017.

[11] B. Klose und H. Klose, Meteorologie, Oldenburg, Germany:

Springer Spektrum, 2016.

[12] R. Wengenmayr and G. Lux, „Wie gut sind Wettervorhersagen?- Qualitätsprüfung beim DWD,“ Deutscher Wetterdienst, Offenbach, Germany, 2008.

[13] W. J. Grünenfelder and T. Juerg, „The use of weather predictions and dynamic programming in the control of solar domestic hot water systems,“ in *Mediterrainian electrotechnical Conference of IEEE Region 8*, Madrid, Spain, 1985.

[14] F. Weißel, Stochastische modell-prädiktive Regelung nichtlinearer Systeme, Karlsruhe: Universitätsverlag Karlsruhe, Germany, 2008.

[15] G. P. Henze and M. Krarti, „Predictive Optimal Control of Active and Passive Building Thermal Storage Inventory,“ in *University of Nebraska*, Lincoln, USA, 2005.

[16] F. Oldewurtel, A. Parisio, C. N. Jones, D. Gyalistras, M. Gwerder, V. Stauch, B. Lehmann and M. Morari, „Use of model predictive control and weather forecasts for energy efficient building climate control,“ in *Energy and Buildings (2012) 15–27*, Zurich, Switzerland, 2012.

[17] A. Viehl, R. Valentina, M. R. Zofka and B. Mühr, „Optimized Utilization of E-Vehicle Range Using Route-Based Online Weather Forecast Data,“ in *24th Aachen Colloquium Automobile and Engine Technology 2015*, Aachen, Germany, 2015.

[18] Y. Zhang and V. I. Hanby, „Short-term prediction of weather parameters using online weather forecasts,“ in *Proceedings: Building Simulation 2007*, Leicester, United Kingdom, 2007.

[19] J. Masino, J. Thumm, M. Frey and F. Gauterin, „Learning from the crowd: Road infrastructure monitoring system,“ in *J. Traffic Transp. Eng. (Engl. Ed.) 2017; 4 (5): 451-463*, Karlsruhe, Germany, 2017.

[20] R. Dittmar and B.-M. Pfeiffer, „Industrial Application of Modell Predictive Control,“ *at Automatisierungstechnik,* Bd. 12, pp. 592-593, 2006.

[21] M. Feindt and U. Kerzel, Prognosen bewerten - Statistische Grundlagen und praktische Tipps, Karlsruhe, Germany: Springer Gabler, 2015.

[22] S. A. Dudani, „The Distance-Weighted k-Nearest-Neighbor Rule,“ in *IEEE Transactions on Systems, Man, and Cybernetics*, Malibu, USA, 1976.

[23] H. S. Fischer and H. Gilgen, „DACHRad – Berechnung der direkten Sonneneinstrahlung in Deutschland, Österreich und der Schweiz,“ in *Bulletin of the Geobotanical Institute ETH*, Zurich, Switzerland, 2002.

[24] V. Quaschning, Regenerative Energiesysteme, Munich, Germany: Carl Hanser Verlag, 2015.

[25] G. P. Henze, D. R. H. and K. Moncef, „Development of a predictive optimal controller for thermal energy storage systems,“ in *International Journal of HVAC&R Research 3(3)*, Boulder, USA, 1997.

[26] G. P. Henze, D. E. Kalz, S. Liu and C. Felsmann, „Experimental Analysis of Model-Based Predictive Optimal Control for Active and Passive Building Thermal Storage Inventory,“ in *HVAC&R Research, Volume 11, Number 2*, Lincoln, USA, 2005.

[27] B. Dong and K. P. Lam, „A real-time model predictive control for building heating and cooling systems based on the occupancy behavior pattern detection and local weather forecasting,“ in *BUILD SIMUL (2014)*, San Antonio, USA, 2013.

Long-Term Environment Prediction for Model Predictive Control in Vehicles:

Pattern Recognition upon Primitive Driving Behavior and Driver Condition

Karl-Falco Storm, Daniel Eckardt
Powertrain & Power Engineering
IAV GmbH
Gifhorn, Germany
email: karl-falco.storm@alumni.tu-clausthal.de,
daniel.eckardt@iav.de

Meng Zhang, Jörg Grieser,
Michael Prilla, Andreas Rausch
Institute for Informatics
Technische Universität Clausthal
Goslar, Germany
email: {meng.zhang, joerg.grieser, michael.prilla,
andreas.rausch}@tu-clausthal.de

Abstract—**This paper evaluates the prediction accuracy of indeterministic environments. The exhaust aftertreatment for vehicles is used as a sample scenario, whose efficiency should be enhanced using pattern recognition techniques. It determines a control strategy to minimize exhaust emissions—whose volume, composition and temperature depends on the load and speed of the combustion engine. Since the engine being controlled by the accelerator pedal, the driving behavior needs to be predicted for adequate horizons. The new approach is simulated on the basis of driving data at different traffic scenarios, including urban, overland and motorway road types. The recorded driving behavior is examined location-based by transferring it into a dynamical number of primitive driving behavior classes. This way, traffic scenarios can be distinguished by using a relatively small set of data. Furthermore, the driving behavior does not have to be labeled, since information about it occurring is not required. In context with the task of vehicle control, possible changes in driving behavior due to a higher stress level have already been proven. Following this finding, driving behavior prediction is investigated in consideration of the driver's condition. In the end, a benchmark is carried out to compare existing prediction methods of location-based pattern recognition. After presenting the findings, an outlook for possible future research is given.**

Keywords-pattern recognition; long-term prediction; driver condition monitoring; primitive driving behavior; model predictive control.

I. Introduction

From the perspective of control theory, ambient conditions are key input factors for a controller's performance. In order to optimize the regulatory strategy of model predictive control systems regarding predefined targets, accurate predictions are needed. While this is very effective for deterministic and completed systems without randomness of future states, indeterministic processes and environments must be monitored closely. The environment is represented by signals of sensors observing it. Nevertheless, not all states and influences can be recognized, as the observation of certain values is impossible or technically too expensive.

Turning over towards driving behavior prediction, the actual state of the vehicle is observed by various on-board sensors. From this point of view, future conditions depend on possible car maneuvers performed by the driver. Besides driving behavior classification, maneuver restricting driving environments are also an ongoing subject of research. These (partly indeterministic) restrictions include course of the road, speed limits, other traffic participants as well as weather and light conditions, for example. So, in order to generate accurate predictions, both factors—human and environmental—are considered. In this research, the predictions of indeterministic environments using pattern recognition techniques are evaluated and differentiated against existing approaches. This is done using driving behavior as a use case, including the driver's condition for the first time.

A. Motivation

In automotive field, slow control circuits like engine cooling, cabin climate conditioning gain efficiency from predictive control systems. The prediction of driving behavior is a key factor to many different applications in the automotive field. In this context, it is understood as the longitudinal and lateral control of a vehicle. Velocity and acceleration are mainly influenced via the accelerator pedal that affects the engine load [1]. To date, driving is mainly linked with human behavior, therefore, it is of an indeterministic nature. In conclusion, the effectivity depends on the driver's pedal control, which represents his driving behavior as a function of the current traffic scenario.

The engine load and speed indirectly determine the amount and composition of the exhaust gas. Its general purpose is minimizing the emission of unwanted exhaust gas components. Each of its modules has got its own optimal operational temperature range, where each catalytic reaction performs best [1].

Looking at diesel engines in particular, an injection angle shift can lead to an increase in the exhaust gas and the exhaust aftertreatment system's temperature. Compared to a cold system, a preheated exhaust aftertreatment system dramatically decreases the amount of NO_x emitted at emission peaks due to better efficiency. But preheating also causes a slight increase in fuel consumption and, therefore, leads to additional CO_2 emission. While this strategy is usually pursued at the engine's cold starting, it might also occur at normal operation [2]. For example, if the engine idles for a certain time (e.g., waiting at a road junction), the exhaust aftertreatment system cools down. Thereafter, at a possible acceleration, a huge amount of exhaust gas may release the exhaust gas system untreated, until the light off temperature of the components are reached again. In this case, the exhaust aftertreatment gains efficiency, if preheating starts punctual. If it starts too early, fuel is wasted because of unnecessary heating. If it starts too late, the aftertreatment efficiency still increases, but fuel consumption is higher than at optimal timing. The regeneration of the diesel particulate filter requires a constant high exhaust gas temperature. Ideal way, this process takes place at the time when a constant (higher) engine performance is present. This way, intensive preheating is not necessary again saving fuel and CO_2 emissions [1]-[4].

Both examples show that detailed knowledge of the upcoming engine load is significantly important for model predictive control. Therefore, improvements in prediction accuracy are investigated in this work.

B. *Content and Structure*

This paper has the following structure: Section II gives an overview about predictive control systems, driving behavior, its prediction and driver condition detection. As a conclusion, a scientific gap is worked out in Section III. Thereafter, the new developed approach is described and explained with the aid of an example scenario in Section IV. Detailed structures and specifications of the algorithm are explained in the implementation part. In Section V, the experiment including test data generation is described. Finally, the findings are summarized and an outlook for possible future work is given in Section VI.

II. RELATED WORK

Predictions of future ambient conditions can be done by using several approaches. A simple approach is the extrapolation of the actual observed status. Taking the vehicle condition as an example, constant speed, acceleration or accelerator pedal position (*KoGaS*-model) are common techniques for short-term estimations in the matter of a few seconds, becoming more inexact for longer horizons [5][6]. But for the shown model predictive control systems, a horizon in the matter of minutes is required. Figure 1 shows a rough categorization of the related work. The different techniques are classified by their methodical approaches, their prediction horizons and their universality for being used at different road classes and traffic scenarios

Long-term predictions can be achieved by conflating navigation data (street type, road course, speed limit and ele-

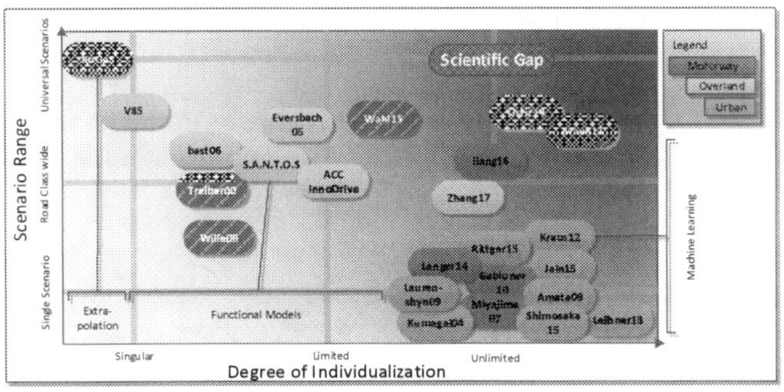

Figure 1. Categorization of driver stress detection methods.

vation profile) of the future route with the driver's average (expected) driving behavior. Following this concept, functional models like *V85* are able to generate a velocity trajectory based on this navigation data. Further development of this concept was done by Müller et al. [7] and Ebersbach [8]. Both references describe functional models that learn the mean velocity deviation (compared to the speed limit) and acceleration behavior of an individual driver. Using this averaged driving behavior, good results are achieved for low traffic density at overland road. But these methods suffer at heavy traffic situation and at built-up areas, where the driving behavior is predominantly influenced by environmental factors like preceding vehicles [7]-[9]. Thus, concepts for taking the driving behavior of preceding vehicles into account have been developed, but they depend on environmental scanning, e.g., using an adaptive cruise control's radar sensor [10].

Numerous authors addressed the prediction topic using machine learning techniques and statistical methods. They are also suitable to predict uncertainty by the distinction of traffic scenarios, e.g., using kernel density estimation [11] and Markov transition probabilities for discrete states [12]. Artificial Neural Networks (ANN) proved to be an accurate way of predicting driving behavior under uncertain conditions [6]. Nevertheless, ANN's high demand of labeled learning data is a downside.

Clustering algorithms are commonly used to distinguish traffic scenarios, thus potentially receiving better results [13]-[15]. Features can be abstracted from the raw signals, their histograms or distributions. Both pattern recognition techniques have almost exclusively been used on single traffic scenarios yet, but they do offer promising possibilities for universal approaches even with small sets of data [10].

So far, driving behavior prediction has commonly been described from a data's point of view. But in this context, the human machine interaction's point of view is another important field of investigation, because each driver has got his individual behavior in different driving situations. Besides physical and legal restrictions, the personal preferences of the driver may depend on a wide field of different factors, giving it indeterministic characteristics [8]. They can be classified into stable (1) and variable (2) factors, depending on the person (a) or a certain situation (b), e.g., sociodemographic characteristics (1a), driving ability (2a), traffic environment (2a) and weather (2b) [14][16]. By observing the mental and emotional state of the driver, some conclusions might be drawn—e.g., a negligent driving behavior while being pressed for time.

Mental workload estimation of humans has been investigated for an even longer period. In general, five different techniques of state evaluation are derived from literature (Figure 2). They include direct measurement and iterative physiologic measurements, self-assessment, observing via attention tests to make assumption from ambient conditions (*Digital Emotions*). All methods can deliver exact results, only if appropriate analysis models are used and calibrated before.

A fusion of different physiological measurements gives good results if the physical impact of the environment can be controlled (e.g., movements, temperature fluctuations). Attention tests and repetitive surveys are not very suitable for continuous measuring, because they affect the actual state of the

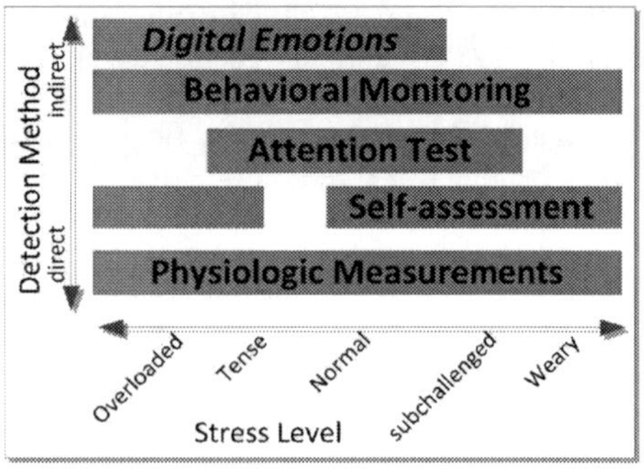

Figure 2. Categorization of driver stress detection methods.

experimentee by giving him an additional task. For self-assessment, slight stress may not be detected by the experimentee. Behavior observing can be done by rating actions, movements and posture. This usually requires a qualified investigator or expertise. Finally, *Digital Emotion* summarizes techniques for making assumptions of the experimentee by observing ambient conditions. For driving tasks, this includes the interpretation of external factors that might affect the driver condition such as intense traffic or aggressive behavior. Of course, a fusion of all five methods delivers highly precise information [17].

While matching workload onto sensor data is relatively easy, this does not count other way around—detecting stress from sensor data. According to the valence-arousal model, stress is a combination of mental workload and negative emotions. A great variety of physiological signals are capable of drawing conclusions about the mental load and the emotional state after setting up a suitable stress model [15][18].

Pulse data and the Galvanic Skin Response (GSR) are easy to measure and frequently used in activity trackers. While studies proofed their reliability for scientific applications, open low-cost platforms for scientific research are yet hard to find. This also applies for the evaluation methods apart from classical methods. In terms of data analysis, features are extracted and interpreted from the respective raw sensor signals. The Heart Rate Variability (HRV) is derived from time difference between two subsequent heart beats, which can be used as a stress measurand. High mental workload and emotional stress usually cause the HRV to decrease. Photoplethysmo Graphic Sensors (PPG) allow the measurement of pulse data by simply recording the capacity of reflection at suitable skin areas. Because this signal is not identical to electrocardiograms, the derivation of HRV is inexact [19][20].

GSR analysis is another approach that is issued frequently. An internal or external stimulus leads to a sudden decrease with slow recovery of skin resistance because of sweat gland activity within seconds. Therefore, the palm of the hand and sole are suited best for measuring. The number and intensity of peaks is determined by a deconvolution analysis [21]. Emotional states are usually detected using non-heuristic methods [22], necessitating a valid emotional model to be established in advance. Relying on physiological measurements alone, sensor accuracy and interpretation accuracy together tend to be around 45-65% [21][23].

In context with the task of vehicle control, possible changes in driving behavior due to a higher stress level have already been proven [16]. Vice versa, stress and traffic scenarios have been related by Heinrich [17] and Yamaguchi et al. [24]. Based on their findings, the prediction of future driver workload is possible after a sufficient training period. But studies also showed that the manner and effects are individual, as the experimentee's driving behavior responds different in complex and stressful situations. Therefore, no general valid conclusions can be drawn [25].

III. Scientific Gap and Research Question

Machine learning techniques for predicting the future environment have already been described in numerous publications, proving their effectivity in certain traffic scenarios. But they have not yet been investigated for a universal usage. Concerning driving behavior, long term predictions are currently generated based on functional models and navigation data.

For an extensive traffic scenario distinction, these models need a wider range of input data about road conditions, weather, the driver's intention as well as other traffic participants. It is not possible yet to gather all the necessary information via sensors, even if cloud services and Car2X technologies extend their *perception range*. High definition map data are an additional cost factor not to be scored, as it needs to be updated frequently. Especially for cars with simple specification, this kind of information is not available yet, leaving traffic guidance-based predictions at an insufficient data situation. Furthermore, a priori distinction of traffic scenarios is needed for functional models, equivalent to labels for training artificial neural networks.

Keeping this in mind, a pattern recognition technique should be developed that relies on simple and limited data input, offering a wider variety of traffic scenarios to be distinguished. Also, location-based predictions allow considering local particularities if a driver travels repeatedly on the same route, learning from the driver individual behavior. The observation of the driver's conditions regarding his emotion and stress level should be evaluated in order to enhance the prediction effectiveness.

IV. Pattern Recognition

For image recognition, patterns are typical detected and assigned based on the training of an artificial neural network with a pre-labeled dataset. For signal paths, labeling can be done analog, describing certain ambient scenarios that need to be defined in advance. Conversely, pattern recognition focuses on similar recurring patterns of an observed value. This implies that certain patterns occur regularly in any similar form and order. Clustering algorithms allow the detection and specification of similar patterns by the comparison of the input data, opening up for a wider set of dynamical defined scenarios (classes). Therefore, the signals need to be split into discrete sections on which clustering is applied. In order to combine the individual patterns for long-term predictions, they need to be connected in any particular order. This can be achieved using transition matrices that keep track of the signals during pattern classification. Afterwards, transition possibilities are derived from that.

For a model-based exhaust aftertreatment control system, the timeline of the engine load and speed are of special interest for estimating the future exhaust volume flow. It is mainly influenced by the driver's usage of the accelerator pedal; for first approximation his input needs to be predicted. Generally, the resolution of the engine load can be reduced into several discrete classes, depending on the respective application.

At this point, longitudinal acceleration is graded into primitive driving behavior classified by the following (see Figure 3, deep-red graph): high (1-2) or medium (3) engine load for an increase of velocity or start-up, lower (4) engine load for constant velocity and idle (5-6) for deceleration and coasting. The velocity is classified in relation to the actual speed limit (or a location-based mean speed, if map data are unavailable) to approximate certain primitive traffic scenarios. The classes include halt or stop and go (0), traffic jam (1), minor slow-down (2), normal velocity (2-3) and faster velocity scenarios (3-4). Furthermore, the driving behavior does not need to be linked to factors causing it [10].

Conclusions are rather drawn by evaluating the location-based likelihood of their occurrence and thus, can be interlinked iteratively for long-term predictions. Driving behavior and prediction knowledge are saved inside map database for it to be used location depended. Figure 3 shows how sample data of a route section is translated into its corresponding primitive driving behavior pattern using the introduced heuristic rules.

For the generation of a knowledge base, all previous observed and recorded trips are separated among identical sections borders to keep them comparable. Useful sectioning can be done by the means of road type transitions and intersections (again, if no map data are available, sectioning should be derived from a batch of recorded data on the same route). Figure 4 shows four sample classes of driving behavior that have been identified via clustering, comparing the similarity between each other. Each class represents the driving through a corresponding traffic scenario on the same route section, e.g., rather clear road (left and mid-left) or an intense traffic scenario (far right). This way, changing traffic conditions between each section are considered just by their impact on the driving behavior.

Table I shows how a route is separated into section (s1-s8) by its map-data properties listed in the second column. In fact, all sections are designed to overlap each other enhancing their functionality close to their fringes. Inside each section, a number of discrete classes (N) describe the observed driving behavior pattern. The number of classes is determined dynamically upon the similarity of the recorded trips; it varies between one and a useful upper limit. For example, on a motorway, only three to four different patterns are distinguished,

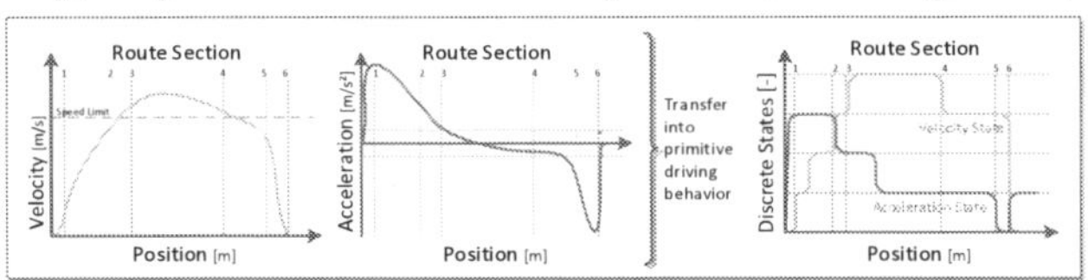

Figure 3. Deriving primitive driving behavior patterns from velocity and acceleration signals; a start-to-stop example.

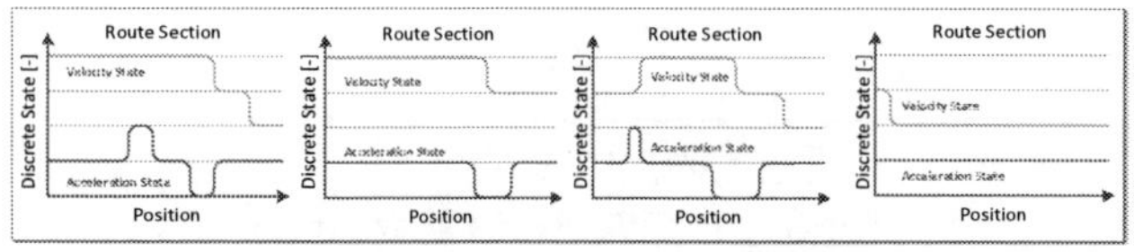

Figure 4. Four discrete traffic scenarios (classes) represented by their corresponding primitive driving behavior patterns.

whereas in urban areas many different patterns may.

Inside each class, the driving behavior (velocity and acceleration) is averaged over all assigned measuring runs. The right side of Table I shows 23 laps being assigned to eight clusters inside section s2. For each pattern-class (and their both section transition), a transition matrix keeps track of the classification flow for each single measuring run (far right). This allows building up statistical transition relationships between the section's classes. Referring to Markov property, the allocation probabilities for subsequent sections only depend on the actual class rather than on the previous classes (see Figure 5). As soon as the knowledge is built for all necessary route sections, prediction is possible. Using the elements with the highest rating, class across predictions becomes possible. Then, when the first couple of meters are passed on the first section (s1), the actual observed driving behavior is matched to its best fitting classes inside the knowledge base. Thus, the algorithm chooses the most appropriate class for predicting. Because of changing transition probabilities, a change of the matched driving behavior class also leads to changes for the interlinked classes of the following route sections.

Regarding the driver, observations of his conditions are also reduced into primitive patterns. They are combined from the self-assessment inside the valence-arousal state space and the physiological monitoring. Figure 6 shows combined ratings matched to the curse of the route. Certain positions show a peak due to brief events (red traffic lights, hard breaking etc.). As a result, pattern recognition methods need to process multi-dimensional input data. Otherwise, a combination of the evaluations needs to be calculated (e.g., by multiplication).

V. SIMULATION AND EVALUATION

A simulation was set up to evaluate the pattern recognition methods shown in Figure 8, with and without the driver's condition consideration, compared to reference methods. In order to make it statistically sound, the overall sample size must reach a relatively high quantity which makes real-time in-car testing impossible. Therefore, a set of training data was recorded to simulate the prediction methods at different traffic environments and scenarios inside a virtual simulation environment. After short explorative research including a basic validation of the approach, the necessary sample size was estimated. Because the size exceeds the number of possible real-time experiments, a MATLAB toolbox was set up for a simulative evaluation. Hereafter, the measuring runs, the data recording and their preparation is described. Afterwards, the implemented methods are outlined, and prediction results are presented.

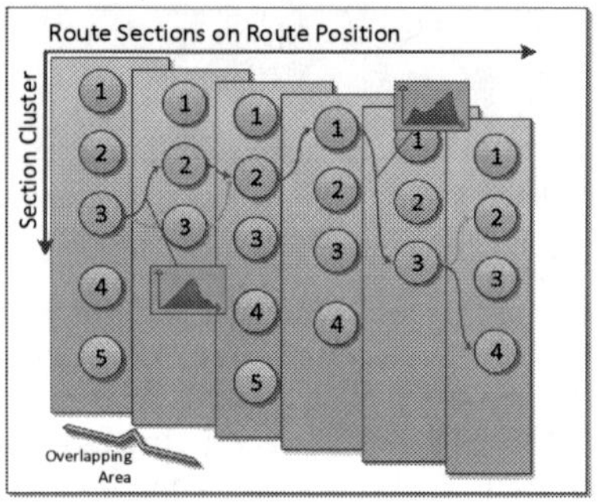

Figure 5. Interlinked driving style classes allow long-term prediction horizons using Markov property.

A. Data Preparation

In order to simulate the reduction of driving behavior, a large pool of real driving data needs to be recorded in advance. This was achieved by utilizing an experimentee that drove repetitive on a predefined test route. The runs were recorded using a position tracker, a physiological recorder and an event logger. Over 60 completed laps of mixed urban, overland and motorway driving environment—a total of 3,400 km—has been recorded, including 31 laps with GSR and Pulse monitoring of the driver. A Volkswagen Golf Mk4 was used as test vehicle. It is equipped with a manual gear shift and a retrofitted cruise control which was used as reference driving behavior.

Physiological data has been recorded using a *Shimmer GSR+* sensor recorder equipped with two GSR electrodes and a PPG fingertip sensor. Figure 7 shows the setup for the measuring runs: The sensor recorder was attached to the left arm to minimize interruption due to finger movements during steering and gear changes (middle). With the help of an event logger software set up, inputs like self-assessment and possible external stimuli are logged (far right). The latter includes temporal stimuli, precipitation, lighting and temperature conditions to contextualize the self-reported emotions.

All measuring data was later mapped on *HERE WeGo* navigation data and interpolated 1 m resolution. Velocity and acceleration data has been adjusted for plausibility considering the vehicle's performance. HRV and skin conductivity features were extracted from the physiological sensor data using the *MATLAB* Toolboxes *Ledalab* (GSR) and Pan-Tompkins (HR) with *KubiosHVR* Standard. They were combined with the driver's self-reports keeping track of the mood and workload. An ordinal evaluation table is utilized for converting the single inputs into an ordinal stress rating (Figure 6).

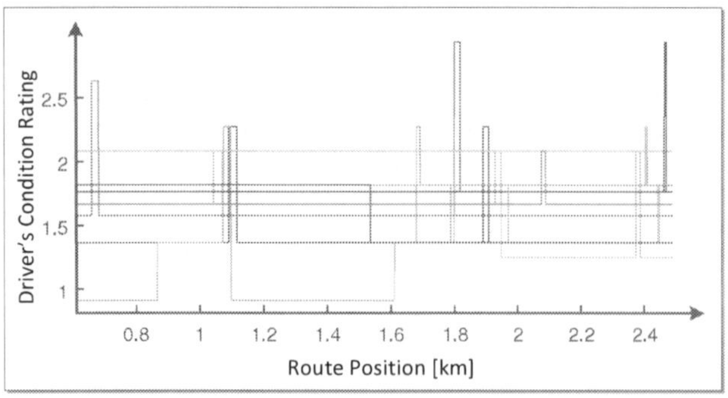

Figure 6. Comparison of several driver's conditioning ratings in relation of the route position. Peaks marking special events of arousal.

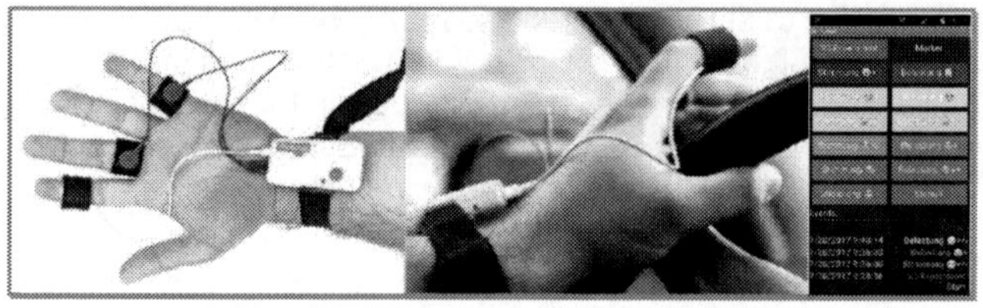

Figure 7. Experimentee with GSR electrodes and PGG fingertip sensor (left and middle); Event logger interface (right).

B. Implementation of the prediction methods

For the final benchmark, five prediction methods were implemented as shown in Figure 8. Two of them were used as a reference: The **Speed Limits** (SL, 1) for the route were retrieved via *HERE WeGo* in advanced. Speed limit transitions were smoothened out using the test vehicle's lateral acceleration capabilities. This way, a rather naïve prediction was generated, representing a minimum solution. Figure 9 shows the speed limit (black line) for a latter part of the test route.

An **Adaptive Functional Model** (AFM, 2) was implemented using *MATLAB Simulink*. It is capable of generating predictions-based on velocity deviation (as a function of the speed limit) and observed acceleration behavior (as a function of the vehicle speed). Every single run is trained in advanced to ensure this method to deliver the best possible outcome. Even though this kind of training would not be possible in real-time evaluation, training the AFM using other recorded laps give detrimental results. Figure 9 shows the speed profiles generated with this model. For better performance at traffic lights and intersection (pink, area of interest), an additional feature was integrated into the functional model to give it further advantages over straight trajectories. Taking all recorded test laps as a basis, statistical information about the chance of stopping were evaluated. If halt probability was over 50 % inside the according region of interest, the average velocity passing it, is added to the trajectory.

Next up, two different clustering methods are described: **Hierarchical Clustering** (HC, 3) and **Growing Neural Gas** using driving behavior (GNG, 4) and additional Driver Condi-

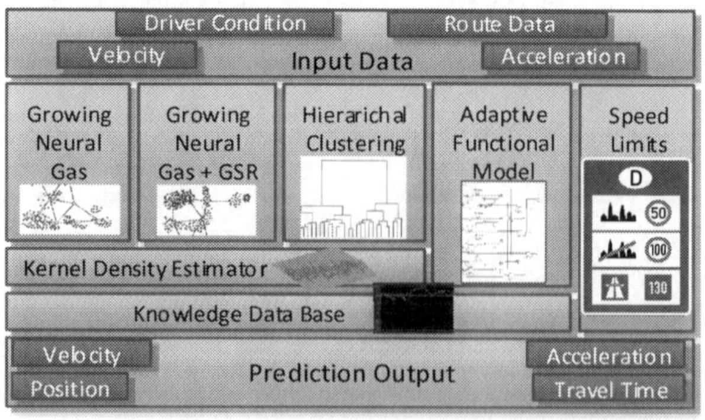

Figure 8. Overview of prediction methods used for the Benchmark.

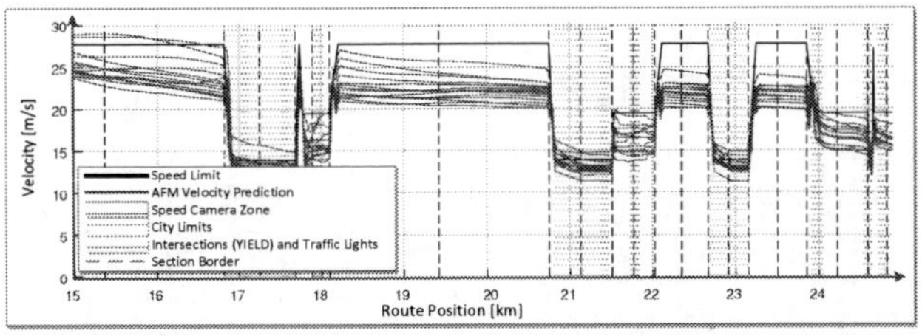

Figure 9. Generation of 14 velocity prediction trajectories using the adaptive functional model (AFM) reference.

tions (DC, 5) as training data. Hierarchical clustering using Ward's Method is-based on the Euclidian distance between each set of features. In this case, the distances are calculated between the primitive velocity and acceleration pattern (see Figure 4). The distances between primitive driving patterns can be visualized using linkage tree. In Figure 10, the corresponding Euclidean distance values of 23 driving profiles mark the border between aggregated and independent clustering classes. The optimal number of classes is determined by minimizing the inter-cluster distances (that is, minimizing the sum of class internal distance values), depicted by the orange bar for $L^2 = 500$. In a last step, all driving profiles that remained linked are merged into a single class.

In order to get predicted behavior for every class, velocity and acceleration data are averaged using a kernel density estimator. Then, the primitive driving behavior is derived from it. A Growing neural gas implementation is used with two distinct data sets. Unlike hierarchical clustering, it allows multidimensional feature sets; A priori combination is not necessary. Also, the dynamical optimization of the class numbers is already integrated [26].

For deciding which class (prediction) to choose, the same distance metrics from HC are used for comparing the actual driving behavior with the knowledge base. At the end of each section, the subsequent classes are determined considering transition probabilities. Figure 11 shows the prediction of a measuring run (solid green line) being iteratively calculated every 10 m (dotted blue line) on the left-hand side. At the 11.5 km mark, the road type changes from two-lane motorway to a single-lane overland road. A change in prediction accuracy is directly visible due to an increased variance. The speed limit (black) is drawn as reference.

C. *Simulation Runs*

First of all, the recorded laps were separated randomly using a lottery, resulting in 75 % (23) training data and 25 % (8)

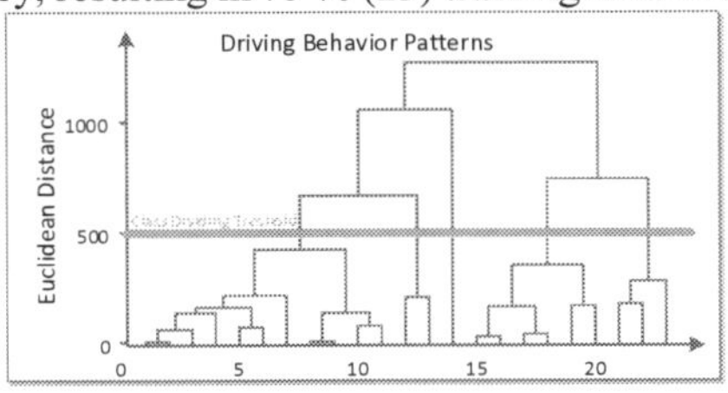

Figure 10. Dendrogram of 23 driving profiles being divided into five classes according their similarity.

test data sets. After separation, knowledge databases were generated for all clustering methods using parallel processing. For benchmarking the methods at different traffic environments, four test areas were defined for all three road types: urban, overland and motorway. Inside each area, the actual start of prediction is then determined randomly for each simulation iteration. The prediction horizon is set to 90 seconds with 150 m being the minimum distance. This way, the horizon usually reaches from 1250 to 2500 m, depending on the actual vehicle speed at the prediction start. All methods then use the same end horizon to keep them comparable. With eight simulation runs in total, the number of simulated predictions reveals to 768 iterations (8 iterations × 8 tested profiles × 12 evaluation areas).

For each iteration, the virtual Volkswagen drives up to the next prediction start point. After arriving, all prediction methods calculate velocity and acceleration trajectories within prediction horizon. Figure 11 shows two sample predictions generated by AFM (dotdashed grey) and HC (dotted blue) on the right-hand side. The point where the prediction starts is indicated by a blue circle, located at the original trajectory (solid green). On the left side, a main road example is shown. AFM prediction is visibly better for the first 700 meters as it is closer to the original trajectory. Looking at the acceleration, HC gets it quite well for position 13.1 to 13.5 km where both trajectories decrease. On the right side, a mixed urban (yellow) and ex-urban scenario are shown. Obviously, a stop-and-go traffic scenario can be identified at distance 22.5 to 24 km when velocity drops below 5 m/s. This time, the pattern recognition method clearly outruns the functional model as it predicts velocity and acceleration behavior quite well. Nevertheless, prediction here is shown on a location-based which is preferable for visual evaluation. Physically correct is a time-based prediction which is harder to depict.

D. *Simulation Results*

After generating all predictions, the respective trajectories are compared to the real driving behavior. For both signals, velocity and acceleration, the Root-Mean-Square Error (RMSE) is calculated according to their time-dependent signal paths (Table II). The best performing values are highlighted. For the driving time, the absolute difference at the end of the prediction horizon is used. After completing twelve iterative runs, the simulation starts over using the subsequent lap. Negligible difference between several simulations proved the sample size of 768 to be statistically sound for this simulation (in fact, within a 95 % confidence interval).

In order to apply statistical analysis, a distribution function has been fitted to the RMSE values and the absolute driving time deviation. It turned out that a log-normal distribution fits them perfectly, allowing a symmetrical boxplot representation of the results. Figure 12 shows the aggregated results of the simulation runs. The boxplots illustrate the logarithmized RMSE distribution of acceleration, velocity and time prediction. The diamond represents the median of all measured values. Outliers are represented by spots outside the whiskers

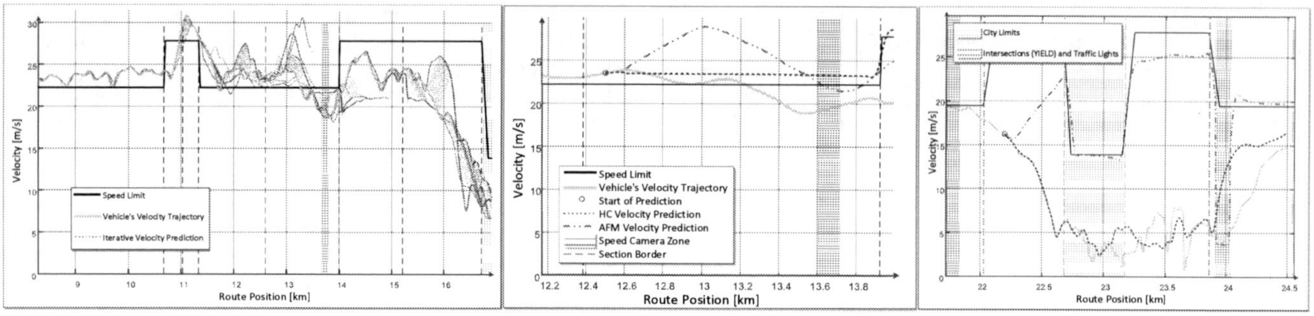

Figure 11. Iterative velocity prediction every 10 m (blue, dotted) using HC and a prediction horizon of 30 s (left figure). Two samples of a single velocity prediction comparing HC and AFM including local features (right figures).

The upper plots show direct comparison between the reference methods (SL, AFM) and the three pattern recognition methods (HC, GNG, DC). All three disciplines are dominated by the pattern recognition methods—they have lower logarithmized RMSE values, and thus, lower mean errors (see Table 2). At urban, ex-urban and motorway scenarios, the mean acceleration difference is 0.076 m/s^2using the naïve speed limit-based prediction. The adaptive functional model-based prediction only improves little by 5 % (0.072 m/s^2). Pattern recognition greatly improves the accuracy by 37.5 % (0.045 m/s^2) using Growing neural gas. Velocity and driving time predictions show a similar picture. While pattern recognition improves velocity prediction by 35 % (0.77 vs. 0.50 m/s for AFM vs HC), driving time, which is the sum of all velocity deviations at the end of the prediction horizon, pattern recognition methods reduce the mean error by 30 % from 8.6 s to 6.1 s.

The lower boxplots show the detailed results for each road type. As pattern recognition dominates, both references methods (HC and SL) are left out now to obtain a better overview.

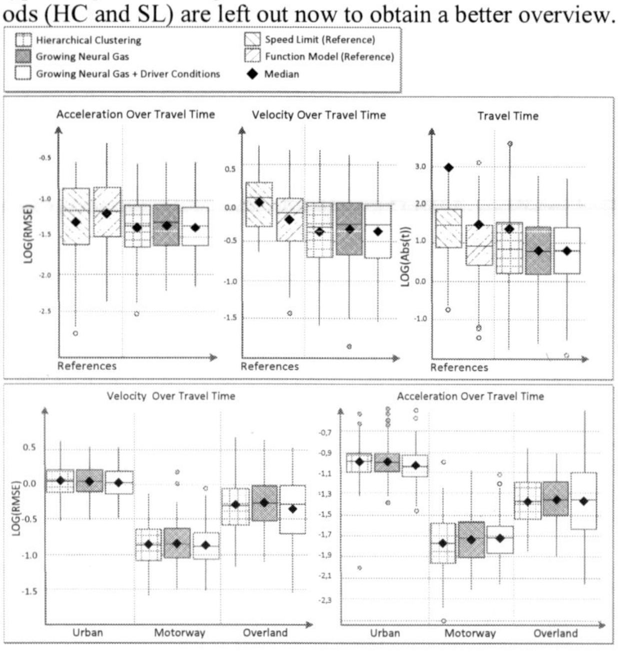

Figure 12. Detailed boxplots of the simulation results (n: 768, 90 s horizon).

On the left third, the logarithmized RMSE for velocity prediction are shown, arranged in urban, overland and motorway traffic environments. On the right, acceleration prediction is shown in the same order. Overall, predictions for motorway scenario got the highest accuracy, being more than 7.5 times better than urban and more than 3.5 times better than at overland scenarios; Five times or 2.5 times for acceleration, respectively. It is worth mentioning that Growing neural gas using driver condition patterns performs best at built-up areas. Velocity predictions are 3 % better, whereas the acceleration performance increases about 8 %. The mean driving time deviation is 0.02 s better, which is an improvement of 2 %. All other scenarios are not dominated by DC.

In terms of computing time, the SL reference uses almost no resources being plausibilized only. Next up, as AFM only learns the actual run, computational time is negligible. The situation for clustering algorithms is quite different. Knowledge base generation using Growing neural gas algorithm uses up a lot of resources and calculation time doubled with every additional driving profile. Hierarchical clustering performed most effective by comparison.

VI. Conclusion and Future Work

In this work, it has been shown that location-based pattern recognition is capable of delivering long term driving behavior predictions. It also shows a significant higher accuracy compared to traditional functional models. Also, the consideration of the driver condition does have advantages at traffic scenarios with great external influences, improving predictions by another 3 to 8 % (Figure 12, lower part).

At this point, it is rather unclear whether the driver's condition really influenced the driving behavior at urban scenarios, or if external factors like traffic intensity influenced the drivers' conditions. In the latter case, ambient conditions may become "visible" for the pattern recognition method. For other traffic environments, benefit from computationally expensive Growing neural gas over Hierarchical clustering algorithm was no issue.

For fürther validation of the concept, the following changes in the experimental designs are recommended: Using a better motorized test vehicle and recording its CAN-Bus data directly. The set-up of a stress model using valence-arousal model, a stimuli session should be completed in advanced, in order to perform a qualitative analysis upon the driver's condition [25]. Five to ten different experimentees should participate in the test run in order to evaluate the prediction performance according their individual driving behavior. Looking at driving behavior in particular, the respective traffic scenarios should be captured and analyzed detailed.

On the algorithm's side, prediction methods based on artificial neural networks should be included into the benchmark as well. Furthermore, the necessary level of detail for model predictive control should be considered in the evaluation. Therefore, the simulation of real physical processes and the effect of variable prediction horizons length may be considered as well.

REFERENCES

[1] S. Pischinger and U. Seiffert, "Handbuch Kraftfahrzeugtechnik," (Automotive Engineering), Springer Vieweg, 2016.

[2] R. Plöntzke, S. Naumov, M.-C. Bartsch, A. Lechmann, and C. Stebner, "Nutzung prädiktiver Streckendaten zur Minimierung von Verbrauch und Emissionen in allen Fahrsituationen," (Minimizing Consumption and Emissions Using Predictive Route Data), Desden: FAD, 2017.

[3] K. R. Neuhäuser, "Entwicklung einer Temperaturregelung und Vorsteuerung für die Dieselpartikelfilter-Regeneration mit experimenteller Bedatung,"(Developtment of a Temperature Control and Pilot Control for the Regeneration of DPF), Berlin, 2016.

[4] T. Grahle, M. Tonne, A. Wiedersberg, and T. Zsebedits, "Regeneration des Partikelfilters mithilfe von Navigationsdaten," (DPF Regeneration with the Help of Route Data), Motortechnische Zeitschrift, vol. 77, no. 1, 2016, pp. 16-22.

[5] D. Heinrich, "Modelling the driver's behavior to investigate the dynamic loads in the drivetrain," Forschungsberichte IPEK, vol. 92, 2016.

[6] S. Lefèvre, C. Sun, R. Bajcsy, and C. Laugier, "Comparison of parametric and non-parametric approaches for vehicle speed prediction," American Control Conference, 2014.

[7] M. Müller, M. Reif, M. Pandit, Staiger, and Wolfgang, "A predictive gear shift system for motor vehicles using environmental data," Automatisierungstechnik, vol. 52, no. 4, 2004, pp. 180-188.

[8] D. Ebersbach, "Entwurfstechnische Grundlagen für ein Fahrerassistenzsystem zur Unterstützung des Fahrers bei der Wahl seiner Geschwindigkeit," (Speed Selection ADAS), Dresden, 2004.

[9] H.-G. Wahl, "Optimale Regelung eines Prädiktiven Energiemanagements von Hybridfahrzeugen," (Optimal Model Predicitve Control for Hybrid Vehicles), Karlsruhe, 2015.

[10] M. Zhang, K.-F. Storm, and A. Rausch, "Recognition and forecast of driving behavior-based on self-learning algorithms," in Hybrid and Electric Vehicles, Braunschweig, 2017, pp. 216.

[11] T. Kumagai and M. Akamatsu, "Modelling and prediction of driving behavior," in 2nd International Symposium on Measurement, Analysis and Modeling of Human Functions / 1st Mediterranean Conference on Measurement, Genova, 2004.

[12] T. Mauk, "Selbstlernende, zuverlässigkeitsorientierte Prädiktion energetisch relevanter Größen im Kraftfahrzeug," (Selflearning, Reliability-Criented Prediction of Energetic Relevant Dimensions), Stuttgart, 2011.

[13] A. Laurenshyn, L. Åström, and K. Brundell-Freij, "From speed profile data to analysis of behaviour—Classification by Pattern Recognition Techniques," IATSS RESEARCH, vol. 33, no. 2, 2009, pp. 88-89.

[14] M. Liebner, F. Klanner, M. Baumann, C. Ruhhammer, and C. Stiller, "Velocity-based driver intent inference at urban intersections in the presence of preceding vehicles," IEEE Intelligent Transportation Systems Magazine , vol. 5, no. 2, 2013, pp. 10-21.

[15] Z. F. Quek and E. Ng, "Driver identification by driving style," Stanford, 2013.

[16] H. Holte, "Einflussfaktoren auf das Fahrverhalten und das Unfallrisiko junger Fahrerinnen und Fahrer," (Treats on Driving Behavior and Crash Risks of Young Drivers), in Berichte der Bundesanstalt für Straßenwesen, no. M 229, 2012.

[17] F. Heinrich, "Vorhersage der Fahrerbelastung während der Fahrt," (Prediction of the Driver's Stress Level During Driving), Stuttgart, 2012.

[18] M. B. H. Wiem, and Z. Lachiri, "Emotion classification in arousal valence model using MAHNOB-HCI database," in International Journal of Advanced Computer Science and Applications, vol. 8, no. 03, 2017, pp. 318-323.

[19] P. Rainville, A. Becharab, N. Naqvib, and A. R. Damasioc, "Basic emotions are associated with distinct patterns of cardiorespiratory activity," in International Journal of Psychophysiology, vol. 61, 2006, pp. 5-18.

[20] M. Rollin, M. Atkinson, and W. A. Tiller, "The effects of emotions on short-term power spectrum analysis of heart rate variability," in The American Journal of Cardiology, vol. 76, no. 14, 1995, pp. 1089-1093.

[21] Y. Shi, M. H. Nguyen, P. Blitz, B. French, and S. Fisk, "Personalized stress detection from physiological measurements," Pittsburgh, 2010.

[22] R. E. W. Jenke, "Static and dynamic methods for emotion recognition from physiological signals," München, 2015.

[23] C. McCarthy, N. Pradhan, C. Redpath, and A. Adler, "Validation of the Empatica E4 wristband," in Student Conference (ISC), 2016 IEEE EMBS International, Ottawa, IEEE, 2016, pp. 1-4.

[24] M. Yamaguchi, J. Wakasugi, and J. Sakakima, "Evaluation of driver stress using biomarker in motor-vehicle driving simulator," in EMBS Annual International Conference, New York City, IEEE, 2006.

[25] M. Soleymani and J. Lichtenauer, "A multimodal database for affect recognition and implicit tagging," in Transactions of Affective Computing, vol. 3, no. 1, 2012.

[26] S. M. K. Heris, "Neural gas and GNG networks," in MATLAB, 2015-08-28. http://yarpiz.com/77/ypml111-neural-gas-network [Accessed 2018-02-02].

[27] P. J. Lang, M. K. Greenwald, M. M. Bradley, and A. O. Hamm, "Looking at pictures: affective, facial, visceral, and behavioral reactions," in Psychophysiotogy, no. 30, 1993, pp. 261-273.

[28] M. Singh and A. Bin Queyam, "Stress detection in automobile drivers using physiological parameters: a review," in IJEE , vol. 5, no. 2, 2013, pp. 1-5.

[29] J. E. Meseguer, C. T. Calafate, and J. C. Cano, "Driving styles: assessing the correlation of driving behavior with heart rate changes," València, 2017.

TABLE I. DIVIDING A ROUTE INTO DISCRETE SECTIONS, SAMPLE CLUSTERING OF 23 MEASURING RUNS.

Map Visualisation of the Route	Map Data	Section Type	Number of Classes per Section	Number of Trips per Class	Transitions' Probability
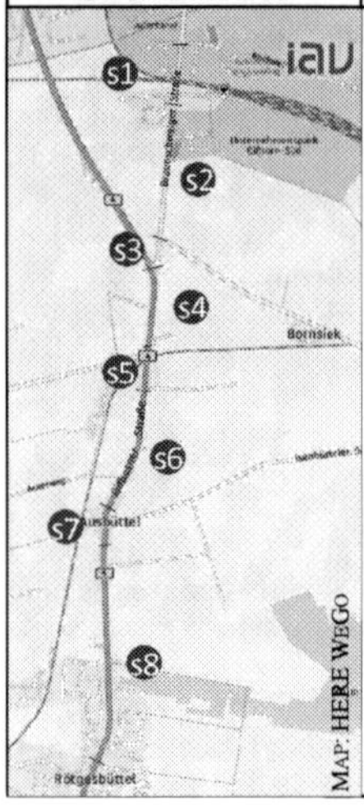	Road Type Speed Limit Intersections Traffic Lights [...]	s1: Urban	N = 9 Classes		
		s2: Overland	N = 8 Classes	Cluster 1: 3	
		s3: Overland	N = 4 Classes	Cluster 2: 2	Previous Section (s1) From Cluster 3: 6/16
		s4: Overland	N = 6 Classes	Cluster 3: 3	
		s5: Urban	N = 9 Classes	Cluster 4: 6	
		s6: Overland	N = 6 Classes	Cluster 5: 1	Subsequent Section (s3) To Cluster 4: 1/6 To Cluster 8: 4/6 To Cluster 9: 1/6
		s7: Urban	N = 6 Classes	Cluster 6: 2	
				Cluster 7: 4	
				Cluster 8: 2	
				∑ 23 Trips	
		s8: Overland	N = 7 Classes		
		[...]	[...]		

TABLE II. MEAN RMSE AND COMPUTING TIME FOR ALL SIMULATED PREDICTION METHODS.

	SL			AFM			HC			GNG			DC		
	$\frac{m}{s}$	$\frac{m}{s^2}$	s	$\frac{m}{s}$	$\frac{m}{s^2}$	s	$\frac{m}{s}$	$\frac{m}{s^2}$	s	$\frac{m}{s}$	$\frac{m}{s^2}$	s	$\frac{m}{s}$	$\frac{m}{s^2}$	s
Urban	2.04	0.157	80.9	1.346	1.193	**24.7**	1.099	0.102	39.9	1.109	0.101	33.7	**1.077**	**0.092**	34.4
Motorway	0.43	**0.013**	7.75	0.21	0.021	2.09	**0.137**	0.019	1.25	0.143	0.019	**1.21**	**0.137**	0.020	1.28
Overland	0.90	0.060	15.6	0.80	0.070	10.5	**0.515**	0.043	7.11	0.543	0.045	7.80	0.533	**0.040**	**6.70**
Combined	1.191	0.076	31.3	0.771	0.072	8.63	**0.502**	0.066	6.98	0.542	0.050	**6.08**	0.533	**0.045**	6.61
Computing Time	*Low*			*Low*			*Medium*			*High*			*Highest*		

a. Sample size: N = 768, Prediction Horizon of 90 s.

Towards Cross-domain Release Engineering - Potentials and Challenges for Automotive Industry

David Inkermann, Tobias Huth, Thomas Vietor

Institute for Engineering Design
Technische Universitaet Braunschweig
Langer Kamp 8, 38106 Braunschweig, Germany
Email: {d.inkermann, tobias.huth, t.vietor}@tu-braunschweig.de

***Abstract*—Product Development (PD) is facing fundamental challenges since the proportion of hardware and software-based functions realized to create innovative products is changing. Performance and enthusiastic attributes of products are more and more based of software providing new functionalities and services to the user. Short innovations cycles of software-based functions result in a decreasing life time of the overall products. Also, it is a trend that products are taken out of operation due to availability of products with new or enhanced functionalities and performance. However, from a technical viewpoint the products retired still provide full functionality. Release Engineering (RE) provides a concept to handle the different innovation cycles of subsystems and maintain or improve the functionality of a product within PD and during the whole life cycle. However, there is a divers understanding and focus regarding RE in the different engineering domains. This contribution discusses the basic concepts in the domains of software and mechanical engineering and highlights the challenges and potentials of RE in the field of automotive engineering. As a basis for further research, different fields of actions are highlighted.**

Keywords–Release Engineering; Release Planning; Innovation Cycles; Cross-Domain System Modelling; Automotive Engineering.

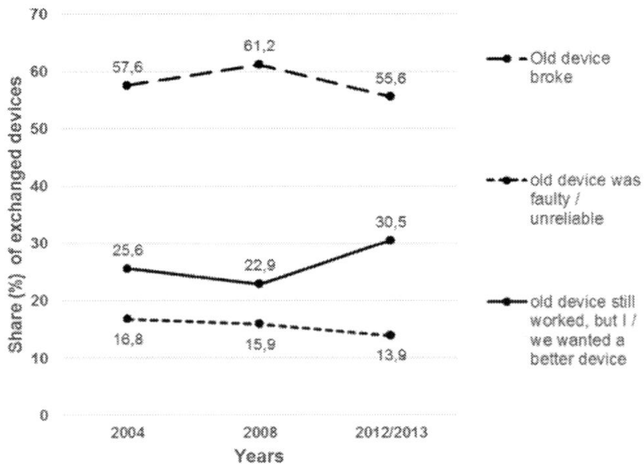

Figure 1. Reasons for the replacement of products and the increasing trend to substitute products with full functionality [2].

I. Introduction

There is an increasing trend to retire products before they reach their end of technical life time. Major reasons for this are that customer's decisions to acquire or substitute existing products are mainly based on enthusiastic attributes like comfort and entertainment functions or connectivity functionalities. These functions are often based on software and are driven by short innovation and technology cycles. However, hardware components are required to fulfil the software functions. As a result of the differing innovation and technology cycles of the hardware and software subsystems, there is an increasing gap between the technical and value life time of products [1]. This fact is highlighted by a study of the German Federal Environment Agency [2]. With focus on consumer products like laptops during the years from 2003 to 2013, there is a clear trend to replace products that are completely functioning because products with better performance and increased functionality are available; see Fig. 1.

On the one hand, this trend leads to a waste of resources since a big amount of material and energy used to produce the hardware is no longer used [1]. On the other hand, shortened product life cycles put challenges to product development. Albers et al. [3] formulates this dilemma by stating *"for economic and risk-minimizing reasons, as few subsystems as possible should be newly developed. Nevertheless, an innovative product with good performance and new enthusiasm attributes has to be developed"*. To address this challenge different approaches are proposed. Albers et al. highlight the need for a consequent product generation engineering by consequently reusing existing product concepts and perfuming variations (principle or geometrical variation) [3] [4]. Other approaches propose upgrades of products during the use phase by introducing new functionalities based on the concept of modular product concepts [5] [6]. Aside from this approaches in the mechanical domain, there are established methods of Release Management (RM) in the field of software engineering. Objective of these methodologies is to plan, develop and deploy releases to provide new features with minimal disruption of the existing product [7].

A. Basic Concept of Release Engineering

The basic concept of Release Engineering (RE) is to maintain and improve the performance and enthusiasm attributes of products by providing additional functionalities during the development and use phase of a product. Major drivers and objectives are (1) the bundling of development, testing and implementation activities during the development phase [7], the (2) consolidation of changes as well as the adaptation of variants [8] and the (3) implementation of innovations for product enhancement and life-cycle-accompanying updates [8]. These objectives are realized by planning and providing release units for the product. The term *release item* or *release unit* is defined in software engineering as the collection of one or more new or changed configuration items deployed into the live environment as a result of one or more changes [7]. Thus, a main task of RE is to define suitable release units in order to address the above mentioned drivers and aims. This highlights the strong interaction with the task of product architecture design [9], configuration management and change management [10]. Based on the evaluation of impact and weakening of releases Schuh [8] introduces a basic categorization of releases units; see Fig. 2. This categorization helps to define a suitable product architecture, determine appropriate release cycles and manage development to achieve the required degree of innovation over the product life cycle.

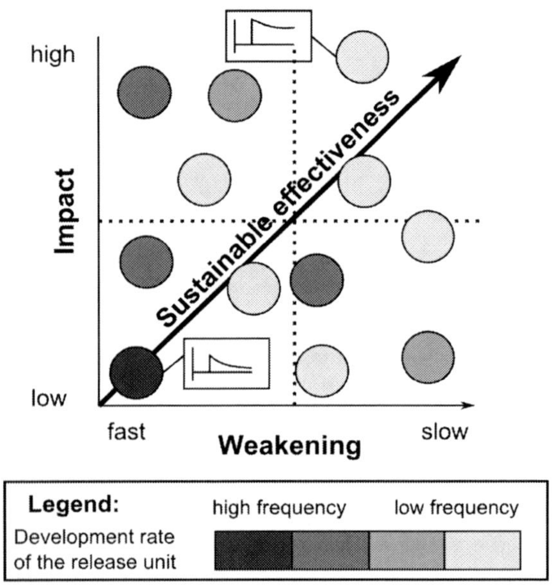

Figure 2. Categorization of Release Entities based on their Impact and Weakening for the Innovation of the overall Product [8].

In the field of software engineering the task of release unit definition is allocated to Release Planning [11]. Based on an extensive literature review Svahnberg et al. [12] highlight the diversity of objective and restriction to be considered when planning release units and frequencies. Aside from customer feedbacks, defects of previous releases, market factors and new customer demands, technical factors like the existing system architecture, interdependencies between requirements and the features to be included have to be incorporated.

To set the focus of this contribution in the following the term Release Engineering (RE) is used and defined following Aleksic [13]: *Release Engineering (RE) is a part of Release Management and defines release units, which are understood as assemblies or modules that can be assigned to specific release cycles.* The tasks and activities covered by this definition match with the common understanding of Release Planning in software engineering, however, the term Engineering is used to highlight the perspective of the mechanical engineering domain.

In order to apply the concept of RE to products inclosing subsystems of different engineering domains like automobiles, it becomes obvious that the definition of release units and cycles is a task involving all domains. To provide support for this interdisciplinary task in this contribution it is analysed how this task is supported in the different domains and which methods and approaches are used. Furthermore, it is discussed which challenges and potentials exist to apply cross-domain RE in automotive industry.

B. Research Focus and Outline

This contribution aims at introducing a basic understanding of cross-domain RE by analysing and comparing existing models and methodologies in the domains of mechanical and software engineering. The research is guided and structured by the following questions:

- Which approaches and methods for RE exist in mechanical and software engineering and what are their main objectives and principles?
- What are challenges in cross-domain RE and which information and product models are needed to support cross-domain RE?
- What are relevant fields for further research to support cross-domain RE?

In order to answer these questions in, Section 2, an analysis of existing approaches of RE is conducted focusing software and mechanical engineering. Based on this analysis, a brief comparison is presented. This comparison serves as a basis to formulate requirements and implications for cross-domain RE in general. In Section 3, potentials and challenges to apply cross-domain RE in automotive industry are discussed. With reference to existing methods and tools for architecture design and change management relevant fields for future research are derived and described in Section 4. Section 5 concludes the contribution with a discussion and brief outlook.

II. EXISTING APPROACHES FOR RELEASE ENGINEERING

Release Management is an established process in software engineering. The common understanding already emphasizes the importance of considering the interrelations between software and hardware systems when planning and developing releases [14]. However, there are different obstacles to overcome when introducing consequent RE into industrial practice. In the following paragraphs a brief overview of existing approaches is given in order to highlight their main differences regarding the objectives, principles and relevant product information and models. Based on a comparison requirements to support cross-domain RE are derived.

A. RE in Software Engineering

Importance of Release Management (RM) in software engineering is highlighted by a number of guidelines and standards for instance described in the IT Infrastructure Library (ITIL) [15]. The process of RM strongly connected to the software engineering process [16] and tasks of service management [14] and covers the superior tasks *defining*, *developing*, *implementing* and *operating* releases. Furthermore, a strong interrelation is given to the processes of configuration and change management since the release units have to be planned based on and extending the existing system architecture.

Different approaches and models exist to plan releases, differing between *ad-hoc* and *systematic* planning strategies. Ad-hoc planning is common in industrial practice [12] and has limited planning scope of one or two releases while systematic release planning considers a number of releases planned for the future. In order to time future releases two basic models stand out, namely time-based and feature-based releases [17]. Time-based release processes aiming at introducing major versions of the software with regular intervals, following a strict schedule. These time related release plannings are often applied in highly modular projects [18]. In contrast feature-based release processes are focussing on delivering a predefined set of features in one release; see Fig. 3. Because of the high percentage of 80% [19] of features being dependent in industrial software systems, it is vital to analyse their interdependencies when planning a release. According to Ruhe eight types of dependencies between features have to be distinguish [11]. In order to assign features to releases different methods exist, taking for instance into account the (subjective) priorities given to features by the different stakeholders and the estimated amount of resources consumed by the features. Established methods are described and reviewed by Ruhe [11] and Svahnberg et al. [12] including the EVOLVE II procedure [20] or the greedy planning algorithm [21] as common approaches. Like highlighted by Ruhe, these methods differ in their objectives spanning from value based to the maximizing the financial value function, the stakeholder involvement as well as the consideration of feature dependencies [11].

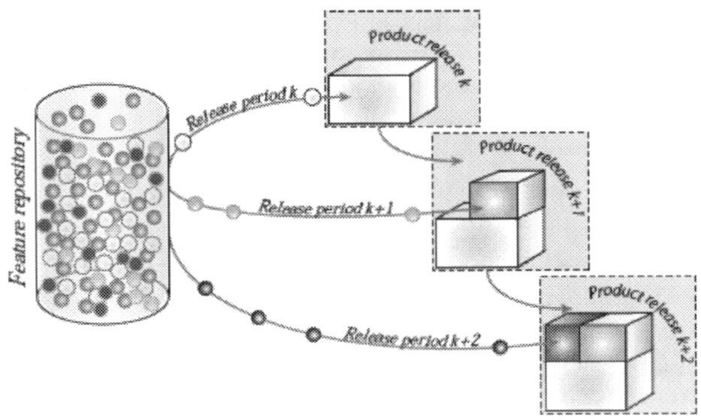

Figure 3. Schematic Illustration of Release Planning as the Selection and Assignment of Features to Releases [11].

Of special interest with regard to cross-domain RE are the models used to define and evaluate the release scope as well as the factors considered. This is often done by pre-selecting and prioritizing of features using methods like the Multiscore method or the voice of the customer [11]. Thus, main preconditions for feature-based release planning are project information including feature set, their description as well as stakeholders nominated for prioritization. Moreover, different soft and hard factors have to be considered during release planning. According to Svahnberg et al. [12], hard constraints include technical constraints, budget and cost constraints, resource constraints, effort constraints, and time constraints. Soft constraints cover stakeholder influence factors, risk factors, value factors, and resource consumption factors [12].

The brief description of RE in software engineering and the related methods on the one hand highlights that there are established approaches and detailed procedures like the EVOLVE II available. On the other hand it becomes clear that features are frequently used to describe the "selling units of a product" and form the additional functionalities to be delivered by a release.

B. RE in Mechanical Engineering

Release Engineering is not a well-established concept in mechanical engineering. Research works around the group of Schuh propose to transfer the principles of RM from software domain to the domain of mechanical engineering. In analogy to the processes in software engineering they emphasize the strong interrelation to the processes and methods of modular product architecture design [5] and technical change management [10]. In addition the importance of anticipating innovations during the whole life cycle and the settlement of product variants are mentioned as major objectives [8]. Essential tasks of RE in mechanical engineering cover the definition of components to be substituted or added in order to provide additional functionalities and value to the customer. To support this task there are numerous methods described in literature addressing the definition of modules with regard to the functional and/or physical structure of the product. For instance the modular function deployment (MFD) proposed by Ericsson and Erixon uses so called *module drivers* to define suitable modules to build up the product [22]. With focus on modular products this approach uses a matrix for mapping functional requirements to certain modules. The Design for Variety introduced by Martin [23], focusses on creating robust platforms for modular products and reducing interdependencies between system elements. By introducing the Coupling Index (CI) that specifies the strength of the connection between the components of a product the importance of the physical system structure to define suitable modules (release units) and evaluate the design effort is highlighted. To represent and analyse interdependencies between components Design Structure Matrices are often used [24]. Here, the system is decomposed into single parts or subsystems and the different interactions for instance *spatial*, *energy*, *material*, and *information* are denoted within the cells. By analysing these interactions clusters with strong interrelations between parts and subsystems can be identified that are suitable to bundle development effort or changes [25]. Other works provide principles to enable changes in systems throughout the life cycle. These principles focus on suitable system architectures to implement changes required for upgrading or releasing new derivate with small impact on the existing product [26]. Major objective of the concept of design for changeability is to increase the changeability of products with regard to the dynamic of marketplaces, technological evolution, and varying environments.

Although, there are numerous methods to support system architecting and technical change management in mechanical engineering there are less approaches that address the timing of releases based on the consolidation and bundling of changes and consideration of innovation gaps. A basic concept to define release cycles and synchronize changes is proposed by Aleksic [13]. He introduces the module change flexibility classification number (MCF) to support future planning of changes. The MCF is a result of the evaluation of the dimensions *market driven requests caused by customer demands*, *production costs*, *one-time complexity costs*, *running complexity costs*, and *module interaction*. Each dimension is evaluated by the classification number D_{MCF_i} with a maximum value of nine. The factor g_i is used to weight the dimensions and adapted the importance of each dimension to the boundary conditions of different companies and targets. The product of the classification number D_{MCF_i} and the weighting factor g_i is normalized by the sum of the g_i and x_i, which is consistently given the maximum value of nine [27].

$$MCF_g = \frac{1}{\sum_{i=1}^{5} g_i \times x_i} \times \sum_{i=1}^{5} g_i \times D_{MCF_i} \quad (1)$$

According to the given equation, the MCF ranges between zero and one. This value is used to locate each module within an onion peel model visualizing the incensement of the MFC from the inside to the outside; see Fig. 4. Modules placed in the inner shell are thus less flexible than these placed at the outer shell.

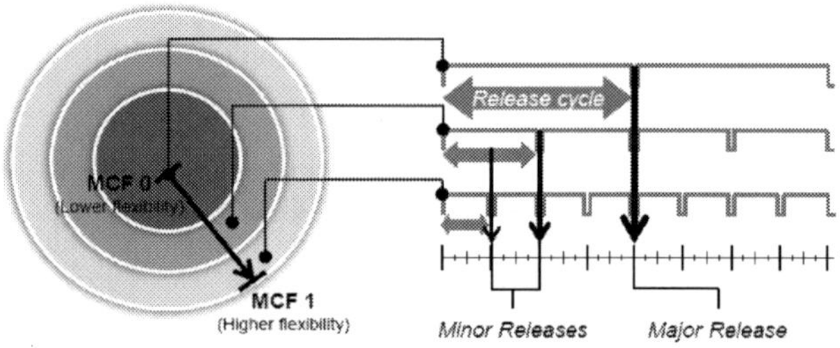

Figure 4. Onion Peel Model to Visualize the Module Change Flexibility Classification Number (MCF) and Resulting Release Cycles [27].

The MCF and the onion peel model help to identify modules that can be changed with small efforts and those that can hardly be changed without affecting other modules. Furthermore, the onion peel model can be used to plan release cycles systematically by defining suitable release frequencies with regard to the MCF. Here, high flexibility modules are chosen to by changed more frequently since they cause lower change effort. Furthermore, the onion peel model gives advices of how to structure the product architecture in order to enable releases.

From the brief discussion of the methods it becomes clear that the content of release in the field of mechanical engineering is defined by modules. These modules contain different parts of the mechanical structure and are defined using established methods considering for instance life cycle and technology aspects. However, there is now established procedure or method covering all activities required for RE.

C. Comparison of RE Approaches

Based on the domain specific methods and approaches for RE described beforehand, this paragraph introduces a brief comparison. The comparison presented in Table I highlights the main differences according to the considered *time horizon*, *main objectives and drivers*, *required product information and preconditions*, *content of releases*, *release cycle definition*, and *considered restrictions*.

From the comparison, it becomes clear that main differences of existing RE approaches in software and mechanical engineering concern the product information used to define releases as well as the content of the releases and the restriction considered. While RE in software engineering is based on features and their relations within the software system, in mechanical engineering modules are used to define release units. This points out that on the one hand in both cases the representation and analysis of the system structure and the included interdependencies between the elements (components or function) is essential when defining release units and on the other hand (changing) requirements and user needs are important for suitable planning of releases. A main deficit of RE related approaches in mechanical engineering is the missing support of adequate release cycle definition. Most of the existing methods focus on the initial definition of the product architecture but do not consider the possibilities of consequently delivering new or additional functionalities by releases. One main obstacle to do this in industrial practice can be found in the high efforts and costs caused by production of hardware parts.

Based on the given comparison the following requirements can be formulated to support cross-domain RE:

- A cross-domain linking between features and components or functions is needed to define suitable release units and provide new and additional functionalities to the users.
- The different interdependencies between features and components of initial and existing systems architectures have to be modelled to support planning for instance of product upgrades.
- An interdisciplinary requirement and innovation management is required to ensure value oriented planning and definition of release units across domains.

While the first two requirements pertain to the activities of interdisciplinary system modelling, the third one is concerning assisting processes and information needed for planning and evaluation activities within RE. Based on these findings and requirements, in the following section, potentials and challenges of RE in automotive industry are briefly discussed.

III. Towards Cross-Domain RE in Automotive Industry

Automobiles are complex mechatronic systems. Due to increasing value creation based on software-based functions like comfort or assistance functionalities there is a trend towards decreased use phases of cars like discussed in Section 1. This results in increasing pressure to shorten development times and coordinate the cross-domain development activities. To cope with the resulting complexity of highly linked organisational structures, requirements, development documents and product structures and processes different approaches exist including RM. Fig. 5 illustrates the hierarchical structuring of systems and organization as well as the correlations between data and processes using electrical and electronic systems as an example. Also here RM processes on different system levels are represented. Major objective of these RM processes is to

TABLE I. BASIC COMPARISON OF RE APPROACHES IN SOFTWARE AND MECHANICAL ENGINEERING.

Characteristics	*Software Engineering*	*Mechanical Engineering*
Time Horizont	Next release (ad-hoc planning) and overall life cycle (systematic planning)	Overall life cycle of the product and single modules
Main Objectives and Drivers	Change requests (errors or upgrades), Bundling of development, testing and implementation activities (temporal and functional)	Implementation of "innovations" for product enhancement, life-cycle-accompanying updates, consolidation of changes and innovations, adaptation of variants
Product Information and Preconditions Required	Features sets of the software system, interdependencies between features, requirements	Functions and components of the product, dependencies between components, requirements
Related Activities	Configuration management, change management, requirement management, service & quality management	Technical change management, product architecture design, requirement management, life cycle management
Content of Releases	Features as value units for customers	Modules as changeability units of the product
Release Cycle Definition	Considered as essential part of RE	Not consequently considered
Restrictions Considered	Technical constraints, budget and cost constraints, resource constraints, effort constraints, and time constraints, stakeholder influence factors, risk factors, value factors, and resource consumption factors	Market driven requests, production costs, complexity costs, innovation cycles, module interactions

release subsystems at specific points of time during the PD process like quality gates or product starts [28]. Necessity and complexity of these RM processes results from the different hardware and software versions as well as for instance electrical control units' development during the PD. The introduced RM aims on ensuring proper functioning of all variants as well as the total car system by initiating tests and changes.

The described understanding and process of RM in automotive industry is basically different from the understanding introduced before since it focusses to support the efficient development a predefined configuration of subsystems and functions. The releases to be delivered in this context are solutions or variants of subsystems of the overall car system. At the same time the predefined point of times serve to consolidate and coordinate required cross-domain changes for following development activities. With regard to the understanding of RE introduced in Section 3 the following basic concepts to handle releases in PD have to be distinguished:

- Releases as *development units* to be delivered at predefined points of time in the PD process in order to handle process and product complexity based on a defined configuration.
- Releases as *value and innovation units* to enable upgrading of the product during use phase including changes and expansions of the system configuration.

Independent from the applied concept of releases, it becomes clear that there is a strong interrelation to the structuring of the automobile system since the content of the releases in both cases is modules of the system including hardware and software. Thus, the illustrated hierarchical structuring of processes, systems and related requirements and data have to be considered when discussing potentials and challenges of RE in context of automotive industry.

In the following paragraphs, essential potentials and challenges of cross-domain RE in automotive industry are described focusing on the concept of releases as *value and innovation units*.

A. Potentials of Cross-Domain RE in Automotive Industry

Based on the introduced understanding of RE the following potentials can be formulated for automotive industry with regard to the vehicle system:

- Consequent RE enables to continuously provide new and additional functionalities to customers by upgrading existing vehicle systems.
- Value oriented RE supports diversification of vehicle systems and innovation leadership of by integration by efficient market launches of new technologies.
- Life cycle oriented RE contributes to the reduction of resources needed for manufacturing of hardware components.

These potentials highlight the use of RE from the external (customer) and internal (manufacture) viewpoint related to the product. At the same time, positive implications of RE can be expected with regard to the PD process:

- Definition of technology and innovation oriented release units enable to prioritize development activities. Release units with short technology and innovation cycles can be developed and implemented late in the PD process while those with longer cycles should be part of the long term development.
- Function and value oriented definition of release units supports cross-domain engineering and coordination of change and integration activities.
- Consequent RE helps to shorten PD time by release a basic configuration of the vehicle system that is continuously extended by further releases.

It is obvious that realization of these potentials requires the definition of release units across domains since there are strong interrelations between the subsystems needed to realize the intended functions. Thus, it is essential to analyse and modify the interrelations between subsystems of the different engineering domains both on the level of system structure and requirements. However, the existing structure of systems and document based development activities established in automotive development projects, as shown in Fig. 5, often hinder to identify and represent domain crossing links needed for release planning. In the following paragraph the major challenges hindering cross-domain RE are described.

B. Challenges of Cross-Domain RE in Automotive Industry

Consequent implementation of the principles in industrial practice of automotive development is hindered by organizational, process and product related issues. On the one hand there are established – in most cases hierarchical– approaches to decompose systems and structure processes in order to handle complexity. Up to now, systems and processes are structured with regard to the engineering domain (mechanical, electric/electronical, and software). This also results in domain specific models and documents to hold product

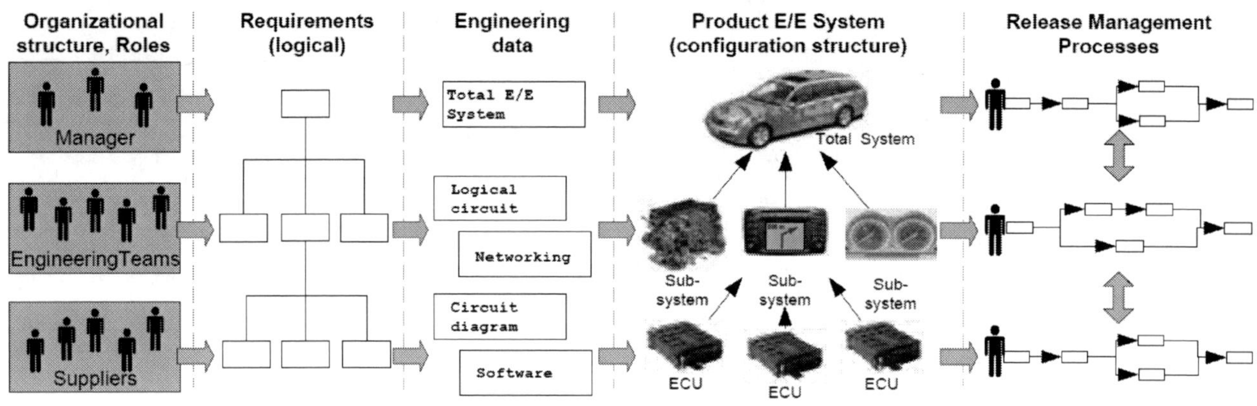

FIGURE 5. Schematic illustration of the structure and interrelation of organization, requirements, documents, product structure and processes in E/E development [29].

relevant information. In consequence there are less models and documents representing interrelations between subsystems across domains. With regard to RE this leads to the following challenges:

- Processes, documents and models of automotive development are structured with regard to components and systems and not value or function oriented.
- Configuration management is often done on the level of components and functions in the single domains using specific documents and models without linking information.
- Definition of suitable release units is complicated since technical constraints cannot be elaborated.
- A consistent requirement management addressing all involved domains and system levels is missing but needed for release planning and definition.

These boundary conditions highlight challenges that have to overcome when introducing cross-domain RE. It becomes clear that required changes to support cross-domain RE address processes as well as the way and structure the emerging products are described by models and documents. In order to overcome challenges and support the changes required in the following section fields of research are introduced.

IV. Fields for Future Research to support Cross-Domain RE

Based on the discussed potentials and challenges to introduce cross-domain fields for further research can be derived. The fields named in the following were identified based on observations in industrial practice and the analysis of existing approaches and principles of RE in the domains of mechanical and software engineering:

- Development of value and innovation oriented descriptions of systems and subsystems (related to requirement management).
- Development of modelling techniques to represent interrelations between components (mechanical domain) and functions (electric/electronical and software domain) on different level of aggregation and with regard to different kinds of relations like geometrical, logical or functional constraints.
- Development of methods to support cross-domain definition of release units with regard to different innovation cycles.

The formulated fields of research highlight the most relevant areas to work on. In order to establish cross-domain RE approaches and principles interdisciplinary research is essential to integrate viewpoints and methods of software and hardware engineering. Thus, the fields of research are closely connected with the area of systems engineering and address the fields of configuration management, requirement management, change management, and life cycle engineering.

V. Discussion and Conclusion

Objective of this contribution was to introduce a basis understanding of cross-domain RE based and the analysis of methods and principles in software and mechanical engineering. Moreover, it aims on pointing out potentials and challenges of cross-domain RE for automotive industry.

The analysis and comparison presented in Section 2 represent a first overview on existing and related methods used to support RE. It points out the main differences between software and hardware engineering for instance with regard to information of the product and preconditions needed to define release units. However, it is limited in its focus and conclusions to be derived because of the small number of methods analysed. The potentials and challenges formulated in Section 4 are based on observations in automotive industry and derived from the general potentials of RE described in literature. In further works potentials have to be analysed in more detail for instance by analysing examples from other industries. The challenges also have to be clarified based on the specific boundary conditions of industry partners.

Further work will focus on the fields defined in Section 5 as well as case studies to refine requirements for modelling techniques and methods to support cross-domain RE. Short-term work aims on applying existing and adapted methods of RE for an interior subsystem of an automobile. Furthermore, research will be conducted to analyse the interrelations and impact of intelligent manufacturing approaches and technologies like Internet of Thinks or flexible production concepts to the aspects of Release Engineering. Here, the focus will be to investigate new possibilities for dynamic planning and agile development concepts in PD.

REFERENCES

[1] Y. Umeda, T. Daimon, and S. Kondoh, "Life Cycle Option Selection Based on the Difference of Value and Physical Lifetimes for Life Cycle Design," in Proceedings of the International Conference on Engineering Design (ICED), August 28–31, 2007, Paris, France, J.-C. Bocquet, Ed. The Design Society, 2007, pp. 145–146.

[2] Umweltbundesamt, "Texte 11/2016: Einfluss der nutzungsdauer von produkten auf ihre umweltwirkung: Schaffung einer informationsgrundlage und entwicklung von strategien gegen obsoleszenz," 2016.

[3] A. Albers, N. Bursac, and E. Wintergerst, "Produktgenerationsentwicklung - Bedeutung und Herausforderungen aus einer entwicklungsmethodischen Perspektive," in Tagungsband Stuttgarter Symposium fuer Produktentwicklung "Entwicklung smarter Produkte fuer die Zukunft", June 19, 2015, Stuttgart, Germany, H. Binz, B. Bertsche, W. Bauer, and D. Roth, Eds. Fraunhofer IAO.

[4] A. Albers and G. Moeser, "Modellbasierte Prinzip- und Gestaltvariation," in Tagungsband 14. Gemeinsames Kolloquium Konstruktionstechnik, October, 6-7 Oktober, 2016, Rostock, Germany, K. Broekel, J. Feldhusen, K.-H. Grote, F. Rieg, R. Stelzer, P. Koehler, N. Mueler, and G. Scharr, Eds. Shaker Verlag, Aachen.

[5] K. Ulrich and S. Eppinger, Eds., Product Design and Development. Irwin/McGraw-Hill, Boston, 2011, ISBN: 978-0073404776.

[6] W. Bauer, "Planung und Entwicklung Aenderungsrobuster Plattformarchitekturen," Ph.D. dissertation, Technische Universitaet Muenchen, 2016, ISBN: 978-3-8439-2778-9.

[7] "Ieee standard - adoption of iso/iec 20000-2:2012, information technology - service management - part 2: Guidance on the application of service management systems," 2013.

[8] G. Schuh, Ed., Produktkomplexitaet managen: Strategien - Methoden - Tools. Carl HanserVerlag, Muenchen, 2005, ISBN: 978-3446400436.

[9] T. Richter, D. Inkermann, and T. Vietor, "Product Architecture Design as a Key Task within Conceptual Design," in Proceedings of the International Design Conference (DESIGN), May 16–19, 2016, Cavtat-Dubrovnik, Croatia, D. Marjanovic, M. Storga, N. Pavkovic, N. Bojcetic, and S. S., Eds. The Design Society.

[10] U. Lindemann and R. Reichwald, Eds., Integriertes Aenderungsmanagement. Springer-Verlag, Berlin, Heidelberg, 1998, ISBN: 978-3-642-71958-5.

[11] G. Ruhe, Ed., Product Release Planning: Methods, Tools and Applications. CRC Press, Taylor & Francis Group, Boca Raton, London, New York, 2010, ISBN: 9780849326202.

[12] M. Svahnberg, T. Gorschek, R. Feldt, R. Torkar, S. Saleem, and M. Shafique, "A systematic review on strategic release planning models," Information and Software Technology, vol. 52, no. 3, 2010, pp. 237–248.

[13] S. Aleksic, "Nachhaltige Weiterentwicklung von modularen Produktarchitekturen durch Release-Management," Ph.D. dissertation, RWTH Aachen, 2015, ISBN: 978-3-86359-397-1.

[14] "Iso/iec 20000 part 1: Service management system requirements. geneva,switzerland: International organisation for standardisation," 2011.

[15] C. Wischki, Ed., ITIL V2, ITIL V3 und ISO/IEC 20000. Gegenberstellung und Praxisleit-faden fr die Einfhrung oder den Umstieg. Carl Hanser Verlag, Muenchen, 2009, ISBN: 9783446419773.

[16] "Iso/iec/ieee 15288: Systems and software engineering - system life cycle processes," 2015.

[17] M. Michlmayr, "Quality improvement in volunteer free and open source software projects - exploring the impact of release management," Tech. Rep., 2007.

[18] H. Wright, "Release Engineering Processes: Their Faults and Failures," Ph.D. dissertation, University of Texas at Austin, 2012.

[19] P. Carlshamre, K. Sandahk, M. Lindvall, B. Regnell, and J. Nattoch Dag, "An industrial survey of requirements interdependencies in software release planning," in Proceedings of the Symposium on Requirements Engineering, August 27–30, 2001, Toronto, Canada, F. Titsworth, Ed. IEEE Computer Society Washington, DC, USA.

[20] D. Greer and G. Ruhe, "Software release planning: An evolutionary and iterative approach." Information and Software Technology, vol. 46, no. 4, 2004, pp. 243–253.

[21] T. Cormen, C. Leiserson, and R. Rivest, Eds., Introduction to Algorithms. McGraw Hill, New York, 2009, ISBN: 978-0262533058.

[22] A. Ericsson and G. Erixon, Eds., Controlling Design Variants: Mudular Product Plattforms. ASME Society of Manufacturing Engineers, Dearborn, 1999, ISBN: 978-0791801505.

[23] M. Martin, "Design for Variety - A Methodology fpr Development of Product Plattform Architectures," Ph.D. dissertation, Stanfort University, 1999.

[24] T. Browning, "Applying the Design Structure Matrix to System Decomposition and Integration Problems: A Review and New Directions," IEEE Transactions on Engineering Management, vol. 48, no. 3, 2001.

[25] U. Lindemann, M. Maurer, and T. Braun, Eds., Structural Complexity Management - An Approach for the Field of Product Design. Springer-Verlag, Berlin, Heidelberg, 2009, ISBN: 978-3-540-87888-9.

[26] W. Fricke and A. Schulz, "Design for Changeability (DfC): Principles to enable Changes in Systems Throughout their Entire Lifecycle," Systems Engineering, vol. 8, no. 4, 2005, pp. 279–341.

[27] G. Schuh, S. Aleksic, and S. Rudolf, "Module-based Release Management for Technical Changes," in Progress in Systems Engineering - Proceedings of the Twenty-Third International Conference on Systems Engineering, August, 2014, Las Vegas, NV. Springer International Publishing, 2014, pp. 293–298.

[28] D. Mueller, J. Herbst, M. Hammori, and M. Reichert, "IT Support for Release Management Processes in the Automotive Industry," in Proceedings of the International Conference on Business Process Management (BPM 2006), September 5–7, 2006, Vienna, Austria. Springer-Verlag Berlin Heidelberg, 2006, pp. 368–377.

[29] K. Rouibah and K. Caskey, "A workflow system for the management of inter-company collaborative engineering proces," Engineering Design, vol. 14, no. 03, 2003, pp. 273–293.

Towards Alignment of Processes, Tools, and Products in Automotive Software Systems Development

Joachim Schramm
Andreas Rausch
and Daniel Fiebig

Clausthal University of Technology
Department of Computer Science &
Institute for Applied Software Systems Engineering
Goslar
Germany
Email: forename.surname@tu-clausthal.de

Oscar Slotosch
and Mohammad Abu-Alqumsan

Validas AG
Munich
Germany
Email: surname@validas.de

***Abstract*—Numerous quality standards impact the lifecycle of software and system development in the automotive industry. Hereby, quality is evaluated through rigorous assessment of the deployed processes, tools and products. Yet, although these three aspects go hand-in-hand, they are typically assessed separately and manually. Moreover, system providers are increasingly challenged by media breaks coming along with the necessity to integrate processes and tools, and to facilitate data exchange among these tools. Consequently, this adds more demands and challenges on certification. This paper presents the TOPWATER approach, whereby a unified metamodel is used to specify how processes, standards and tools are linked. We introduce TOPWATER from the conceptual as well as from the technical perspective. Shown also in particular is the integration of the approach into the Validas' qualification methodological framework, which is used for qualification and classification of toolchains; a requirement of safety standards imposed on all tools used to develop safety-related products/items. This example from the Automotive Software Engineering field is used for evaluation, where outputs from the TOPWATER method supported Validas process assessment by TÜV. In this pretest, TOPWATER has demonstrated its feasibility. The approach supports the integration of new sustainable and resilient mobility concepts in existing infrastructures and saves costs through early deviation detection.**

***Keywords*–Process-Tool Integration; Toolchain; Software Process; Standards; Certification.**

I. Introduction

Today's software engineering of automotive software systems is impacted by a number of safety standards, such as ISO 26262 and IEC 61508. Hereby, quality and safety are assured through rigorous assessments of the processes and tools used, and the final product. For instance, process quality is achieved by formulating and assessing requirements, e.g., test procedures or code coverage levels. Likewise, tools and particularly critical tools must be classified [1]. Finally, the product's quality is evaluated by checking, e.g., if the product development followed a defined process and process steps and tools involved were developed and used according to the respective standard's requirements. However, even though these three aspects are highly interrelated, they are mostly implemented and assessed individually and manually. This can lead to issues regarding consistency and completeness, e.g., a process that was not implemented as defined, or use of tools not appropriately qualified. Currently, available assessment tools mostly cover these aspects in an isolated manner, such as process modeling (e.g., Eclipse Process Framework) or toolchain analysis (e.g., Validas Toolchain Analyzer). If at all, integration of these aspects is done manually using Microsoft Excel.

A. Problem Statement & Objective

In certification of automotive software systems/items/products, tools, processes, and products need to comply with the relevant standards. Yet, most process-tool ecosystems are loosely coupled thus challenging certification. The approach presented in this paper aims at providing a solution that allows for seamlessly integrating software system development processes and the tools used to perform, enact and track these processes. Our approach particularly aims at closing content-related and semantic gaps that hinder a seamless integration by monitoring across-tool artifacts and products of the different processes.

B. Contribution

In this paper, we present the TOPWATER (german acronym for: Entwicklung einer ontologiebasierten Software zur integrierten Prozess- und Werkzeugkettenplanung und validierung für die Automotivesoftwareentwicklung) approach to support a seamless integration of development processes and tools. TOPWATER was a German government funded project, which requires at least one industry partner. Our approach is grounded in a metamodel, which allows for linking software process models and development tools. Notably, to support automotive software systems development, our approach is integrated into the Validas' qualification methodological framework, which is used for qualification and classification of toolchains. We present our approach as a conceptual model, which is translated into a technical metamodel (based on the Eclipse Modeling Framework), and we show the implementation of our approach in the toolchain of Validas AG that is primarily used in Automotive Software Engineering projects. The Validas members are experts in the field of toolchains and the university members are experts in the field of processes.

C. Outline

The remainder of the paper is organized as follows: Section II presents a short background supported by some practical observations (Subsection II-A) and further provides a short review of selected related work (Subsection II-B). Section III presents the approach from a conceptual and technical perspective (Subsection III-A), shows the feasibility based on a TÜV pretest (Subsection III-B), and critically discusses the results achieved so far (Subsection III-C). We conclude the paper in Section IV, including the limitations (Subsection IV-A) and the future work (Subsection IV-B).

II. Background & Related Work

This section provides the background and the motivation of our research using observations from practice. Furthermore, we present the work related to our research.

A. Observation from Practice

Aligning processes and tools in automotive product development is challenging, since heterogeneous ecosystems introduce media breaks and a multitude of data formats. As such, this puts a strain on the product development process as a whole since consistency and completeness, e.g., of models and software, must be ensured as a prerequisite for certification. Aiming at gathering some field information with respect to process-tool alignment, the authors have interviewed nine practitioners from six different divisions within a large German car manufacturer. These interviews were part of a joint automotive process-development workshop. Table I lists the questions which were asked and a summary of the respective answers. Yet, for confidentiality reasons, we can only provide summaries of the interview findings. All information about the respective persons, company and project contexts were removed prior to extracting the information presented hereby. In a nutshell, the results highlight two main factors for causing process- and tool-chain breaks: technical (e.g., isolated incompatible tools) and Human factors (e.g., too extensive and/or complicated processes are ignored, and complex tools pose great challenges to users).

TABLE I. Summary of findings from interviews with six divisions of a large German car manufacturer on experiences concerning process- and tool-chain breaks.

Question	*Summary of Findings*
What do you consider a tool-chain break?	Practitioners consider an employee that is acting as a "man in the middle", i.e., who transfers data manually from one tool to another, a tool-chain break. Another potential break is seen in situations that disturb the normal workfow, e.g., where employees try to familiarize themselves with a new tool that has replaced a previously used one. In addition to these human factors, communication and data transfer issues constitute tool-chain breaks. For example, an integration of DOORS and JIRA, or Vector Software's PREEvision and Excel can—if at all—convert data from tool A to B, but not vice versa.
What do you consider process-chain break?	Practitioners consider potential discrepancies between defined (standard) processes and their implementation and/or enactment as breaks in the process-chain. Particularly, undocumented process deviations might impact compliance checks that take place at subsequent stages, and therefore are considered as a source of risk.
What is the main source for such breaks?	Practitioners point out two major sources for breaks, of which the Human stands as the first and obvious one. Humans might be overwhelmed by documentations, do face the need to interpret process descriptions, and/or do struggle with the complexity of the tools at hand. All this may lead to sloppiness in the process implementation/enactment as well as to going for shortcuts, notably in projects under time pressure. The second major source is concerned with technology. For instance, different tools assembled in a toolchain might cause data exchange complications. Also, expert tools, which are typically used by a restricted number of persons, can cause breaks if many other employees want to consume or provide data, which these tools respectively generate or consume.
Do you have support available or counter-measures defined to deal with such breaks?	The interview revealed contradicting answers by the different divisions. Three divisions argue for working according to the book, i.e., an employee has to read the process description before performing activities/producing artifacts, and involved people should not (only) rely on other 'experienced' people that explain their ways of work. On the other hand, the other three divisions opt for the exact opposite way. In general, the interview participants name external consultants as a countermeasure to avoid process- and toolchain breaks. At the tool-level, participants express their intentions to intensify tool evaluation towards bidirectionally compatible tools to avoid issues with data transfer/exchange.

B. Related Work

What basically renders the alignment of process- and toolchains challenging is that it involves different problem fields, such as data exchange formats, process integration, workflow management, and process enactment. Moreover, in highly regulated domains, such as automotive, integrated process-toolchains, which are used as a part of the product development process, usually require a certification.

To the best of our knowledge, the approach presented in this paper is unique, yet it is built upon concepts and solution approaches for different problems. A major issue addressed by TOPWATER is the systematic design of a toolchain in which different tools are assembled to create an integrated work environment. Among other things, the variety of tools available challenges companies across the Globe. For instance, Portillo-Rodríguez et al. [2] provide an overview of tools used in globally distributed software development. They classified 132 different tools, yet mentioned that only a small percentage is practically relevant.

Different platform providers offer solutions to consolidate the "tool zoo". In particular, two approaches can be identified: (i) open platforms like the Eclipse platform and (ii) commercial tools/toolchains such as Microsoft's Team Foundation Server or Rational's Team Concert. The latter approach usually provides interfaces that can be used by third-party developers. These platforms remain, however, closed to a certain extent and additionally impose high expenditure and infrastructure requirements. On the other hand, open platforms like Swordfish [3], agosense.symphony [4], ToolNet [5], or ModelBus [6] provide mechanisms for technical integration only. These platforms require specific adapters for the tools to be integrated—in the worst case, data is transferred as plain XML (Extensible Markup Language). Nevertheless, both open and commercial platforms have in common that adapters have dependencies to the respective platforms, which requires effort to keep them up to date and operational. TOPWATER aims at addressing this issue by providing a model-based mapping approach. A model connects the different tools and, in the best case, allows for generating the required connections. From this perspective, the approach followed in TOPWATER is comparable with the SPRINT (Software Platform for Integration of Engineering and Things) platform [7]. SPRINT aims at providing a unified view on the different components of complex systems developed in an interdisciplinary manner. It connects the different domain-specific expert tools by providing means to design and transform data to be exchanged among the different tools. The actual connection is realized using OSLC (Open Service for Life-cycle Collaboration) [8], which connects development artifacts and adds semantics to these artifacts and their relationships.

Aiming at facilitating process modeling and enactment, TOPWATER is built on several concepts. Other than business processes, software development processes are hard to enact. For instance, Rozinat and van der Aalst [9] show how conformance checking for business processes is realized using actual behavior. Furthermore, in his keynote, van der Aalst [10] presents the current state of (business) process mining. However, different from business processes, development processes are way less predictable (e.g., due to developers' creativity, situation-specific problem solutions, changing requirements). Nevertheless, different approaches exist to prepare and implement process enactment. Similar to the TOPWATER approach, transformation of process models to allow for process execution or document generation is quite common [11]. Furthermore, rule-based execution of processes using explicit modeling languages is a well-established concept, e.g., [12]. However, approaches proposed so far primarily address the conversion of process models into a format that allows for automating their respective processes. Integrating the processes into a complex conglomerate of processes, products and tools that have to be certified, so far, received little attention. In order to support the aforementioned situation, checking process properties is key (see also Cobleigh et al. [13]). TOPWATER addresses these requirements by utilizing a metamodel to integrate the different aspects and, moreover, to allow for formally evaluating consistency, compliance, and so forth. In particular, TOPWATER helps addressing the determination of the so-called *Tool Confidence Levels* (TCL; as defined by ISO 26262 [14]). An assessment is performed automatically using formal methods. Further details on the tool classification and qualification approach for ISO 26262 can be taken from Conrad et al. [15] in which authors share experiences concerning implementing an approach for development and verification tools. Given by the context, TOPWATER so far supports Validas' *Tool Chain Analyzer* (TCA; [1]) [16]. However, TOPWATER is designed with flexibility in mind that other tools, such as *RapiCover Aero* or *RapiTime Aero* can be targeted [17]. These tools help assessing the compliance with the DO-178B or DO-178C requirements, which are relevant for aerospace applications.

III. THE TOPWATER APPROACH

We present our approach to support developing seamlessly integrated processes and toolchains. In Section III-A, we present the approach at conceptual and technical levels. Section III-B presents the validation, and Section III-C critically discusses our approach.

A. Solution Approach

The TOPWATER approach comprises two parts: a conceptual generic solution and a technical approach for direct implementation in the context of particular toolchains. In the following, we introduce both parts with more emphasis on the technical solution and its concrete implementation.

1) Conceptual Model: TOPWATER is a collection of metamodels and tools, which are illustrated in Figure 1. In its core, TOPWATER allows for

- modeling software development processes (Figure 1; *Process Layer*),
- modeling tools as part of a toolchain (Figure 1; *Tool Layer*), and
- modeling use-case-based mappings between processes and tools. (Figure 1; *Mapping Layer*).

Following the modeling of tool- and process-chains step, three major steps may take place. These are represented with partitions and shown in Figure 1 as vertical "swimlanes".

- validation step: in which process engineers validate the different interconnected models before a project starts.
- operation step: in which different concrete process artifacts (or artifact instances) and project results are created.
- controlling step: project managers use the generated models to implement a quality-gate-based controlling to check the fulfillment of the process- and tool-related requirements, and to check whether such requirements are likely to be fulfilled in future project stages or not.

Grounding TOPWATER in a metamodel provides manifold options to support the models' quality assessment—at design time and during the different project phases alike.

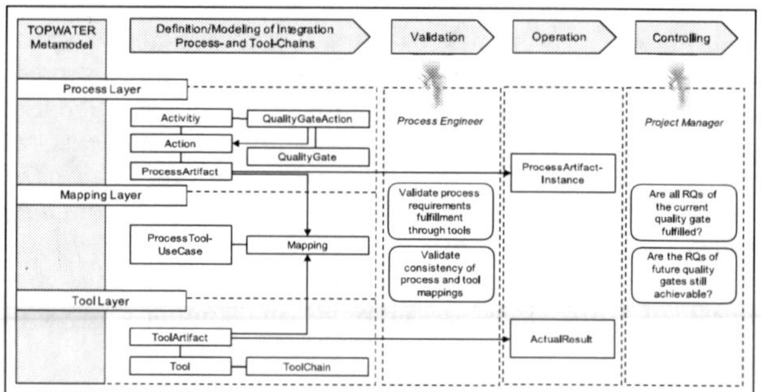

Figure 1. Overview of the conceptual model of the TOPWATER approach including the different metamodel layers, the project phases and selected model elements and project-related activities.

2) Implementation: As a proof of concept, TOPWATER is integrated with the Validas toolchain, which is usually used for formal tool qualification [1], i.e., a tool can be qualified according to safety standard requirements and a tool can be mapped to an assessable process to create a certification-ready work environment. To allow for easy integration in different toolchains, TOPWATER's metamodel is developed in the Eclipse Modeling Framework (EMF), which additionally allows for generating a modeling tool from the metamodel. Figure 2 provides an overview of the key elements in the metamodel, of which certain data types for standards or requirement classes are used to manifest the transition from the generic concept (Figure 1) to the actual practical implementation.

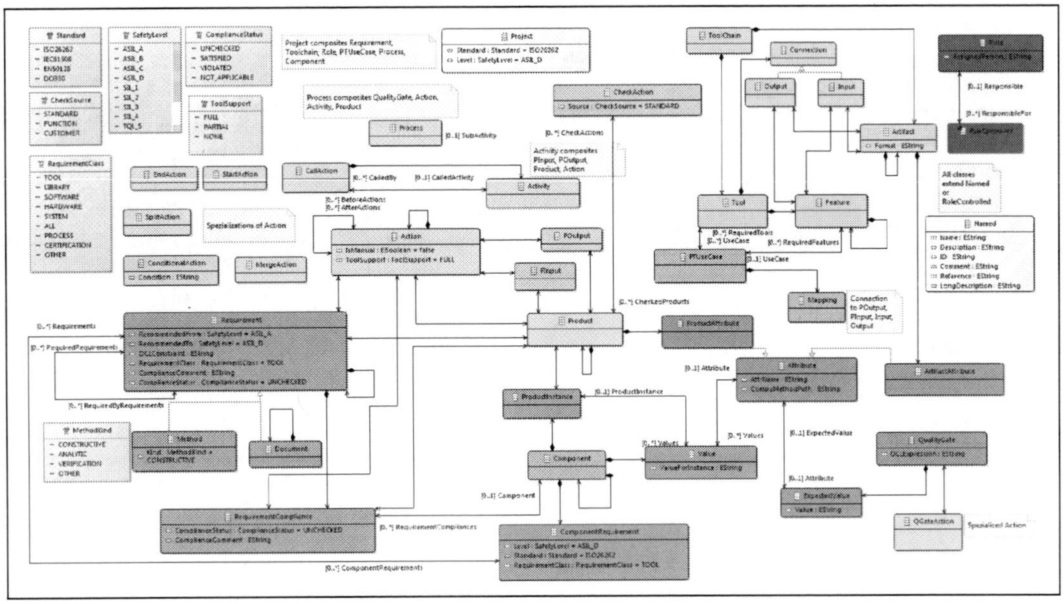

Figure 2. Key elements of the TOPWATER metamodel, developed in the Eclipse Modeling Framework (EMF).

From the technical perspective, a TOPWATER project comprises `Components`, `Processes`, and `ToolChains`. Products and components, in particular, are mapped to `Requirements`, e.g., concerning the targeted standard or required safety integrity levels by the tool qualification. `Products` together with `Actions`, define a `Process`. The actions allow for designing the process to be checked. Process modeling follows the UML principles (including, e.g., start-, split-, and conditional actions) and, hence, the users can model object and control flows alike. For instance, the products can be inputs (`PInput`) and outputs (`POutput`) of activities. Similarly, toolchains contain `Tools`, `Artifacts`, `Features`, and relations, e.g., artifacts are inputs/outputs of tools.

A key feature of the TOPWATER tool is the ability to provide mappings. A mapping serves the requirement to be able to link tools and processes, such that the development process can be tracked and, thus, aids the different certification requirements. Mappings are part of the so-called `PTUseCases`, which link process inputs and tool outputs (and vice versa), i.e., process steps are connected to tools that realize them.

The metamodel allows for several validation operations and quality assurance activities, which in turn can aid certification needs. TOPWATER uses a validation model based on quality gates. A `QGateAction` is a specialized action, which has one or more `QualityGates` assigned. By design, a quality gate is a predicate expressed in OCL to define product states and product attribute values at certain project stages. Quality gates represent critical steps in the evolution of artifacts and, within this evolution, several product-specific expressions must be true for the project to continue.

For the actual validation in the context of a quality gate, TOPWATER provides two views, to which we refer as

- *closed world view* (CWV)
- *open world view* (OWV).

The CWV focuses on supporting completeness checks of artifacts. To this end, an artifact-specific expression is assumed `false` (i.e., a quality criterion is not fulfilled yet) whenever it is not evaluated as `true` for a certainty. Thus, performing a validation on a quality gate and all products assigned to it provides an overview of all incomplete artifacts and, particularly, the attributes that cause the tests to fail. On the other hand, the OWV assumes an expression to be `true`, regardless of its actual evaluation. Consequently, this view provides a broader picture of the modeled project and, to a certain extent, supports prediction. This is achieved by checking which subsequent quality gates might be fulfilled given the current project status. The prediction allows for identifying quality gates that can be reached according to plans, as well as identifying those quality gates that cannot be reached anymore, should the process be executed as planned and without modification. Such predictions can be used for early deviation detection, and therefore enable project managers to initiate counter actions as early as possible.

3) Integration into the Validas Environment: Figure 3 provides an overview of the compliance methodology of the Validas AG. The model-based *Validas Qualification Methodology* (VQM) is used for classifying and qualifying tools and toolchains according to safety standards. The VQM is informally described with an informal process description. Central to the VQM is the *Tool Chain Analyzer* (TCA), which is a modeling tool that is developed by Validas AG and is used to develop the so-called *Qualification Support Tools* (QSTs). QSTs are shipped to customers, so that qualification can be performed within the customer environment to automatically generate work products relevant to the target safety standards, such as the Tool Qualification and Tool Criteria Evaluation Reports in ISO 26262. Evidence is generated for each developed QST to assure that (i) procedures are compliant with safety standards, and (ii) procedures were adhered to. The former is typically covered by a compliance report (CR), whereas the later is typically done by performing *Verification & Validation* (V&V) and generating the V&V report. The QST and the quality assurance documents (i.e., CR and V&V report) are altogether referred to as *Qualification Kit* (QKit).

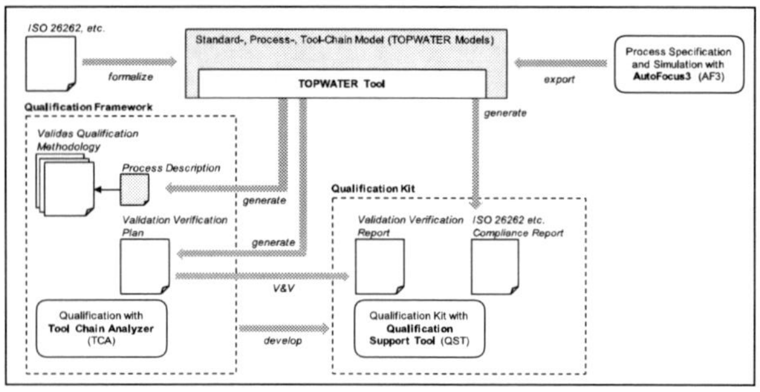

Figure 3. Overview of the Validas compliance methodology.

Figure 3 additionally shows the TOPWATER's integration into the otherwise isolated steps of the VQM. As a prerequisite, however, the VQM process is formally modeled using *AutoFocus3* (AF3; [18]). AF3 is an open source modeling tool that allows for model-based development of embedded systems, with support for formal modeling and rigorous quality assurance of the models (including, e.g., validation, verification, model checking and simulation). By using AF3 for modeling the processes of the VQM, these processes can be formalized and checked using the quality assurance mechanisms of the tool. The formally modeled and checked VQM processes can be easily imported into the TOPWATER tool. The TOPWATER tool additionally receives the targeted standard(s) as input. The target standard(s) is/are used to create the mappings of the different processes and tools (which happens here to be the tool chain modeling tools; see Figure 2). Using the different standard-, process-, and tool models, the TOPWATER tool can automatically generate: (i) the compliance report of the developed/modeled processes (ii) the V&V plan as a checklist, according to which V&V can be performed and V&V reports can be generated (iii) a formal description of the processes, which when combined with the informal description is used to guide involved people in creating QKit projects.

B. Validation by Example

This section presents a validation of the TOPWATER tools by example. The validation presented hereby is based on an audit performed by TÜV (TÜV = Technischer Überwachungsverein, engl: Technical Inspection Association); a certification body that provides independent inspection and product certification services (in Germany and worldwide). The audit aimed at evaluating if the generated files from TOPWATER are adequate to support process/product certification. In this pretest the TOPWATER approach was preliminarily evaluated for certification readiness. At the TOPWATER tool side, this involved:

- Modeling of the tool qualification process
- Mapping of standards' requirements and their mapping to tools
- Mapping of processes and tools
- Generation of compliance reports and V&V plan

Figure 4 shows an excerpt of the VQM process modeled in AF3 in which the qualification component of the process is shown. This component takes a QKit and the tool (model) to qualify and executes the qualification process. The component shown in Figure 4 contains the three actions `classify`, `plan`, and `validate`. The `validate` action creates the *Tool Qualification Report* (TQR; to be delivered to the safety manager for review) and the *Tool Safety Manual* (TSM; to be delivered to the tool user). The result of importing the VQM AF3 model into TOPWATER is shown in Figure 5 showing the manifestation of the different metamodel elements from Figure 2. Specifically, the figure shows the aforementioned actions `classify`, `plan` and `validate`, and the products QKit, TSM, TQR, TCS, and TQP. Also, the input and output relations are shown that illustrate the workflow. For example, the element `POutput Validate_to_TSM` connects the action `validate` and the corresponding output product TSM.

Figure 4. Excerpt of the VQM modeled in AF3 to be exported to TOPWATER.

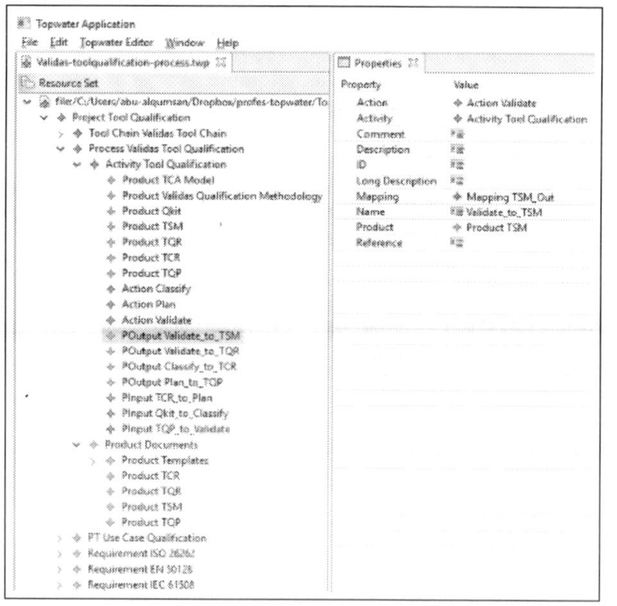

Figure 5. The TOPWATER tool after importing the VQM from AF3 (node *Activity Tool Qualification*, which includes the activities and products involved in a qualification).

Providing the formalized VQM process to TOPWATER allows for integrating all tools involved in the tool qualification process into one framework. Among other things, Figure 5 shows *Requirement* nodes, which contain models of the target standards for which the compliance must be checked. Figure 6

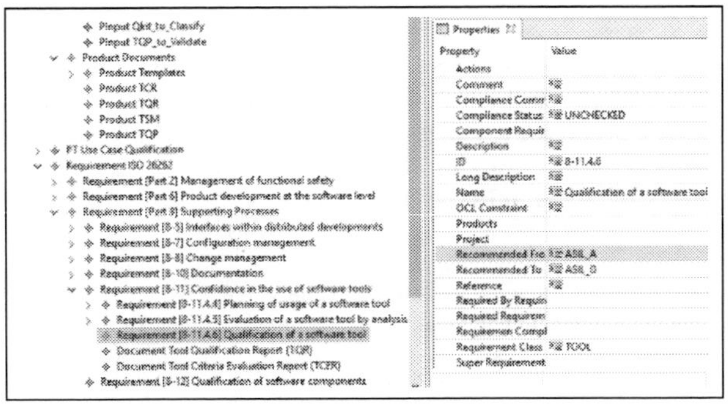

Figure 6. Expanded nodes for requirements in the TOPWATER tool.

shows a part of the ISO 26262 [14] standard used for the TÜV audit mentioned at the beginning of this section. The selected item *8-11.4.6 Qualification of a software tool* demonstrates how requirements are modeled within TOPWATER. It shows, inter alia, that requirements have compliance status, requirement class, and recommendations concerning their application with respect to the different ASIL levels—in this particular case, the selected requirement must be checked for all levels (i.e., from ASIL A to ASIL D).

To carry out the actual tool qualification as required by standards, it is necessary to explicitly state which tool is used to perform a specific process step (including the specification of the artifacts involved). For this, the TOPWATER metamodel (Figure 2) defines the class `PTUseCase`, which handles the mapping of processes, products, and tools. Figure 7 shows the expanded node *Qualification* that realizes this mapping. In particular, the *Qualification* use case maps process inputs to tool/toolchain inputs and, respectively, process outputs to tool/toolchain outputs. For example, the mapping *TQP_Out* connects the `POutput` *Plan_to_TQP* from the validation process with the output *TQP Output* from the toolchain. The metamodel ensures that only valid mappings can be made, e.g., `POutput` elements can only be mapped to other `POutput` elements, which is ensured by a just-in-time filtering and type validation.

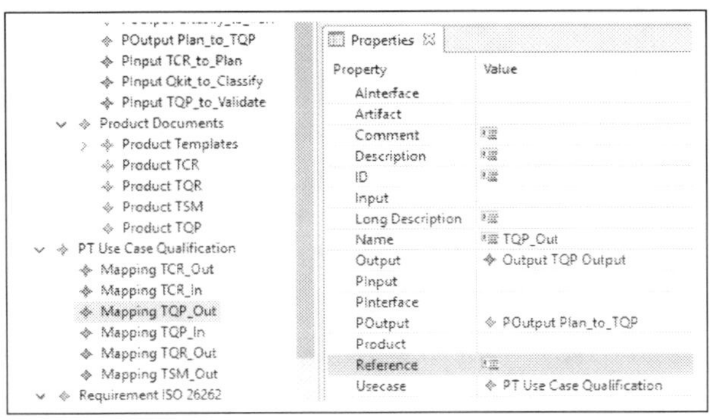

Figure 7. Expanded nodes for PTUseCases and the process and tool mappings.

Beyond the type-based standard validation, the TOPWATER tool also checks the models for completeness and inconsistencies. The platform allows for defining required rules, i.g., check if all requirements have names and descriptions provided, and if the provided names are unique.

The previously shown steps give an overview of the activities necessary to develop the different models for processes, products and tools, and how to connect them to modeled standards for which the compliance must be checked. The tool further helps performing the required activities to a large extent and allows for documenting the mappings appropriately, i.e., the V&V-related documents. Here, the *V&V Plan* contains a description of the V&V strategy, which, inter alia, includes the supported safety standards, the tool adequacy, and a description of the different checks for standard compliance or the components involved. Complementing, the *V&V Report* contains the check results. Notably the *V&V Report* shows the sheer mass of documentation that needs to be delivered for a certification process thus underlining the benefits a model-based approach offers.

C. Discussion

The previous sections have presented the TOPWATER approach and its first implementation within the Validas processes and tools. This section discusses the benifits and the limitations of the current state of TOPWATER. As a first step, we highlight in Table II the extent, in how far TOPWATER addresses the challenges mentioned by practitioners, which were summarized in Table I.

TABLE II. DISCUSSION OF THE CURRENT STATE OF THE TOPWATER APPROACH FOLLOWING THE STRUCTURE OF TABLE I.

Question	*Summary of Findings*
What do you consider a tool-chain break?	Practitioners consider project employees or "man in the middle" and data exchange/transfer as major issues. In the current implementation, TOPWATER does not address tools with automation interfaces. Yet, TOPWATER makes a first step by providing an integrated and uniform model that allows for connecting the different parts. Automation, however, remains subject for future works.
What do you consider process-chain break?	Practitioners consider discrepancies between "as-planned" and "as-is" processes as a major problem. TOPWATER addresses this aspect through its manifold process modeling and model checking options including options that check compliance against the targetted standards, such as ISO 26262 or DO 330.
What is the main source for such breaks?	Practitioners consider human factors and technological aspects as major sources for breaks. TOPWATER partially addresses these problems. The human factor is addressed by the manifold process modeling and checking capabilities, e.g., importer from Microsoft Visio or AF3, and process enactment with quality gates based on process constraints. The technological aspects are initially covered by the ability of TOPWATER to model tools and toolchains. Given that the respective tools provide sufficient options for data exchange, this exchange can be modeled accordingly and integrated with the process-, product- and tool mapping.
Do you have support available or counter-measures defined to deal with such breaks?	See previous comment. Furthermore, the TOPWATER tool provides users with comprehensive guidance and different quality checks to guard against possible breaks, e.g., type-based constraints or more comprehensive validity checks.

The current implementation of the TOPWATER approach has been run through a TÜV pretest and demonstrated its feasibility. Furthermore, the current implementation solves several of the challenges identified (Table II). Specifically, the problem of proving that a defined process has been performed is addressed. The TOPWATER tool allows for importing process models, i.e., the development process of the companies running a development project targeting an automotive application.

The imported process is connected with the tools used to enact the process and the standard requiring certain activities executed to be eligible for certification. The mapping provided by TOPWATER allows for creating an integrated model that can be evaluated for consistency and compliance and, furthermore, supports the generation of reports as requested by the certification authorities. Moreover, the TOPWATER tool can also be integrated with the project as such. By continuously maintaining the state of the process through constraint-based quality gates, project progress can be tracked and, to a certain extent, predicted such that early plan deviation is possible. Finally, the qualification method implemented using TOPWATER is able to validate itself. Using AF3 as process modeling tool, the qualification process is formalized thus allowing for formal validation of the process (which is also possible for any other method that is incoming via the AF3 interface). Nevertheless, several practical requirements are not (yet) implemented, which we further discuss in the Section IV-B.

IV. Conclusion and Future Work

The present paper has presented TOPWATER, a methodological approach that allows for joint and integrated modeling of processes, products, and tools. The objective of such modeling is to reduce breaks in process- and toolchains, and hence to reduce friction in the development processes. In industries, where such breaks may have a high impact on efficiency, like automotive, the proposed approach might be of great interest. The integrated approach helps companies to ease and accelerate certification (and recertification) efforts. Specifically, we have shown the integration of TOPWATER into Validas AG qualification methodology that supports the classification and qualification of tools and toolchains, a key activity required by automotive safety standards. An initial evaluation of the presented approach was carried out, where the TOPWATER tool was exploited to automatically generate documents that supported Validas AG process assessment by TÜV. This evaluation has successfully demonstrated the feasibility of the approach.

A. Limitations

Within the current state of the TOPWATER tool, several standards are already modeled or still under development. Furthermore, different converters/adapters are implemented, e.g., to integrate formal process models generated by other modeling tools. However, the TOPWATER approach and the respective tools still have some limitations (Table II). For instance, despite the fact that the modeling approach is per se accurate and correct, the modeling activities, in its current form, remain a complex activity that requires expert knowledge in the field. Moreover, several practical problems identified throughout the project are currently only partially addressed by the tool, i.e., the concept is developed, but the tool does not deliver its features fully. For example, several aspects that are part of the automation engine still require manual work and checks.

B. Future Work

Future work comprises the completion of the automation engine to implement and, eventually, provide all TOPWATER features to its users. In the present work, we have also shown the feasibility of the approach for the tool qualification methodology. Hereby, however, the scope of the safety standards which is covered by projects of this nature is relatively limited. For future work, evaluation with other applications, with large number of tools and large scope of targeted standards are planned.

References

[1] M. Wildmoser, J. Philipps, and O. Slotosch, "Determining potential errors in tool chains: Strategies to reach tool confidence according to iso 26262," in Proceedings of the 31st International Conference on Computer Safety, Reliability, and Security, ser. SAFECOMP'12. Berlin, Heidelberg: Springer-Verlag, 2012, pp. 317–327.

[2] J. Portillo-Rodríguez, A. Vizcaíno, M. Piattini, and S. Beecham, "Tools used in global software engineering: A systematic mapping review," Information & Software Technology, vol. 54, no. 7, 2012, pp. 663–685. [Online]. Available: https://doi.org/10.1016/j.infsof.2012.02.006 [retrieved: January, 2018]

[3] [Online]. Available: http://www.eclipse.org/swordfish/ [retrieved: January, 2018]

[4] [Online]. Available: http://www.agosense.com/agosense.symphony [retrieved: January, 2018]

[5] [Online]. Available: http://www.es.tu-darmstadt.de/forschung/overview/ [retrieved: January, 2018]

[6] [Online]. Available: http://www.modelbus.org/en/modelbusoverview.html [retrieved: January, 2018]

[7] [Online]. Available: http://www.sprint-iot.eu/ [retrieved: January, 2018]

[8] M. Saadatmand and A. Bucaioni, "Oslc tool integration and systems engineering – the relationship between the two worlds," in Proceedings of the 2014 40th EUROMICRO Conference on Software Engineering and Advanced Applications, ser. SEAA '14. Washington, DC, USA: IEEE Computer Society, 2014, pp. 93–101. [Online]. Available: http://dx.doi.org/10.1109/SEAA.2014.64 [retrieved: January, 2018]

[9] A. Rozinat and W. M. P. van der Aalst, "Conformance checking of processes based on monitoring real behavior," Inf. Syst., vol. 33, no. 1, Mar. 2008, pp. 64–95. [Online]. Available: http://dx.doi.org/10.1016/j.is.2007.07.001 [retrieved: January, 2018]

[10] W. v. d. Aalst, "Big software on the run: In vivo software analytics based on process mining (keynote)," in Proceedings of the 2015 International Conference on Software and System Process, ser. ICSSP 2015. New York, NY, USA: ACM, 2015, pp. 1–5. [Online]. Available: http://doi.acm.org/10.1145/2785592.2785593 [retrieved: January, 2018]

[11] M. Kuhrmann, G. Kalus, and M. Then, "The process enactment tool framework-transformation of software process models to prepare enactment," Sci. Comput. Program., vol. 79, Jan. 2014, pp. 172–188. [Online]. Available: http://dx.doi.org/10.1016/j.scico.2012.03.007 [retrieved: January, 2018]

[12] G. E. Kaiser, N. S. Barghouti, and M. H. Sokolsky, "Preliminary experience with process modeling in the marvel software development environment kernel," in Twenty-Third Annual Hawaii International Conference on System Sciences, vol. ii, Jan. 1990, pp. 131–140, vol. 2.

[13] J. M. Cobleigh, L. A. Clark, and L. J. Osterweil, "Verifying properties of process definitions," SIGSOFT Softw. Eng. Notes, vol. 25, no. 5, Aug. 2000, pp. 96–101. [Online]. Available: http://doi.acm.org/10.1145/347636.348876 [retrieved: January, 2018]

[14] ISO TC22/SC3/WG16, "ISO/IEC 26262:2011: Road vehicles – Functional safety," International Organization for Standardization, Tech. Rep., 2011.

[15] M. Conrad, G. Sandmann, and P. Munier, "Software tool qualification according to iso 26262," in World Congress, Society of Automotive Engineers, SAE Technical Paper 2011-01-1005, Detroit, MI, USA, 2011. [Online]. Available: https://doi.org/10.4271/2011-01-1005 [retrieved: January, 2018]

[16] [Online]. Available: http://www.validas.de/TCA.html [retrieved: January, 2018]

[17] [Online]. Available: www.rapitasystems.com [retrieved: January, 2018]

[18] Fortiss, "AutoFocus3 Modeling Platform, v2.11," Online: https://af3.fortiss.org [retrieved: January, 2018].

Barcelona Virtual Mobility Lab

The multimodal transport simulation testbed for emerging mobility concepts evaluation

Lídia Montero, Mª Paz Linares, Juan Salmerón, Gonzalo Recio, Ester Lorente, Juan José Vázquez
Universitat Politècnica de Catalunya - BarcelonaTECH
Barcelona, Spain
email: lidia.montero@upc.edu, mari.paz.linares@upc.edu, juan.salmeron@upc.edu, gonzalo.recio@upc.edu, ester.lorente@upc.edu, juan.jose.vazquez.gimenez@upc.edu

***Abstract*—New sustainable mobility concepts and smart resilient ideas are arising every day. However, there is not an easy way to bring these ideas into reality, or to test how good they are as mobility solutions. Virtual Mobility Lab offers the opportunity to evaluate the impact of new mobility concepts before taking them to the real world. In this work, a multimodal macroscopic traffic simulation model of the Barcelona Metropolitan Area is developed, including both public and private transport network. This paper explains the remarkable features developed for this model, such as the network hierarchy and the multimodal public network interchangers, allowing demand to exchange between public transportation modes along their origin-destination paths.**

Keywords—multimodal; public; transport; network; macroscopic; traffic; simulation; model.

I. Introduction

Nowadays, changes in urban networks and proposals of new mobility concepts are not easy to evaluate. They cannot be assessed directly in the real life, either due to the unknown effect on the real traffic or due to new infrastructures that are not yet built in the city. An option is to apply a pilot test, but it is often difficult, expensive and hardly configurable. Another option simulates the impact of the change or proposal applied to the real environment.

The simulation is used in many contexts in order to measure, in a virtual environment, the impact of applying modifications on the real-world. It requires a previously developed model that represents, as precise as possible, the key characteristics and behaviors of the selected real scenario. In this case, any new mobility concept that wants to be tested should be recreated first in a simulated scenario, instead of spending time and money evaluating it with real fleets in the streets (if possible) [1][2]. In order to perform a good transport simulation, it is necessary to develop a model that represents accurately the real transport network. For this, it is important to have knowledge about the real scenario, as for example the multimodal details, a well-defined network hierarchy and an updated information of the public transport system.

Thus, this paper presents the Barcelona Virtual Mobility Lab (VML), which uses a multimodal macroscopic simulation model developed in inLab FIB at Universitat Politècnica de Catalunya using PTV Visum Platform [3]. This project models a transport system to assist in the design and evaluation of impacts of new mobility concepts.

The paper is organized as follows. Section II describes how the study territory area is divided and Section III and IV explain how private and multimodal public transport networks have been modeled, respectively. For Section IV, some indicators obtained from the model are described in addition to some guidelines of how the built model can be exploited on its potential applications. Finally, the document shows some final conclusions.

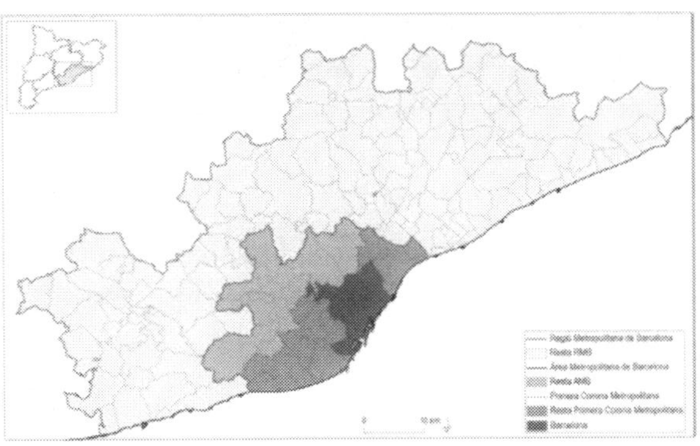

Figure 1. Areas of metropolitan region of Barcelona.

Figure 2. Zoning system of the study area.

II. STUDY AREA ZONING SYSTEM

The study area included in this model is identified as the first crown of the metropolitan area of Barcelona. This area (delimited by the green line in Fig. 1) is composed by Barcelona city and 17 municipalities placed around it and they represent a population of more than 2.8 millions of people.

Zoning system divides the study area into homogeneous Transport Analysis Zones (TAZ) according to socioeconomic features and access to transport facilities. Demand matrices model the number of trips between TAZ zones. In the zoning system, the area is represented by 628 zones that cover the study area and the contiguous territories (identifiers from 700 in Fig. 2).

The used demand data is provided by KINEO [4] who uses mobile phone data to extract the origin, destination and trip time tags. The demand is represented separately by hourly Origin to Destination (OD) matrices. This allows studying the different situation of the transport network depending on the time of the day.

III. PRIVATE TRANSPORT NETWORK

The private transport network is the representation of the urban network geometry. In order to simulate the behavior of the private vehicles in the network, it is needed to model a road network and their private transport systems. In traffic simulation modeling, the network geometry is usually constructed street by street to obtain a first model. This is a hard work task since even for small traffic models can have thousands of streets.

This methodology is not a feasible solution for such a huge metropolitan area, thus geographical maps from HERE [5] have been imported into the platform to simplify the model building process. It also imports the available transport system in the modeled area for private and public transport (imported from General Transit Feed Specification (GTFS) files [6]).

To support this, the traffic simulator VISUM allows a fast transport network modeling through HERE Maps to obtain a first approach model. The updated road network from HERE has been imported to VISUM that generates a traffic model with all the nodes and links (Fig. 3).

This procedure helped to construct a first network model, but there are more concepts that needed to be modeled like the representation in detail of the road network hierarchy. This hierarchy created to distinguish between transport road types is shown in the Table I.

This allows to model different types of streets depending on the speed limit, number of lanes, etc. in the road network for each of the transport systems (e.g., if allowed, the velocity limit, etc.) in a general mode. Then, manual edition of network characteristics imported from HERE maps has been done for specific areas.

IV. MULTIMODAL PUBLIC TRANSPORT NETWORK

As mentioned before, a multimodal network allows generating OD paths exchanging public transport modes when doing a demand assignment. In our model we considered the following modes:

- Train
- Underground
- Bus
- Tramway

Accordingly, building a multimodal public transport network implies introducing all these modes and, for each of them, all the transport lines (e.g., Fig. 4 and 5). For this, it is necessary to know the topological route of each line, the number of stops, which sections have reserved lines in case of buses, and the number of travels each day

Figure 3. Private vehicle network road hierarchy.

TABLE I. PRIVATE VEHICLE NETWORK ROAD HIERARCHY

Type Name	Lane-capacity per hour	Free-flow Speed (km/h)
Motorway	1500	120
Urban motorway	1200	80
Coordinated Arterial (Aragó)	900	50
Uncoordinated Arterial	650	50
First Level Collector	700	50
Secon Level Collector	500	50
Road	800	80
Street without Traffic Lights	300	40
Unpaved rural road	100	30
Side/Access Lane	600	40
Roundabout	350	40
Bike	100	15
Pedestrians	60	5

Figure 4. Public Transport network: underground.

Figure 5. Public Transport network: buses.

considered: headway based journey based on frequency. For this macroscopic model, frequencies were used to model public transport services, adjusted to current transport operators.

One of the main peculiarities of this macroscopic model is the approach of joining these transport modes. To achieve this, some logical components were introduced: *stop points*, *stop areas* and *global stops*:

- *Stop points* define the topological position in the private network (urban map) where a station or bus stop is located.
- *Stop areas* are useful for grouping stop points that lead to the same public line (e.g., an underground could have more than one entrance to the platform).

Global stops gather all *stop areas* where it is allowed to perform transfers between different transport modes (blue circle in Fig. 6). Changing costs between lines or modes can be configured in these *global stops* (Fig. 7).

V. RESULTS

Just having into account the integration of all transport modes with almost all operators is a magnificent achievement, especially considering the context of Barcelona's network complexity. As a result, the macroscopic model obtained is the unique intermodal built until now with all transport modes.

The methodology followed to build the Barcelona VML model can be applied to any other model building process for other geographical areas. The Barcelona VML model also can be extended. Portability and extensibility of multimodal models through the proposed methodology is a trustingly success key. The model can be applied to other cities and also can be extended to larger areas.

Also, accurate model calibration has to be taken into account in following working steps to obtain a stunningly realistic model. This implies collecting real data to validate measurements from the model and contrast them with reality (e.g., data from counting sensors vs results from an assignment). The more data sources implied in the calibration process, the better for the model's accuracy. Besides that, on the early first version of the model (without any accurate network refinement), public and private transport assignments brought to light very reliable results (assignment results shown in Fig. 8 and Fig. 9). To perform this calibration, more real data from business key partners is needed, such as direct network measurements in the real world.

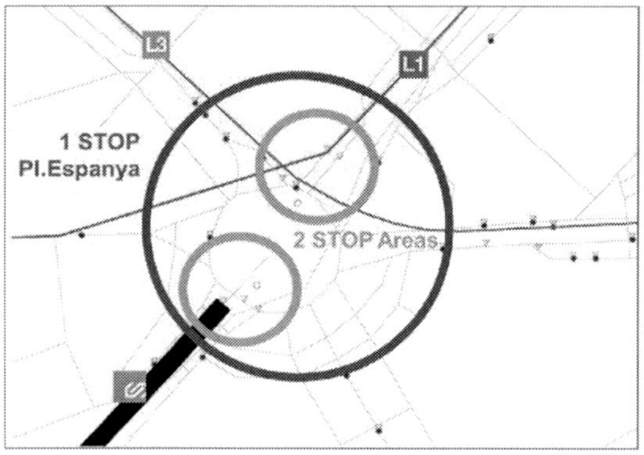

Figure 6. Modelization of Pl. Espanya Multimodal Transfer Area.

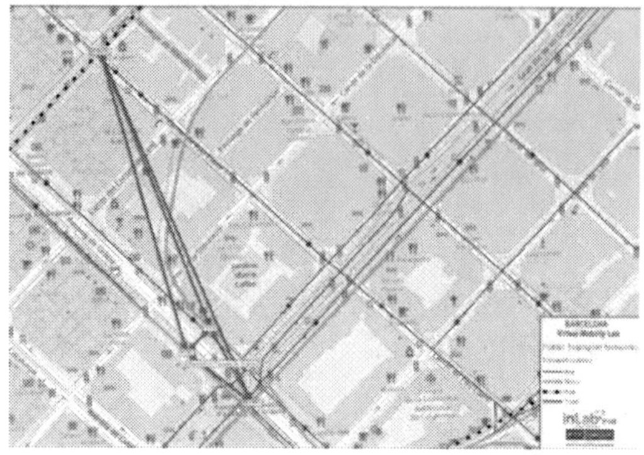

Figure 7. Modelization of Pg. de Gràcia Multimodal Transfer Area.

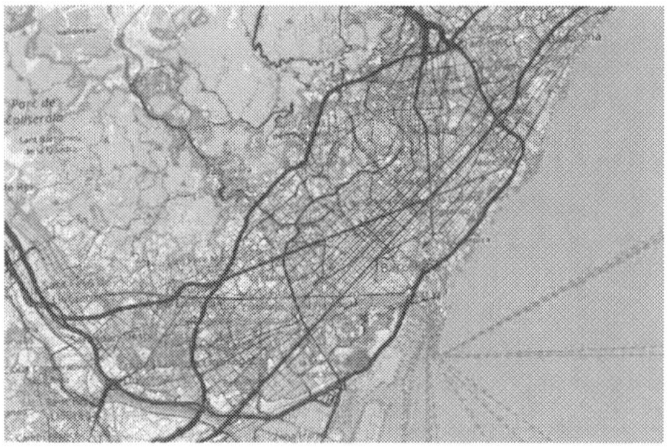

Figure 8. Private transport assignment 8h - 9h.

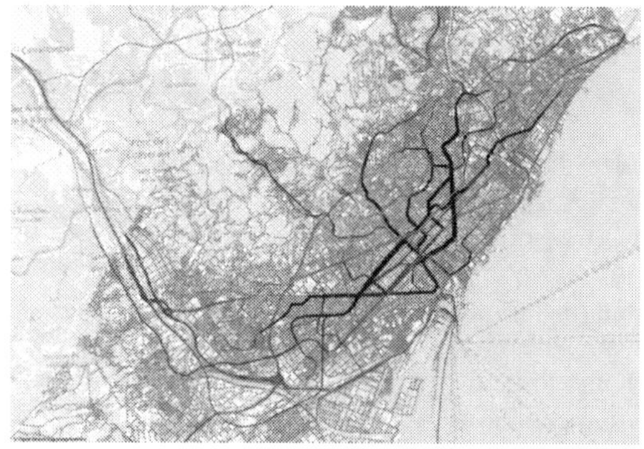

Figure 9. Public transport assignment 8h - 9h.

VI. Applications

The developed simulation model offers a lot of possibilities in order to correct, to update and to improve the mobility scene of the contained scenario. It allows studying how the current mobility plan is working, identifying the demand patterns and how they evolve and, detecting possible shortcomings in the current or future system. This information helps public organizations to take political decisions about the future modifications in the city mobility plan. Beside public organizations, the public transport operators can also take advantage of a complete vision of the scene and apply improved action plans depending on the demand behavior.

With regard to this panorama of smart mobility, this model can be very useful for evaluating new concepts or ideas, as well as having a complete analysis of all possible parameters involved, before launching them to the real world.

VII. Conclusions

The Barcelona Virtual Mobility Lab is the first detailed multimodal model of the Prime Crown of the Metropolitan Area of Barcelona. It integrates all modes of public transport as well as the private vehicle roads that would support future projects in traffic design and planning. A systemic scope consisting of all transportation modes and services is the added value of the developed model.

The next step will be to calibrate the model. Otherwise, it will not be useful as a Decision Support System tool. The model will help supporting future scenarios involving new transportation modes, vehicle types and urban developments.

Acknowledgment

This research was funded by TRA2016-76914-C3-1-P Spanish R+D Programs and by Secretaria d'Universitats-i-Recerca -Generalitat de Catalunya- 2017-SGR-1749.

References

[1] L. Montero, M. P. Linares, O. Serch, and J. Casanovas-Garcia, "A visualization tool based on traffic simulation for the analysis and evaluation of smart city policies, innovative vehicles and mobility concepts.," in Proceedings of 2017 Winter Simulation Conference, WSC 2017, Las Vegas, NV, USA, December 3-6 ISBN 978-1-5386-3428-8, 2017, pp. 3196 – 3207.

[2] M. P. Linares, L. Montero, E. Lorente-García, O. Serch, G. Navarro, and J. Salmerón-Moya, "Analytics tool for assessing innovative mobility concepts, vehicles and city policies (CitScale)," in Proceeding of the 5th IEEE International Conference on Models and Technologies for Intelligent Transportation Systems (MT-ITS) Napoli (Italia), 26-28 June ISBN: 978-1-5090-6484-7, 2017.

[3] PTV Vision Traffic, "PTV Visum." Karlsruhe.

[4] "KINEO," [accessed: 2018-02-03]. [Online]. Available: http://www.kineo.com.

[5] "HERE," [accessed: 2018-02-03]. [Online]. Available: https://www.here.com.

[6] "GTFS," [accessed: 2018-02-03]. [Online]. Available: https://developers.google.com/transit/gtfs.

**International Academy, Research,
and Industry Association (IARIA)**
412 Derby Way
Wilmington, DE 19810

ISBN 978-1-5108-6135-0

9 781510 861350

Fourteenth International Conference on Information, Process, and Knowledge Management (eKNOW 2022)

Held at DigitalWorld 2022

Porto, Portugal
26-30 June 2022

IARIA